Learning Peace

SUNY Series, Global Conflict and Peace Education
Betty Reardon, editor

Learning Peace

The Promise of Ecological
and
Cooperative Education

edited by
Betty Reardon
and
Eva Nordland

with the assistance of
Robert Zuber

STATE UNIVERSITY OF NEW YORK PRESS

Published by
State University of New York Press, Albany

For information, address the State University of New York Press,
State University Plaza, Albany, NY 12246

Production by Berndine Dawes
Marketing by Fran Keneston

Library of Congress Cataloging-in-Publication Data

Learning peace : the promise of ecological and cooperative education /
    edited by Betty Reardon and Eva Nordland ; with assistance from
    Robert Zuber.
        p. cm. — (SUNY series, global conflict and peace education)
    Includes bibliographical references (p.) and index.
    ISBN 0-7914-1755-7 (alk. paper) —ISBN 0-7914-1756-5
(pbk. : alk. paper)
    1. Education—Social aspects. 2. Environmental education.
3. Social ecology—Study and teaching. 4. Peace—Study and
teaching. 5. Critical pedagogy. I. Reardon, Betty. II. Nordland,
Eva, 1921– . III. Zuber, Robert William. IV. Series.
LC191.L37   1994
370.19—dc20   93-731
                                                          CIP

1 2 3 4 5 6 7 8 9 10

Contents

Preface

In 1988, American, Russian, and Norwegian scholars launched the Project on Ecological and Cooperative Education (PEACE). Later we were joined by educators from Ukraine and Canada; new members continue to join our group.

The background in 1988 was the cold war between the two superpowers and the imminent threat of nuclear war. The members of our group shared the conviction that more than everything else our planet needed an ecologically conscious culture that might overcome the fragmentation and specialization that is typical of the worldview dominating societies of today. We shared the conviction that humankind needed to cultivate the attitude of caring and cooperation instead of encouraging competition, confrontation, and threats of violence.

From these considerations our main questions arose: What are the consequences for education of our knowledge about the problems of the planet at the end of the twentieth century? The Earth is fast deteriorating because human beings have too powerful tools, too little understanding of the impact of our operations and transactions, and too little caring. What are the consequences for education when we realize that fatal threats to our planet are the result of rivalries among powerful individuals, cultures, and states?

The first task of our group was to get to know each other as persons and as scholars. We felt that we were first and foremost family people; our children, nieces, nephews, and grandchildren were a powerful reminder of our responsibilities as adults.

We enjoyed coming to know each other as teachers of education at universities and teachers' academies in our different countries. Together we were contemplating the birth of a new era, a historic transition that required from us new modes of thinking, acting, and organizing.

We started with a wish to contribute to the creation of a field of cooperation between the two—at that time—hostile superpowers; together we might take one of the countless important steps in the direction of building a new world. Was it conceivable that Norwegian scholars, representatives of a tiny country, might serve as bridge builders between representatives of two huge countries?

Our growing group of scholars meets once a year, presenting to each other follow-up studies of ecological and cooperative education in our several local communities. In this book, authored by nine members of our group, we present American and Russian thinking and experiences in new education, edited by one of the Norwegian members of the project. The nine authors of the book have met several times, in the United States, in Moscow, and in Norway, after our first meeting in Oslo in 1988.

We have worked together, given expression to our values, fears and hopes, and shared our knowledge. We have listened to each other and come to enrich our outlooks by solving problems together. We have become close friends, communicating with each other by letter, fax, and telephone—even by traveling in times of crisis, as for instance during the attempted coup in Moscow against the Gorbachev reform regime in August 1991. Repeatedly we have asked one another, "What is happening in your country, and how are you all?"

It is a unique part of our collaboration that as a group we have been following at close quarters the enormous changes in the former Soviet Union. Some of the participants have even taken a direct part in the drama. During the years we have worked together, the Soviet Union has collapsed as a superpower and dissolved into a large number of very different countries. It is impossible at present for anyone to forecast the next stages of development. When our group started its cooperation in 1988, Gorbachev had made known the main political ideas of the new perestroika era: openness (glasnost), democracy, and nonviolence in solving conflicts.

People in the Soviet Union were not really able to believe in the new democratic ideas; they were especially unsure whether they could safely voice their opinions. We knew that Soviet friends, even leaders of the Soviet peace movement, were asked by the authorities "to withdraw from their positions" and that they were accused of "disloyalty" when they criticized Soviet institutions (e.g. that elections were not organized in a democratic way). How could we dare in our project to encourage Soviet members of the group to be publicly critical of the Soviet Union?

As late as the summer of 1991, when Anatoly Golovatenko, one of the Russian members of our group, strongly criticized Soviet society in his work, the other members of the group made him aware of the risk he took and asked him to consider the implications for himself as a Soviet citizen. His answer was the same as that of so many others: Gorbachev's government had changed the law on this issue, if not yet the practice; no legal action could be taken against people who criticized their country, "even if they did so abroad." The non-Soviet members of our group were uncomfortable with this attitude, knowing that for decades it had led to imprisonment, even to being sent to Siberian prison camps.

Several chapters in this book describe the many initiatives in the Soviet school system and in organizations for children and youth that are important parts of the work by Soviet educators for democratization and humanization. These attempts had attained important results in parts of that enormous country. The general attitude of private citizens in the Soviet Union during the eighties was to express their opinions freely in the family and among trusted friends, and to be cautious in public. They might lose a lot if they were careless. The values they were fighting for, such as peaceful relations with the United States, might lose ground if they did not look before they leapt. Soviet citizens and people from the West were in this way able to have open discussions on all important topics as long as both parties knew "the rules of the game": a Soviet citizen was not supposed to make public criticism of the Soviet Union. During the sixties, seventies, and eighties, friendship and openness were cultivated on the basis of the need for communication with reliable friends. Friendship became a vital part of peace work for a great number of Soviet citizens and persons in Western countries belonging to the peace movement. It was unavoidable, though, in cold war years that Western peace workers were labeled "KGB agents" and criticized in the Western media as persons serving "the interests of Moscow."

Privately and with some caution, for several decades, people East and West were discussing all the main issues of a peaceful world development: the danger of testing, production, and storage of nuclear material and nuclear weapons; the need for nuclear weapon-free zones; the plans for step-by-step disarmament; nonviolent conflict resolution; and the many concepts of developing a democratic world, with freedom, equality, and justice. Shevardnadze, the foreign minister in Gorbachev's government, told me (at a reception at a world women's congress in Moscow,

1987) that he and Gorbachev had been influenced and inspired by the ideas and concepts of the peace movement in the West when they developed the ideas of perestroika and glasnost.

The Soviet participants in our project group from 1988 were all among the peace activists who joined the peace campaigns, meetings, and peace marches when East and West met during the eighties in the Soviet Union, in the Eastern European countries, and in Western Europe when possible (given Eastern restrictions on visas and currency). Soviet citizens had serious difficulties getting permission to go abroad; each had to belong to an organization and be accepted as "a reliable person" by that organization. In this way the Soviet Peace Committee became an essential part of the network of contacts, East and West, even if it had to be careful not to provoke state authorities.

Many members and employees in the Soviet Peace Committee became well acquainted with the way of thinking among peace activists in the West, just as Westerners came to appreciate the enormous work many Soviets did toward East-West bridge building.

Later, during August 1991, after the revolution, the situation changed drastically for the Soviets (later the citizens of the CIS countries—the Russians, Ukrainians, Byelorussians, and so on). One vital step forward was formal democratization; another was that in principle it became much easier to cross borders between countries and to travel abroad. However, after the attempt in January 1992 to make the ruble a convertible currency, it became virtually impossible to pay the travel expenses. Rubles lost enormously in value abroad. Also, the salaries of ordinary citizens were very low compared to those of their friends in the West. Prices for plane tickets became prohibitive, especially after January 1992; a thousand dollar round trip between Moscow and London was *several years salary* for a Russian citizen. Earlier, Russians and Ukrainians needed peace friends abroad to invite them to important events; today they need *rich* friends who can both invite them and pay all expenses.

In this way the situation in 1992 became increasingly more dangerous—and tragic—because general poverty is connected with increasing corruption and criminality. Ordinary Russian citizens are so poor that they have to sell their personal valuables, such as books, crystal, and textiles. Unscrupulous people take advantage of the needs of others. Our Moscow friends today advise us not to take taxis in the metropolis; they arrange for friends to drive us and ask that we pay the fare in dollars.

During the twenty-year Brezhnev era, from the mid-sixties to the mid-eighties, the school system provided many opportunities for open-minded teachers and parents. Art, music, theater, sport, mathematics, physics and languages were well-developed fields that good teachers who wanted to use the openings of the system could adapt in order to include peace studies in their students' education.

When the Gorbachev era started, the fifteen republics of the Soviet Union organized a state committee for democratization of the educational system. Reform-minded people from all over the country came together, told each other about initiatives, and inspired each other; support was organized by well-educated and democratically minded leaders in state and university systems. I was invited in 1991 to become an external adviser to the (then Soviet, today Russian) system of education.

Since the 1991 disintegration of the Soviet Union into separate states, school reform work has gone national. But it is severely hampered by the general poverty of the whole public sphere since the collapse of the public and private economy in Russia and the other new states.

This, then, is the practical background for the work of the project—and for the present book, which has been developed and written in what has been, especially for the Russian and Ukrainian members of the group, a time of turmoil. Some chapters had to be rewritten several times, as even the names of some of the writers' countries and basic educational issues changed during the period of our collaboration.

At the moment we are launching what we call "the second stage" of our work: the use of our ideas in practice. In this phase, Russian, Ukrainian, American, Canadian, and Norwegian teachers have started pedagogical reforms with great enthusiasm, using ideas and concepts developed during the first stage. With the collective intention of using our ideas of *an ecological and cooperative education* in various new and practical ways, and in different countries, we present in this book aspects of what we call *Learning Peace: The Promise of Ecological and Cooperative Education*.

Eva Nordland

1
New World—New Thinking—New Education

Eva Nordland

A PERIOD OF TRANSITION

The authors of this book have worked together during the worldwide changes around 1990, which present both threats and new possibilities. During our three years of cooperation, the idea of cold war between two superpowers has vanished; instead of the USSR, we have the various CIS countries, which are in extreme difficulties socially and economically. Through the "movements" in the international stock market during these years of instability, everyday life has been changed dramatically world-wide, with a marked widening of the gap between rich and poor. In many industrialized countries, such as the Nordic countries, the general nature of the welfare state has changed. Ethnic conflicts in Eastern and Western Europe have flared up; the former Yugoslavia is torn by civil war; thousands of families are fleeing from their homes without knowing where to go. Developing countries, like Sudan and Somalia, suffer from war and ecological crises; whole families are starving to death. The world of the nineties is crying out for alternatives.

We are at the same time witnessing the birth of a new era—a historic transition that requires new modes of thinking, acting, and institution building. We suggest throughout the chapters of this book ideas and initiatives, in our various fields of work, based on experiences in our different countries: Russia, Ukraine, the United States, Canada, and Norway.

The Global Context that brought about Our Project

We started our work with a view of today's world as interconnected and interdependent. As educators we focused on the increasing number of

1

people who are without security or influence in their everyday lives, people in whom passivity and the habit of being "onlookers" are being bred.

The widening gap between poor and rich is an extremely dangerous sign of the ill health of our global society. Long-standing resentment in many poor countries against the Western powers leads to continuous preparations for war.

People in the rich countries have acquired a life-style characterized by buying, using, throwing away. Money and property have become the symbols of rank, marking off as misfits those who do not "make it." Increasing numbers of children and young people all over the world expect to grow up as "second-class" citizens; they lose hope in the future, lose the sense of value in their lives. People of all ages in such situations tend to seek distraction and oblivion, to get away from themselves.

The Global Village

Ecology and economy are increasingly interwoven—locally, nationally, and globally—into a seamless net of causes and effects. When the local resource base is impoverished, wider areas are affected. Deforestation of highlands causes flooding of lowlands. Factory pollution depletes the local fishing catch. Acid rain and nuclear fallout spread and pollute across national borders. Threats are emerging on a global scale: global warming is changing the climate, gases are depleting the ozone layer. Hazardous chemicals enter foods that are traded across continents, causing illness among exporters as well as importers.

In international trade, powerful forces are in a position to decide who is going to produce what and how, and how much is going to be paid on either side. The current approach requires the poor to remain in poverty while they provide increasing amounts of scarce resources for export. A Tanzanian producer must work 150 hours or more to pay for goods that cost a Scandinavian producer 15 hours' work—as is the case when Tanzania trades its cotton for Scandinavian bicycles. Senegal produces carnations instead of wheat, because international decision makers have the power to regulate what the country produces. Senegal gets foreign currency in the exchange, but the food that must be imported to compensate for not growing wheat is so expensive that the population is left poorer than ever. The soil is abused and in twenty years may be exhausted; erosion sets in.

Hundreds of millions of people are denied basic human rights. Growing distrust and injustice are becoming a time bomb of resentment and hate. In Peru, 80 percent of the population do not have enough food. Crime is all-pervasive; three thousand abandoned "street children" roam the streets of the capital, Lima, getting what they need for the day by attacking unprotected people in the back streets. A fifteen-year-old leader of a gang, asked by a journalist what his future as an adult will be, replies: "I hope to be a terrorist, a thief, or a kidnapper, and so do most of my comrades."

The deterioration of the Earth's life-support system is threatening, as is the potential human toll from failing to act. With increasing awareness of the scarcity of resources, people in power will increasingly monopolize those resources to benefit their own circles, firms, families. If we fail to act to protect our resources for the benefit of all, we will lose confidence in ourselves, in the establishment, and in the future—hence breeding a general sense that our ability to direct our destiny is slipping away.

Ecology and Economy are Interlocked

Inequality between human beings is the planet's main "developmental problem." Economic inequality is the planet's main "environmental problem." The debt of the Third World, now at one trillion dollars and increasing by some hundred billion dollars a year, has grown beyond all reasonable hope of repayment, in a sort of irresponsible international pyramid game.

Interest payments of a hundred billion dollars per year have reversed the traditional situation, leading annually to a net capital transfer from poor to rich countries. In many heavily indebted Third World nations, the economic and social progress that normally lowers birth rates has been replaced by falling incomes. Hence, populations continue to grow rapidly, destroying the environmental support systems on which future economic progress depends.

A characteristic of the production system is the use of large-scale technology and enormous amounts of chemicals. On huge *monocultures*, owners grow one commodity such as coffee, cocoa, or cotton; they earn as much as possible and abandon the land when the soil is impoverished. The capital, earned over a short period, can then buy new land for a new round of short-term use.

The natural resources of clean soil and water are thus rapidly depleted.

The resulting environmental pressures cause the millions who are most severely hit to seek new places to live. Increasing numbers move to the cities, hoping for new opportunities. If today's trends continue unchanged, Mexico City, with sixteen million people in 1982, will have twenty-six million by the year 2000, and Bombay will increase from eight to sixteen million over a twenty-year period (UN projections).

Globally, military expenditures total about one trillion dollars a year and may continue to grow. Even in many developing countries, military spending adversely affects the struggle for development. At the UN World Summit in Rio in June 1992, detailed information about the issue was distributed to the world's NGOs (nongovernmental organizations). Various global programs for solving major human needs and environmental problems were presented, together with the annual costs for each program. Their combined total costs were shown to be approximately 25 percent of the world's total annual military expenditures (World Game Institute 1991).

It has become evident that the notion of "security" must be expanded to include the growing impacts of environmental stress. In all parts of the world, the arms race preempts resources that might be used more productively to diminish the security threats and resentments that are fueled by widespread poverty.

Over some decades a lawless interdependent market has generated dangerous global forces that are devastating local development and perpetuating injustice. These forces are rapidly becoming stronger, threatening the world with economic collapse and destroying the environment.

In a short period of time our human world of five billion must make room for five billion more. Ninety percent of the increase will occur in poor countries; 90 percent of that growth will be in already bursting cities. Industrial production has grown more than fiftyfold over the past century, and four-fifths of this growth has occurred since 1950.

Such figures presage profound impacts upon the biosphere, as the world invests in buildings, transportation, farms, and industries. Much of the economic growth draws raw material from forests, soils, seas, and waterways.

We are forced to concern ourselves with the impacts of economic growth on the environment. We can see before our eyes the degradation of soils, water, the atmosphere, and forests. There is a growing realization that it is impossible to separate economic developmental issues from environmental issues. Many forms of development erode the environmental resources upon which they must be based.

Environmental degradation, in turn, undermines economic development. Poverty is a major cause and effect of global environmental problems. It is futile to deal with environmental problems without addressing the factors underlying world poverty and international inequality.

A SHIFT IN PARADIGM

Our Beautiful and Fragile Planet

When in 1982 the Scandinavian peace movement organized a peace march from Stockholm to Moscow, we focused on the idea of the unity of our world. Valentina Tereshkova, the first woman cosmonaut, told us how she had been awakened to the feeling of caring for the planet when she was circling around it. "I marveled," she said, "at the beauty of our Earth, looking at it from space. I realized how tiny and fragile it is, suspended in the darkness of space; suddenly I knew that all of us belonged to *one* independent life-support system. The boundaries I knew when drawn on the map were just artificial; however we have hurt each other— the differences between us are insignificant—*compared to what we share.*"

Today an increasing number of people share this idea. More and more of us know that we are one human species belonging together on a fragile planet. We, as humans, must find a way of life that satisfies our basic needs *and* gives our life meaning and purpose. We have to learn to *care for* the integrated system that we belong to.

For tens of thousands of years, human beings were few on the planet. We were able to produce and transport what we needed without doing much damage to our environment. We had modest tools; we could burn, deforest, deplete, pollute, and even go to war over the best pieces of land. Families and cultures might become insecure, but the system as a whole was not threatened (Capra 1982, 1988).

Near the year 2000 now, we number five billion. Some of us have an enormous ability to destroy; many more of us do damage to our environment through our life-styles. At this moment in the history of Earth, humans can no longer choose whatever life-style they please. To violate others, or to violate nature, is to violate the system and therefore ourselves. Gradually we have started to acknowledge the idea that the value of education must be judged in relation to health and well-being for all humankind and for the planet as a whole. So, in the nineties we start to call for a new type of education.

The Old Way of Thinking

At this point in our history we have to learn new ways of understanding the present and future world. We have started to see that we are threatening our common future, and that something is fatally wrong with the values we cherish, and with our thinking and acting as well. Historically, the breakthroughs of natural science in the seventeenth century may explain the development of the Western educational system. Galileo, Descartes, and Francis Bacon established a way of thinking that made us separate intellect and understanding from emotion, creativity, humor, and wholeness, and separate a person from his or her surroundings.

Bacon established the alliance between *knowledge* and *power* that today, three hundred years later, has become an alliance between knowledge, government, and business. Natural science from the 1700s till now has laid the foundations for the way we cultivate the analytical human being and reward those who work in their various sectors in a "thought" world.

The worldview that emerged with Newton, Bacon, and Descartes includes these ideas:

- The universe is a mechanical system composed of elementary building blocks
- The human body functions like a machine and can be treated without understanding the human being as a whole
- Society is in a constant competitive struggle for existence
- The different human cultures are natural enemies; even more so are the different species
- Material progress is unlimited and may be achieved through technological and economic growth
- Human beings have a right to be in control of nature

In the seventeenth century the basis was established for what Paulo Freire prefers to call "modern education." Modern education is connected with an abstract and value-neutral tradition of knowledge that promotes the cultivation of certain habits of thought. Thinking sharply and clearly came to mean

- understanding problems and issues by dividing them into fragments,
- specializing in sectors of knowledge, and
- seeking for chains of cause and effect. (Freire 1970)

The British-American philosopher Gregory Bateson (1972) has characterized this worldview—which he calls the "old way of thinking"—by depicting a vicious circle, the dynamics of the ecological crisis: famine, population growth, war, high technology, pollution; all interconnected. He shows us that an important driving force in this vicious circle is the hubris, or arrogance, of the concept that human beings can and should be in control of nature (Bateson 1972, figure 1).

The Turning Point

Fritjof Capra writes in his book *The Turning Point* about a necessary "shift of paradigm" from an old way to a new way of thinking. The word *paradigm* means a shift in understanding; it concerns much more than "new thinking"—it concerns our whole world outlook and way of life. "A paradigm for me," he says, "would mean the totality of thoughts, perceptions and values that forms a particular vision of reality, a vision that is the basis of the way a society organizes itself" (Capra 1988). To Capra it is vital at this point in the history of human beings that we should have a new model of understanding when analyzing our problems. This model is characterized by *unity* and *interconnectedness* (Capra 1982).

New Thinking

In *Steps to an Ecology of Mind* (1972) and *Mind and Nature—A Necessary Unity* (1979), Bateson goes into the concept of "new thinking," basic alterations in all we think and do. This concept involves assuming a feeling of personal and historic responsibility for everything that lives on planet Earth. We can no longer do anything we choose. We must reject life-styles not compatible with the sustainability of nature. We need to cultivate our abilities to see the interconnected world, generated by our love of fellow human beings and of nature. *Ability to love* must be the core of education.

Gregory Bateson is among those who have laid the basis for a new tradition in thought better suited for the tasks of our time. The crises that threaten humans and the planet with collapse are better understood and dealt with by using as our tool *system thinking* and *ecological thinking* (Bateson 1972). This means to study phenomena

- as wholes instead of as fragments,
- as belonging together instead of as parts, and
- as circular instead of as chains of linear cause and effect.

From the start of our project we also studied the ideas of Mikhail Gorbachev, which at the time were expressed in his UN speeches and published in his book *Perestroika: New Thinking for Our Country and the World* (1987). Gorbachev outlines his views on new thinking in politics in terms of global systemic thinking, the emergence of thinking that perceives an interrelated and integral world. Efforts to solve global problems require "cooperation, co-creation and co-development." "The use or threat of force can no longer be an instrument of foreign policy" (Gorbachev, UN speech, 1989).

In the early seventies, Arne Naess made a distinction between "shallow" and "deep" ecology. *Shallow ecology* thinks of humans as above nature and the source of all value. Nature is something to be used by human beings, respectfully, but still for their own purposes. Deep ecology sees the world as a network of phenomena that are basically interconnected; all living beings have intrinsic value, and human beings are just one particular species in the web of life. The human spirit is understood as a consciousness in which the individual feels connected to the world as a whole (Naess 1988; see chapter 2, this volume).

Also in the seventies, Gregory Bateson wrote that the core of personality is the habits, attitudes, and expectations that have unconsciously been established through the ways we have been learning. These habits of thought continue to function as long as we do not make an effort to change them. Such habits may be transmitted down through the generations, just as we are "cultivated" in the way our parents and grandparents thought. When we as a later generation thought about the importance of competition and specialization, we might never have questioned these concepts, which then became the very ideas with which we thought. It is said that we as individuals are "cultivated" when we have "forgotten what we have learnt" (Bateson 1972).

According to Bateson, some of our "illusions," as he calls them, are unconscious parts of our culture. David Orr (1991) claims that the foundations for modern education laid down by Bacon, Galileo, and Descartes are "enshrined in myths that we have come to accept without question." Fritz Schumacher (1974) lists "leading ideas" in our present culture, all stemming from the nineteenth century, that still "dominate the minds of educated people today" (Schumacher 1974).

EDUCATION FOR A NEW WORLD

Throughout history the main idea behind education has been to introduce the existing culture to children and young people and stimulate them to take over and advance along the same lines. Education was to encourage work with concepts, knowledge, and values that were basic for the society of the time as well as find methods to help the new generation carry this on for future generations and make further progress.

Today we have abundant reason to view the dominant culture with skepticism. Do we dare to ask the young generation to go on developing our knowledge and life-style? It becomes more and more clear that the health of Earth is in danger; she may even collapse altogether. Our way of living threatens the stability of our climate, the vitality of the biosystems, and the health and beauty of nature. When we study the tragic effects of our civilization and our way of life, it is important to remember that the problems cannot be explained by lack of information, knowledge, schools, and education. The people who have been the leaders in the various fields of society—the academicians, the top politicians, the directors of production and trade, the leaders of our military systems—have had the best education available to them in their respective countries.

In 1990 Elie Wiesel made this point in a speech to the Global Forum in Moscow when he talked about how the designers and perpetrators of Auschwitz, Dachau, and Buchenwald—the designers of the Holocaust— were the heirs of Kant and Goethe. In most respects, he said, the Germans were the best-educated people on earth, but their education did not serve as an adequate barrier to barbarity.

What was wrong with their education, according to Wiesel? "It emphasized theories instead of values, concepts rather than human beings, instruction rather than consciousness, answers instead of questions, ideology and efficiency rather than conscience" (Wiesel 1990). Wiesel challenges modern education on the same basis as other contemporary critics, such as E. F. Schumacher, Paulo Freire, Wendel Barry, and David W. Orr. One recurring theme is that something must be wrong with an education that substitutes knowledge of technology for the understanding of human beings; substitutes inquiry into fragments for the study of nature in its complexity; substitutes efficiency in producing things for caring about living beings; and stresses the importance of competition instead of encouraging cooperation between human beings.

We can see these priorities when we are looking for the type of knowledge that is rewarded in the industrialized world. Most often our pride concerns education as the basis for amazing progress in science and technology; it has opened up new opportunities in the material field that we could not even imagine a hundred years ago. Today we also see that some of the results are far beyond what we might call "progress." We have technology that gives individuals and groups tremendous power of destruction. We can observe how individuals as well as firms rank efficiency in their own sector above what serves society and nature as a whole. For instance, consider the production of colossal machines to reshape landscapes that were developed over thousands of years; they use enormous amounts of harmful chemicals in vast areas, destroying land, rivers, and seas for future generations.

Gradually we are starting to look for a new mode of education that may benefit the health of human beings and the health of the planet as a whole. We have started to understand that human beings, with their needs and desires, must be recognized as an integral part of all life on Earth. In the 1990s we may see more clearly than before that it will be of vital importance to focus on such questions throughout the decade and into the next century.

We have started to suspect that education cannot save us and our planet merely by being extended. We have started to think that the only way to save the future for our children and grandchildren, and save the planet, is to restructure our system of education. We are beginning to look for *better* education.

HABITS OF THOUGHT

All through childhood and youth, before our conscious minds are developed, ideas seep into our minds, multitudes of them, in what Schumacher calls "the dark ages," during which we are only inheritors of ideas. When we begin to think, we can do so only because our mind is already filled with ideas with which to think (Schumacher 1974, 80).

We often notice that other people have more-or-less fixed ideas—ideas they think with without being aware of doing so. We call these "prejudices," which may be correct because these ideas have merely seeped into the mind and are in no way the result of judgment. They may be dangerous ideas, such as *Human beings are the superior species;* or *If this is my property, I can do with it whatever I like;* or *I used to be the best student, so I have the right to a higher salary.*

If ideas like *I ought to be superior* or *I ought to control others* seep into our minds in early childhood, we may go on believing in them, especially if we are never encouraged to reflect on our habits of thought or to discuss differences in basic ideas. Some nineteenth-century ideas are firmly lodged in the minds of most everybody who has had what Paulo Freire calls "modern education"—specific ideas about property, competition, power, efficiency. People who have not had much education receive such ideas all the same, if they do not have their own basis of understanding through everyday experience. We might talk about *the knowledge of experience*: the farmers' wisdom, fishermen's wisdom, women's wisdom, the wisdom of those who have reflected on their everyday lives. For anyone who is uneducated and also lacks the knowledge of experience, the "big ideas" of yesterday will not make the world intelligible. Such people long for an education that will help them find meaning and understanding; but modern education provides them with no guidance. It may be important to take a look at some of the habits of thought that are cultivated in traditional education.

Knowledge is Power

We tend to believe that knowledge is important because it gives us power. We tend to believe that when we get knowledge it should be used to get *power over* other people and over nature. This way of thinking directly intensifies the crises of our time. People who are trained in this habit of thought seek to maximize profit and exploit nature, just as we see being done in our superindustrialized world. In Bacon and Descartes's tradition we have accepted the belief that human beings can and ought to dominate other species and nature; that they can—and ought to—be able to control other humans.

The major part of higher education is constructed on this habit of thought. We have come to think that theoretical knowledge can eradicate ignorance and make it possible for us to have full knowledge of nature. With our huge machines, we are today in full swing of destroying living conditions for plants, animals, and humans on the planet, and of ruining the future by trying to dominate nature.

Gradually we are being forced to admit that theoretical knowledge will always lag behind when it comes to understanding reality in development. Living nature is always changing; we have to struggle to understand what has been and what is today, and we *never fully understand what is to come.* The insight we gradually get about the connectedness, the wholeness, that we are part of, helps us to discover our lack of knowledge, again and again. This continuous discovery makes it possible to become not only knowledgeable, but also *wise.*

We can never control the planet, in its ever-transforming complexity. If, like Goethe's wizard's apprentice, we live in the illusion of having such power, we may start processes that we cannot stop when they have gotten into their stride.

Instead of trying in vain to get control over nature, our main objective as human beings should be to learn how to control ourselves, our own wishes, our life together with others, our local community, our society. We may then, as time passes, learn to live together and learn to live in peace with nature. We cannot risk the future of the planet by trusting in a game, however well we think we know the rules of the bargain.

Technology as Problem Solver Number One

A dangerous habit of thought is the belief that technology can solve our problems. We have seen how technology can do what we tend to call "miracles." Today a powerful trend seems to support the idea that we can pollute rivers, seas, and oceans, cut down enormous rain forests, transform huge landscapes—and rely on future technology to repair the damage done to the planet.

Today we tend to believe that we can restore, even reconstruct, a living system, such as a destroyed rain forest, with the help of technology. We tend to believe that if we understand the different parts, the whole may be taken to pieces and put together again at will. We cannot know what future technology will be able to achieve; but to act as if we know is stupendous irresponsibility.

Young people today can go through modern education and reach their twenties without ever gaining an understanding of the connection between the various disciplines of knowledge. We train economists who do not, in their evaluation of welfare, take into account elementary ecology. They are not aware of the costs that are handed over to the next generation when resources are exploited, the soil destroyed, air and water polluted. They do not take into account that the use of resources may damage an ecoregion. This is not because they do not know the facts, but because they work inside an artificially limited sector.

Gregory Bateson is among those who take a stand against these habits of thought arising from life in a sectorized society. He writes about an obsolete way of thinking that is characterized by these basic beliefs:

- it is us against the environment, it is us against other human beings;
- it is the individual (individual firm, nation) that counts;
- we can control nature and always achieve new ways of controlling;
- we live within limits that can always be extended;
- it is primarily economic laws that decide developments;
- technology can solve our present and future problems;
- book knowledge surpasses knowledge developed from experience.

(Bateson 1972)

The Illusion that Book Knowledge is Superior

A third habit of thought—or illusion—is the idea that knowledge arrived at through books is more important than knowledge arrived at through personal experience. This way of thinking is cultivated in our educational system even though it has met with skepticism throughout the centuries (for instance, in Molière's comedies about people who understand everything "in heaven" but nothing in everyday life).

It is a deeply rooted perception that book education is the number one bearer of culture. Specialists are expected to have a decisive word when decisions are made, for instance, with regard to child care, illness, and death, as well as national politics. We forget that a specialist is one who knows more and more about less and less. We have come to believe that less formal education means greater ignorance.

This perception of education has lost sight of the basic knowledge that every person has—knowledge we get through our own experience throughout life. Through experiences in our families, at play, at work, in nature, through perceiving ourselves being together, working together, talking together, we learn basic skills, learn what responsibility is, what happiness is, what creativity is, what it means to manage to give and receive help and to solve problems together with others. We learn that we ourselves are part of the wonderful nature around us, and that animals and flowers, like human beings, have their own specific value and beauty. All this human knowledge can be lost if nothing but formal education is given throughout childhood and youth. "For what shall it profit a man, if he shall gain the whole world, and lose his own soul?"

Competition Is the Main Motivation

A fourth habit of thought basic to our educational system is that a person learns more and better through competition. Our world does not need more people competing with each other. Reaching the top in riches and success is definitely not needed as an aim of education.

What the planet needs is an increasing number of people working for a healthy natural environment, healthy values, healthy political systems, a healthy economy, and healthy living conditions for everybody. But the system of education as it has developed throughout the last few hundred years does not contribute to justice, care, cooperation, or sound living conditions. Instead the educational system focuses on grades, notes, marks, competition, a ranking system.

Our Culture Leads to Progress

Another dangerous habit of thought, or illusion, is that our civilization represents the pinnacle of human achievement. Such a view shows a frightening lack of insight into the history of humankind and makes us close our eyes to dangerous fallacies in our civilization. It is the fashion nowadays to talk about the West as having won the cold war between East and West, and to claim that capitalism has shown its superiority to communism.

It is clear enough that the authoritarian communism of the former Soviet Union and in many countries throughout the world has collapsed because neither human beings nor nature can exist under an autocratic control system for long periods.

But the capitalist system has failed as well. It has also destroyed nature; it stands for injustice and exploitation of resources. The capitalist system is also trading with our future. The system fails also because it destroys our values and sets the demand for "economic freedom" as its highest value. The capitalist system has built a world of profit for the few and a world of poverty for hundreds of millions of people. Capitalism today is a culture in disintegration; it does not cultivate ethical values, beauty, or compassion, nor does it encourage responsibility and cooperation (Orr 1991).

It does not bode well for our collective insight into nature that people over large parts of the planet are being driven from the countryside into the big cities, driven from responsibility for soil, forest, and water into the slum areas of the metropolis and skyscrapers. Those who take over the deserted areas of the countryside and manage soil, forest, and water today are increasingly the far-off firms and directors who do not themselves experience the effects of their operations (Orr 1991).

It is possible to go on listing habits of thought like those mentioned above, key concepts in our educational system; in the current context the five ideas mentioned may suffice to show that we take ideas for granted just because they are *habits of thought*. They were leading ideas of the nineteenth century that claimed to do away with metaphysics, but were themselves a life-destroying type of metaphysics. We are suffering from them as from a fatal disease, one that may bring unlimited sorrow in the third and fourth generations. The errors are not in science, but in philosophy (Schumacher 1974, 88ff.).

THE MAIN ISSUES

As we approach the twenty-first century, we realize that an "economistic" worldview is dominating our world. The human species is divided into a small minority participating in managing society and an ever-increasing majority who are onlookers. Too few people are participants outside their close family groups. The result is that, unintentionally, we humans are poisoning and destroying our world. Too few have authority and training when it comes to protecting living systems. Life on the planet, plants and animals, children and adults, get too little care and too little love. The question presents itself with increasing force: How can the educational system prepare the young for the most important of all tasks— responsibility and caring? What are we looking for in an educational system of today? Let us mention just four urgent tasks.

Better, Not More, Knowledge

Up to the present time we have believed that if the amount of knowledge increases, human beings will be better equipped to solve problems. But most of the knowledge "exploding" around us does not at all increase our insight into important issues. Most of the flood of knowledge concerns more and more limited sectors that do not improve our insight and understanding. We get too little of the knowledge that can help us to understand our lives and the connection between ourselves and nature.

There are more and more people in authority who know a lot about specialties, who "are famous all over the world among those three that understand what they are talking about." What we need is more people who know a lot about human beings and about society as a whole, the local society, the country, nature.

Learning for Life

Education is not first and foremost to master academic disciplines. Every subject ought to be a tool for mastering oneself as a person in the society one belongs to. A knife is a dangerous tool for those who cannot master themselves; a knife is indispensable for those who can. We stop a two- or three-year-old who wants to handle a sharp knife. Slowly, through information and training, the small child gets to know how to use the knife. The training begins with a knife that is not dangerous and continues with sharper and more pointed ones, as the child's ability to be responsible increases.

The learning of knowledge and skills, learning to use tools, must be combined with the possibility to learn how the tools are to be used in the environment one belongs to. This principle is valid for all types of knowledge and training. The person who is learning has to practice and get training in responsibility: *how to use one's knowledge and skills.* Education must therefore be organized as *a combination of theory and practice.* A learning program is not finished until the content of it is put into use.

We have dangerous examples of how technology is used in irresponsible ways, as in the case of radioactive materials and harmful chemicals that poison the soil and destroy the ozone layer. The Chernobyl accident, the desertification of Africa, and the destruction of the rain forests in the Amazon are disasters caused by people who have power to use the tools without having learned to take responsibility. The accidents will continue and increase in size until we get a new mode of education that combines knowledge and skills with training in responsibility and consciousness of values.

Ecological Responsibility

Education must further ecological responsibility. All students must learn to see themselves as part of nature. In earlier times, each generation had to learn that drinking water should be protected against pollution and the resources of the local society should be protected against exploitation. Today we must learn that nature as a whole must be protected. We must learn that we are not allowed to use tools for our own benefit if that use of tools destroys part of nature today or in the future. During the decades ahead we will not avoid these ecological demands. They concern curricula at all levels. Students must learn ecology in theory as well as in practice. To learn a discipline—economics, for instance—without studying the ecological implications of the production of goods can never be useful training; on the contrary, such training is dangerous.

Learning through Examples

Education for our time means education for a new life-style, *experiencing* the connection between theory and practice. The South American educationist Paulo Freire liberated new cultural forces by encouraging habits of learning through personal experience and change of life-style.

In the education that Paulo Freire organized, the adult students worked in their jobs and at the same time chose their own themes for study connected with their everyday lives. They were learning theory that was useful in connection with their own praxis. To practice on the basis of theory that concerns one's own problems means to acquire knowledge that develops independence and self-respect.

The opposite happens when, in the system of education, lessons about threats against nature and about human responsibility do not lead to the use of the knowledge in practice. Protection of nature may be taught at the same time as the school itself contributes to wasting resources and polluting the surroundings. Through this procedure the educational system demonstrates hypocrisy and apathy. The students then learn first and foremost that society and they themselves are helpless with regard to the future. It is vital that education combine information with ways of *using* that information. Education must organize action in accordance with the message, combine words and deeds—the first and second orders of communication. This is not done in today's schools, the most visible lesson of which is to acquiesce and be resigned.

The setting of the learning program becomes decisive; methods and ways of learning are just as important as content; the process is just as important as the product. A text or a theme that is handed over to the students to learn by heart or to study at their desks becomes training in passivity—or even apathy. When classrooms are not connected with possibilities for practice, the whole school design announces that the content and material of knowledge are isolated from reality.

Such students study maps about deforestation and statistics about chlorofluorocarbon emissions, get information about the depletion of the ozone layer, and see pictures of starving children in Somalia, but the students themselves are left standing outside the picture. They are not invited to join in any action to improve the situation or to take a step to contribute to an alternative development.

The architecture of buildings for this type of formal education announces that the students are onlookers and are expected to stay with their books. The buildings would look different if they were organized for cooperation, initiative, participation, responsibility, and ecological projects.

CONCLUSION

Today humanity has arrived at a turning point in its history; the educational system must, as must all facets of society, redefine its task. Taking into account the knowledge we have about the health of the planet, the task is nothing less than to bring about—during the coming two or three decades—manifest changes in our cultures and life-styles. The basic need is for the new generations to learn how to combine crucial knowledge with the power to act vigorously on the basis of common values, universal human rights, cooperation, and harmony with nature.

Together the generations must redefine their collective work for the health and welfare of nature and human beings. Students need to develop ways of thinking based on insight into connectedness and the fact that their actions have impacts like rings in the water. To eradicate destitution all over the world is our common cause. To prevent global warming, erosion of the topsoil, and the thinning out of the ozone layer are concrete and practical tasks here and now. Through education, students should be able to see what they can do to protect nature and take care of their fellow human beings. In work with practical tasks they should be able to learn stewardship and develop the courage to make changes.

A new type of education will organize for participation in protecting the environment. Through education, students will learn to see that they are part of the living network of society and nature itself. Gradually, as a majority gets this type of education, a transformation of life-style and culture will establish a safer basis for life on Earth and a future for humankind.

An ecological and cooperative education encourages human beings to learn the *habits* of interaction and cooperation, the *attitudes* of searching for knowledge and taking initiative, and the *expectations* of choosing action on the basis of sustainable values. At this point in our history it is vital to remind ourselves that we have enough knowledge and better means than ever before to change our system of education into global cooperation for a better future.

REFERENCES

Bateson, Gregory. 1972. *Steps to an Ecology of Mind.* New York: Ballantine Books.

———. 1979. *Mind and Nature: A Necessary Unity.* New York: Bantam.

Berry, Wendell. 1987. *Home Economics.* San Francisco: North Point Press.

Capra, Fritjof. 1982. *The Turning Point.* New York: Simon and Schuster.

———. 1988. *Uncommon Wisdom.* New York: Bantam.

Drew, Naomi. 1987. *Learning the Skills of Peacemaking. An Activity Guide for Elementary Age Children on Communicating, Cooperating, Resolving Conflicts.* Rolling Hills Estates, Calif.: Hjalmar Press.

Erikson, Erik H. 1969. *Gandhi's Truth: On the Origins of Militant Non-violence*. New York: Norton.

Freire, Paolo. 1970. *Pedagogy of the Oppressed*. New York: Herder & Herder.

Gorbachev, Mikhail. 1987. *Perestroika: New Thinking for Our Country and the World*. New York: Harper.

Macy, Joanna Rogers. 1983. *Despair and Personal Power in the Nuclear Age*. Philadelphia: New Society.

Miller, Ron. 1990. Editorial in *Holistic Education Review*, Spring.

Naess, Arne. 1988. *Ecology, Community, and Lifestyle: Outline of an Ecosophy*. New York: Cambridge University Press.

Orr, David W. 1991. "What is Education For?" *Trumpeter*, 3 August.

Schumacher, E. F. 1974. *Small is Beautiful: A Study of Economics as if People Mattered*. Great Britain: Abacus.

Wiesel, Elie. 1990. "Global Education." Speech presented to the Global Forum, January, Moscow.

World Game Institute. 1991. *What the World Wants—and How to Pay for It*. Philadelphia, Pa.: World Game Institute.

2
Learning Our Way to a Human Future

Betty Reardon

The ideas and arguments set forth in this essay summarize a variety of learning experiences, each of which has contributed to broadening the conceptual framework within which I view peace education, and each of which has moved me from a systemic structural view of the world and education to a process, organic view.

Many of us now consider our work in terms of pre- and post-*ecological consciousness*.

For me my work with PEACE (Project on Ecological and Cooperative Education) was, and for the moment continues to be, an experience of the awakening of ecological consciousness. Certainly I had factored the global environment into the diagnosis of problems threatening human survival when considering the content to be addressed by peace education. However, although even in the earliest stages of my work in the field I applied a global perspective and a systematic analysis of world society, the anthropocentrism pointed out by Sergei Polozov was, I believe, for many years an unrecognized barrier to the prescriptive tasks I advocated as an element of peace education. I have long believed that the prime requisite of being an effective peace educator is to be, as well, an intentional learner.

My years of work in developing theoretical bases for peace education and in the design and execution of a graduate program in the field have reinforced this belief. My deepening acquaintance with ecological thinking has been an exceptionally rich learning experience.

It has helped me in achieving a paradigm shift that when applied to a global perspective can best be described as a shift from a "spaceship Earth" view of the world as a mechanical (if unified, closed-system) structure controlled by human society, to a *Gaia* view of Earth as a living organism with human society as a living subsystem within the whole, responsible but certainly not in control. That, it seems to me, is a learning to be further pursued and disseminated.

THE NEW MOMENT: THE EDUCATIONAL CHALLENGES AND OPPORTUNITIES

To those of us who have been involved in peace education for several decades, the last years of the twentieth century have been the most surprising, frequently the most hopeful, sometimes depressing, and unfailingly the most challenging.

Over the years, while some have tried to take a positive stance and educate *for peace,* most have found it necessary to spend much of our efforts to educate *against war* in order to define and describe the actual and potential consequences of weapons and violence, often to the detriment of education about other global issues and problems. Rarely were our students' minds opened to the real and potential possibilities of peace. Consequently we all know a good deal more about what we don't want and how it is affecting the quality of our lives than about what we do want and how our lives can be directed toward achieving it. We in North America watched in surprise and awe as the peoples of Eastern Europe took action to shake off what they did not want; and we reflected, in the same confusion and uncertainty as our European brothers and sisters, on what should replace it, with little or no notion of how to deal with the problems and conflicts of the transition from one system to another.

Many of us believe that neither of the economic or political systems that dominated the twentieth century are truly adequate to a viable, just, and attainable common future, but little has been done to develop authentic alternatives.

The challenge then for all, but most especially for educators, whose main social responsibility is preparing people for the future, is to envision such an alternative and to devise the educational means to learn to achieve it.

What the New Moment Means for Learning: The Responsibilities of Educators

In virtually every nation of the world, and most certainly in the industrial nations of the North, contemporary educational systems have been organized around two major purposes: keeping the respective system or nation ahead of its competitors, and keeping the managers of the system in power by popular support or repression or a combination thereof. None have fully succeeded. While the early nineties saw the Western "industrial democracies" engaging in an orgy of self-congratulation on the defeat of Communism in the "former socialist states," the truth is that both systems had exhausted their capacities to maintain a limitless arms race, manipulate the destinies of the rest of the world, and at the same time satisfy the authentic needs of their own peoples.

All the industrial states, both capitalist and socialist—even intensely rich Western Europe and Japan—emerged from the period of the cold war with larger portions of their populations in poverty than was to be admitted freely. They also experienced spiritual poverty, with unprecedented levels of alienation, widespread feelings of emptiness and meaninglessness, among all income groups. Worldwide, educational systems were in deep crisis.

What was most disturbing about the crisis in education was that it was almost universally misinterpreted as a cause of, rather than as the consequence of, the inadequacies of the general social systems. All societies, particularly in the industrialized democracies, failed to acknowledge that the schools were but a reflection of the failure of the entire society to recognize that it was not focusing its learning processes on what people most needed to know and understand, and not taking into account the severe alienation and despair among the most deprived classes who depended upon public schooling.

Once again schools were scapegoated for larger societal shortcomings. Unlike their socialist counterparts, they did not quickly recognize that they, too, were in a new moment. The task of calling it to their attention fell largely upon peace educators.

What peace educators saw in the new moment was an opportunity to at last come to terms with the shortcomings of the society, to take a leaf from the Eastern European book and assess needs and possibilities in a new light. Most especially, I would argue, the major need was to come to terms with the damage done to others in the world system and to the most vulnerable in their own societies by the obsessive competition with the other industrial states, particularly those aspects of competition manifest in the cold war. While the decade opened with a new awareness of the fragility and abuse of the natural environment, the degree to which that fragility was exacerbated and the abuses allowed to run rampant through the behaviors of the agents carrying out the economic, ideological, and strategic competitions of the international system was hardly recognized by either the environmental or the peace movements, or even by the budding ecological education movement. Coming to terms with the environmental and human rights abuses of the cold war thus was taken up as a learning task of PEACE.

Learning to understand the nature and consequences of the abuses, to take responsibility for them, and to find alternative possibilities for education, personal behaviors, and public policies became a central concern of the project. The project tries to focus on positive alternatives: not just on what it means to be *against* war, injustice, human rights violations, and environmental deterioration, but what it is to be *for* peace, justice, the realization of human rights, and ecological balance. The task it assumes is to give concrete form to a peaceful, just society that respects human rights and protects the environment, and to educate people to achieve and maintain a global social order of such form.

We seek to move educational inquiry from the questions of what are the dangers of war, injustice, and environmental abuse, and how they can be avoided, to what are the advantages and forms of peace, justice, and ecological balance, how they are inextricably interrelated, and how they can be achieved and maintained—a seemingly simple but profoundly transformative shift of learning focus.

The Particular Responsibilities of the United States and the Countries of the Former USSR for New Learning

If we conceptualize the human species as a family and this century as a generation, we can begin to understand the human and historic consequences of nearly half a century of superpower competition. The human family has been through a painful and devastating experience not unlike that suffered by families parented by addicts (to alcohol, drugs, gambling, or whatever). The family resources are laid waste by the addiction while the family members suffer from lack of care and mutually enhancing, supportive relationships. The coaddictive parents engage in mutual recrimination while the children and other family members must endure the atmosphere of tension, of potential and actual violence. The parents abuse their power, abjure their responsibility, and seek to impose their own will on each other and all others in the family system without regard to the immediate or the long-range consequences.

Such behavior usually continues unless there is a crisis or an intentional intervention by those affected. In terms used to describe approaches to therapy in addictive families, "an intervention" is an occasion on which those suffering "the fallout" from the addiction gather around the addicted member or members and describe in full and frank detail their own suffering while acknowledging the value and potential of the addicted ones. In essence the message is this: "Look, we are all one family, part of one system, we have received much from you that is positive and nurturing (i.e., economic support, defense, etc.); but your addiction is inflicting damage on us we can no longer bear. We may not survive as a family, or group of friends or associates. You have to stop if you want to maintain a relationship with us."

The Soviet and Eastern European crises, the emerging integration of the European Community, the multiple continued regional conflicts such as that which produced the war in the Persian Gulf, and the growing recognition of the environmental crisis—together these offer the opportunity for such an intervention. Some peace educators seized the opportunity. The participants of PEACE were among them.

The intervention message to the former adversaries of the cold war (and perhaps to the newly emerging power constellation first demonstrated by the Gulf War) from such peace educators is this: "Look, you must take mutual and respective responsibility for what you have done to the world. You have to reconstruct your relationship to each other and to the rest of the world. You are no longer able to control either your own people or other peoples. You and other great techno-industrial powers must construct a relationship that is based on the values of planetary health, an ecologically viable system that attempts to meet human needs equitably and respects human rights universally. You have much learning to do, but you have rich and varied learning resources. You can learn from each other, and from other peoples, particularly the primal peoples who have lived in harmony with the Earth. Above all, much can be learned from Earth itself, particularly about balance, restraint, and renewal. You must acknowledge now that you must be learners from rather than instructors to the world."

An Emerging Paradigm for Security and Community: Learning for a Transformed World Order

The new moment provides an unprecedented opportunity for the two former superpowers that emerged from World War II to bring to actuality many of the values that informed that particular struggle and that formed the basis of a vision of the world the peoples of the two nations had embraced together as their soldiers embraced each other at the Elbe, a vision they sought to enact in the founding of the United Nations. We now have an opportunity to view the four decades from 1949 to 1989 as an aberrant interruption in the history of humankind on the brink of recognizing and experiencing its fundamental unity. The human liberty of any people cannot be achieved within the context of a debased environment or reduced quality of life for other humans. While we were preoccupied with our competition with each other, we stepped up without reflection our common competition with the Earth, and equally carelessly ignored the consequent impoverishment and oppression of our brothers and sisters in the South.

Thus we are challenged by still another common learning task, a radical restructuring of our relationship not only to the planet, but also to the majority of those who inhabit her, the poor of the Earth. As nations we need to learn our responsibility to world society; as educators we need to prepare our students to carry social responsibility at all levels, from local to global. Social responsibility requires that we recognize ourselves as members of a world community held together by concepts of common security, liberty, and humanity.

The peace movement has indeed been proven correct in its insistence that the arms race, the major dynamic of the cold war, has eroded security, and that true security involves much more than the capacity to defend against or prevent military aggression. Authentic security lies in the welfare and dignity of people, in relationships that reduce conflict and prevent violence, and in a viable environment that can sustain life on this planet. The task of building a world community involves the design and adoption of a security system that gives equal attention to all four elements of authentic, viable human security: environment, justice, dignity, and nonviolence.

The attention of research centers, educational institutions, and all other learning groups must be turned to learning to design and achieve such a global system. In short, we need to learn how to transform the institutions and relationships that comprise a world of violence, inequity, and environmental devastation.

PROJECT ON ECOLOGICAL AND COOPERATIVE EDUCATION:
A RESPONSE TO THE CHALLENGE OF LEARNING TO TRANSFORM

PEACE emerged out of the common recognition of a small group of Norwegian, Russian (later also Ukrainian), and American educators of the urgent need for this kind of learning. The essays in this book, our first reflections on the task, are one step toward developing appropriate common learning processes centered on the transformational tasks as we mutually define them.

We worked together first in Norway to define the problems and approaches; then in New York to share practical workshops in specific educational methods; and later in Moscow to elaborate the plans for this volume. We continue to work together to move the learning process forward by learning from and with each other and, where possible, from and with educators from other parts of the world. While we seek to define common approaches and concepts, we also recognize and try to fulfill the unique and special responsibilities of our respective societies.

The Task and the Goal for the
North American Educational Community

If American peace educators designate a healthy environment, economic equity, human rights, and nonviolent conflict resolution as the major needs for a transformed world order, then we must accept some very challenging goals for the American educational community. These challenges arise in large part from the role the United States has played in the creation of problems of environmental degradation, global poverty, human rights abuses, and armed conflict.

Our schools should study the nature of the resource exploitation and the flow of primary resources from South to North that gave rise to American affluence at the cost of increased poverty for many in the developing countries, a consequence of terms of trade negotiated to the advantage of "Northern industrialized" over "Southern developing" nations.

A curriculum on the consequences of the cold war should certainly include a global review of the history and condition of human rights concepts and abuses, including consideration of American support for policies that resulted in such abuses as apartheid and the military repression of liberation movements. And study of the history of armed conflict in the twentieth century must offer the facts on the technological achievements of the American defense industry that fueled the cycles of the arms race, as well as American interventions in other nations. Such interventions were often viewed as serious threats to world peace by allies as well as adversaries.

An Ecological Framework

It has become very clear that the substance of our first phase should be derived from issues and concerns about the environment. In the eighties, with the rise in tensions between the two nations, public concern centered on the threats to world peace, human survival, and global security posed by nuclear weapons. At the beginning of the nineties, with the decrease in cold war tensions and the greater openness to nuclear arms control, it came to focus on "ecological security" and the threats to human survival posed by the degradation of the biosphere.

As the peace researchers of the late sixties and seventies extended the *problématique* of violence beyond armed conflict and war to include the problems of the structural violence of poverty and oppression, broadening the concerns for peace studies and peace research, so violence against the Earth now has taken a significant place in the field. Peace with the planet is seen as inextricably interwoven with peace among and within nations.

The field of conflict resolution is applied to environmental disputes at all levels, from international to local. Environmental issues give rise to actual and potential international conflicts. "Environmental security" is a major issue before the United Nations. The environmental damage caused by the Persian Gulf war is significant evidence of the ecological costs of those hostilities and of all war. The environment is a "hot topic" for peace educators, and ecology is a theme linked with many other issues of global concern.

For PEACE, however, ecology has meaning beyond the study of environmental problems, and beyond the broad study of organisms in their environments. By "ecological education" we mean, of course, those two areas, but even more. For this project the ecological approach emphasizes relationships and interlinkages. It is a way of thinking that is grounded in *holism*, in the consideration of an issue, a topic, or a problem in the broadest possible context—where possible, within the largest system of which the topic at issue is a part. In most cases this means bringing a planetary perspective to bear on the themes of study.

There are a number a characteristics of an ecological approach that serve to illuminate much of the value base of the project. Perhaps the most central concept of the approach is balance, or *harmony within a whole*. Among the fundamental ecological concepts, this one also reflects the aspirations we as educators have for the world system of nations and for human-Earth relations. We see the desirable goal as the achievement of a mutually enhancing balance of relationships and functions within the whole system concerned. This idea relates to political, economic, and learning processes that maintain living systems. Thus we can see several important value-reflecting balances in an ecological approach: among them, fragility and resilience, vulnerability and sustainability, anticipation and avoidance, extraction and replenishment, and even conflict and security. Exploring ways of maintaining these balances within social and economic as well as ecological systems reveals some of our hopes for what ecological learning can contribute to the achievement of a just, peaceful global social order.

The Meaning and Promise of Cooperative Learning

Balance as a characteristic of ecological thinking also connotes *interdependence*. While it has appeared to the human observer that there are elements of competition in natural systems, this seeming competition is in essence a component of the succession and sustainability of the entire system. It is the form that interdependence takes, and it is kept in balance for the health of the system.

Components of natural systems do not encounter each other's existence as threatening the survival of the system. Predators prey upon other life forms, but the intent is their own survival, not the weakening and destruction of the life form represented by the prey. Indeed, in some cultures the reflective predator, the human who hunts for food, offers prayers of thanksgiving to the prey and observes the hunt as an act to sustain not only human life but the great chain of life itself. Far from being an act of competition, so observed, the hunt is a reflection of interspecies cooperation. Yet we humans have brought the hunt, and other modes through which we have come to seek to sustain *only our own survival,* to the ultimate stages of competition, modern warfare, in which humans can wipe out entire groups of our own species, even the species itself, in the name of their own survival.

That competition and aggression are intractable attributes of human nature was long upheld by popular wisdom and even by scientific treatises. However, in recent years we have come to learn that it was more likely the attributes of cooperation and association that enabled the human species to survive and culture to evolve (Howell and Willis 1989). Unfortunately, more of the former assumptions than the latter notions still characterize educational practice, especially in those industrial nations in which the market determines production.

In these nations a high value is placed on competition, and preparation for success in competition is seen as a major task of education and socialization. Individual and group competition pervades the Western and, to some degree, other educational systems, from sliding-scale grading to often potentially dangerous physical contact sports. Some have interpreted these educational practices as being as much preparation for warfare as preparation for the marketplace. Even in some socialist societies there has been the element of preparing to compete against other systems. Creativity and cooperation, two human capacities essential to the survival and development of the species, have traditionally been given little role in the educational systems of most industrialized countries.

Over the past decade this condition has been not only the subject of criticism by educational reformers, but the theme of a growing movement in educational practice, *cooperative learning.* This practice has thus far been used more in the elementary grades than in secondary and higher education, but among some peace educators, at the more advanced levels, some aspects of cooperative learning are now being adapted to broaden and intensify the learning of high school and university students.

Cooperation is a basic component of all sustainable social systems, even those of authoritarian dictatorships, for without the cooperation or the acquiescence of the majority of a population such systems could not maintain themselves.

In essence, any system is a set of interrelated parts operating together to perform a function or achieve a purpose. Even if that purpose be the repression of some of the parts, those parts, just like the others, must work together, "cooperate," else the function cannot be performed or the purpose achieved.

Refusal to cooperate is a major form of passive resistance that has weakened and sometimes crippled systems as effectively as have rebellions. All systems can tolerate some dysfunctional parts for some time, but none can sustain themselves when dysfunctionality extends over long periods of time or involves multiple components.

Indeed, we can say that the world political system found the competition between the United States and the former Soviet Union to be dysfunctional and weakening. The two powers, themselves part of that system, suffered in some ways equally seriously. Both paid a high price in long-range economic well-being, social integration, and cultural development.

Each had viewed the other as being so threatening that they interpreted the threat as one to the entire system, and behaved accordingly, to the point where they brought the entire system to the possibility of collapse. Predation without reflection, or thanksgiving without the authentic purposes of balance or survival, destroys interdependence, often decimating essential parts of a system. The hunting of North American buffalo for "sport" contributed to the devastation of the native American population, whose way of life depended upon that animal; similarly the predatory interventions of the two superpowers in the internal affairs of other nations, when each feared that the rival power was making some gain in the area, weakened and in some cases virtually destroyed the possibilities of freedom in the prey countries while eroding that precious political commodity in their own countries. Predatory intervention endangers the entire system, destroying it or transforming it into another system. The competition between the United States and the USSR brought the world to such a point.

The potential for freedom and democracy that emerged at the end of World War II was transposed into worldwide militarization and repression. We of PEACE believe that the new moment, the possibilities offered by the end of the cold war between the two superpowers, is one of potential positive transformation, a *climax condition* that can move the world to a new political system that is less predatory, less competitive, more peaceful, and more just. We believe this to be possible primarily because of the human capacity to cooperate. Our project is an experiment in such cooperation; we educators are ourselves engaging in cooperative learning.

Cooperative learning as an intentional teaching mode gained wider attention and new adherents in the United States in the late 1980s. Developed out of a theory that acknowledges the significance of personal interaction in learning and emphasizes the variety in learning styles to be found among any group of learners, it advocates setting common learning or problem-solving tasks to be addressed cooperatively by groups of students working together.

It is argued that most of the common learning goals pursued in schools can be achieved by cooperative methods, and further that the learning experience is more rewarding to the participants, whose individual strengths can be applied to the task while their weaknesses can be substituted for by the capacities of others. It is a mode that uses human diversity and complementarity in a mutually advantageous way. It also provides experience that teaches appreciation of diversity and community building in the most practical way, by involving the learners in setting and striving for a common goal approached from diverse perspectives within a context of multiple possibilities.

In this new moment in which we must learn, as nations and as a species, to work together as one system, cooperative learning is probably the most effective educational method. Our greatest need is for all peoples to learn to function together as a single social system whose purpose is to create circumstances that, as Willard Jacobson (chapter 4) observes, allow "all to be the best they can be"—at the inequitable expense of none. That groups, individuals, even ideologies and whole and varied societies can cooperate, functioning together toward a common end, has been demonstrated within nations by the formation of coalitions around some common national goal. Similarly, it has been demonstrated internationally with alliances and in some regional arrangements. It must now be manifest at the global level. The two major issues that urgently call for such integration of goals and collaboration in efforts to achieve them are saving the natural environment and the abolition of war.

Both of these goals require full, integral, global cooperation, and neither is possible within the present structures, institutions, and policies that comprise the world's sociopolitical system, the international system. Indeed, this system of nation-states is premised upon the sovereign right of each state to do as it wills in its own interest without restraint or consideration of others or the whole system, and most are prepared to do so. This system has been called "the war system." Each nation can at will take up arms against others. Even the United Nations Charter, which was drafted to prevent war, cannot restrain member states from taking up arms against others if they deem it necessary for their "defense." And even though the United Nations peacekeeping forces were awarded the Nobel Peace Prize in 1988, all states are still basically responsible for their own "national security."

Neither can any agent or institution in the system legally restrain others from polluting Earth's atmosphere, destroying her forests, dumping wastes into her waters, or overcultivating her topsoil. Such actions are physical assaults, forms of aggression against the life and health of the planet. All states are still basically irresponsible toward Earth's "ecological security" and the human species' "environmental security."

Indeed, nations still think and behave in terms that give primacy to "national security" over all other human concerns. Such a view of security has become dysfunctional and dangerous. Its heavy emphasis on the military not only results in the tragic social consequences of military expenditures (see chapter 1), it results in many other system-damaging consequences that come from the competitive view nations or alliances of nations have taken of each other. Such a view, like the concept of national security itself, is based on a fundamental fallacy: that nations are separate, autonomous entities, systems unto themselves. While the common public discourse now incorporates the concept of interdependence, and the global economy is built upon that concept (though not on an equitable and mutual form of interdependence, as Eva Nordland points out in chapter 1), respect for interdependence has not been the primary characteristic of international relations. Nations still conduct foreign policy as though they were independent and as though other nations are more likely to harm than help them, for such is how they perceive the "real world." This situation has profound implications for education. As implied in the previous remarks on the dominance of the competitive mode in our schools, education has reinforced the "realist" view both in the content of what is taught about world politics and in the way it is taught.

The deep entrenchment of these notions in the way we think now represents one of the great challenges to education. This challenge, we believe, can best be met through ecological and cooperative education, organizing and presenting content in a holistic, integrated, and interrelated form, following an instructional process in which learners work together to seek understanding and work to build both individual and communal knowledge. Such content and process emphasize both the uniqueness of the components of the content and the capacities of the individuals in the process, in ways that orchestrate these differences for the benefit of the whole and the mutual enhancement of all.

PEACE is attempting to engage in such learning itself as it advocates and facilitates ecological and cooperative education in the schools of our respective countries.

TOWARD GLOBAL COOPERATION AND SOCIAL RESPONSIBILITY: LEARNING FOR RESPONSIBLE CITIZENSHIP IN A PLURALISTIC WORLD

Just as *ecology* and *cooperation* are the two key concepts that characterize the pedagogy we believe most likely to facilitate learning toward a human future, *pluralism* and *responsibility* are key concepts that characterize the type of global society that we believe would assure a human future. Just as functional collaboration and diversity of life forms are essential to the life-assuring balance of living systems, so too pluralism and responsibility are essential to a just, peaceful, and viable social system. Social systems, to maintain viability and vigor, must nurture human variety of all kinds.

In ethnically homogeneous societies, this variety may be said to be adequate if various individual capacities and talents and other forms of human diversity and viewpoints are nurtured. In ethnically (and, we might also argue, ideologically) mixed societies, the varieties of cultures and modes of thought must also be intentionally cultivated. Such conditions are essential to our notion of democracy that derives from the belief that the broader and more varied the human resource base, the more successful a society is likely to be. Above all, a successful democracy encourages full and responsible participation of all citizens.

Our Vision of a Democratic World Society: The Observation of Comprehensive, Universal Human Rights

A world society in which universal ethnic, cultural, and political pluralism and active social responsibility are seen as central to the success of the society, in our terms, would be authentically democratic. Most significantly, it would be ecological, in this sense: it would be understood that the true health, welfare, and sustainability of all the component parts would be fully interdependent, and neither the whole nor any single component or multiple components would take primacy at the expense of others. For should such occur, it would be recognized that the system would no longer be the same. While there may be times when some parts may need primary attention, such temporary attention would signify that the component in need has interests superseding those of other parts. So, too, we recognize that system changes intentionally made for the good of the whole will likely be necessary from time to time.

Indeed, we argue here that such is the case for the present system— that it must be so drastically altered as to constitute a transformation to an essentially different system. The members of PEACE are themselves participating in a process of struggle to articulate a vision of a transformed global society. We hold that this process of diverse entities struggling toward a common vision is an important aspect of an ecological and cooperative approach to peace education. Throughout the world, instructors and learners together should be collaborating in multiple processes of envisioning a transformed world order that is truly democratic, participatory in its origins and its functioning.

As we engage in such a process, we also embark upon the redefinition of many fundamental social and political concepts. Many have lost their authentic meanings in the stagnation of the ideological orthodoxies that have defined and divided the world into competitive interests struggling for dominance in a conflictual system. Thus, what we mean here by "democratic" is not adequately defined by the standard definitions previously applied by the East or the West. Differences in ideology have produced contrasting notions of democracy characterized by such standards as full employment (as opposed to universal suffrage), or economic and social (as opposed to civil and political) rights. These differences have certainly fragmented and destructively prioritized the realization of *universal human rights* (meaning comprehensive as well as applicable to all). For us, a democratic society is one that strives to fulfill both sets of rights for all the people, economic and social as well as political and civil, and *all the* categories of *rights* the world has defined and continues to define since the Universal Declaration of Human Rights was set forth in 1948.

Democracy should mean more than voting and representation. It even means more than the assurance of the wherewithal (learned or provided) to meet basic needs. It should mean, above all, broad, meaningful participation in all public decisions, cultural, economic, and social as well as civil and political. Further, authentic participatory democracy can only exist in a global system where it can no longer be limited "in the interest of national security."

A shift from an international system of win-lose competition and destructive conflict to one of genuine cooperation and collaboration would make the present exclusionary, fragmented notion of national security obsolete. Just to seriously work toward such a system would increase democratic participation and certainly would require more participatory education. The ecological and cooperative notions of security noted earlier can best be put into operation in a fully participatory form of democracy, one that, properly structured, could work at all levels of social organization, even the global. For example, the proposal for a "third house," as an addition to the United Nations Security Council and General Assembly, for the world's peoples or nongovernmental organizations, demonstrates such possibilities (Boulding 1988). The notion of authentically participatory democracy calls for a redefinition of power as well as an education for empowerment.

From Domination to Mutuality:
Power as Synergy, a Cooperative Learning Task

Power in the present system has come to mean primarily military might, the capacity to arouse fear and to achieve "the national interest." Power, then, has operated as the means to persuade or force others to acquiesce in the policies of the powerful. Clearly, as demonstrated by the Persian Gulf war and its devastating aftermath, this system of deterrence can neither maintain the peace nor provide global security. At other levels of social organization, in communities and within nations, power used in such a way is perceived as a lack of civility, lawlessness or criminality. Only recently have some begun to recognize the lawlessness and barbarity of the international system itself. From the ecological, holistic perspectives taken here, the lawlessness in the larger system, in fact, makes possible much of the barbarous behavior within nations, most especially that of states against their own citizens. Again the Gulf War of 1991 offers an instructive example; nations coalesced to wage war against Iraq with far greater alacrity than they responded to the plight of the refugees resulting from the internal Iraqi strife engendered by the war. It is evident that we still live in a world in which the state *dominates* rather than *serves* its citizens.

The recognition and application of the imperatives of interdependence among nations would do much to bring authentic democracy to the world society. As power is redefined, the respective governments of the world of nations must learn to relate to each other, in the spirit, and within structures and policies, of mutuality, rejecting the drive for dominance in favor of a struggle toward authentic, fully functioning interdependence.

The formulation of and striving toward mutual goals carries a notion of power now advocated widely by feminists as *power with* rather than *power over*. Sharing power, it is argued, can increase the total capacity of the parties involved to achieve the common goal. Such *synergetic capacity* deriving from cooperative efforts has been demonstrated in the positive educational consequences of many experiments in cooperative learning introduced in the recent past into American schools.

Energy from multiple sources brought to cooperative efforts is often greater than energy from one source, and it is more likely to be renewed or enhanced as the parties involved are increased. In that a purpose of cooperation between the two former superpower rivals is to enhance the possibilities for international cooperation in general, it is hoped that others will soon be brought into the new approach to power as shared capacity, in positive constructive efforts more conducive to authentic security and democracy than the waging of war that has involved many nations.

Developing multilateral, cooperative, international efforts is a learning task, the foundation for which needs to be laid in the schools of the nations involved. Cooperative learning as a standard practice in formal educational systems around the world could be a significant factor in enhancing cooperation in the international system. It would be a significant acknowledgment of the need to enhance interdependence at all levels—to not only teach *about* interdependence but to teach *for* interdependence. Authentic interdependence requires renewed and renewable energy—not only the industrial energy we need to fuel economic production and maintain the world economy, but also, and especially, the human energy to learn and to achieve goals, to carry out equitable, ecologically designed, and environmentally healthy international policies.

Ecofeminists tell us power should be defined as energy (Diamond 1990). Within the content of ecological and cooperative education, power then is also energy directed toward the implementation of an international process of learning for change. Herein lies the vital task of educators, particularly peace educators committed to learning toward the achievement of nonviolence and the promotion of justice.

Our goal then is the conceptualization of and the struggle to implement an educational system and a pedagogy that can enable us to identify, release, and renew the various sources of energy necessary to transform the present system into the democratic world society we have begun to envision.

The competitive individualism of our present classrooms reifies and reinforces the competitive individualism of the nation-state system. Thus change in the classroom is crucial to change in the world.

Education for a Healthy Planet, Healthy Society: A Future Worth Hoping for, a Goal Worth Struggling for, a Task Worth Learning

As noted earlier, our concept of a democratic society is, among other things, that of *a secure society*. Security, it has been argued, derives in large part from the expectation of well-being, and well-being is measured in terms of the environment, justice, dignity, and nonviolence (Reardon and Scott 1990–91). A secure society is a healthy society, physically and psychologically. Health is the realization of well-being. During these years of the environmental crisis we have learned how much the health of the human species depends upon the environment; as the ecological imperative becomes clearer, we are also learning how much the health of the environment depends upon the human species.

Indeed, the relationship between humanity and planet Earth is emerging as the most significant of all global security issues. The most urgent security need of all is that all human beings see themselves as part of the ecosystem, elements of the biosphere, as well as creators of the sociosphere. Helping learners to grasp that urgency and the nature of that relationship is a paramount task for ecological and cooperative education, one that can only be properly conceived and implemented within a global framework. What the PEACE group is working for is a common educational program as well as a joint vision of an environmentally healthy planet.

Energy and attention should be applied to the task of envisioning and struggling for human and environmental well-being. Hope can be kindled in addressing this task. Because security derives so largely from expectations, we can understand now how significant a role hope plays in human well-being. Without hope, there can be no energizing vision of a transformed world, nor is there a source for renewing the physical and psychic energies that will need regular replenishment in the struggle. For PEACE, then, the inspiration of hope is a significant learning task and goal, inspiring (i.e., "breathing in") the energies and igniting the possibilities of faith in our capacities to change ourselves, our systems, and our relationships. It represents for us the spiritual dimension of our project.

We recognize that any movement, educational or political, that seeks to transform the human condition so fundamentally as does the change we seek in the Earth-humankind relationship must nurture the human spirit as well as the mind. Perhaps the role of the arts and artists in the changes sweeping the world today more than any other factor instructs us in the spiritual nature of our task. Our classrooms need to become places in which such envisioning is part of the curriculum.

As we help to release the creative imaginations of learners in the imaging of their own preferred futures and the kind of social order that might make such futures possible, we will help to kindle hope and to dissipate the despair that envelops the minds and spirits of so many of the young.

Hope arises from awareness of positive possibilities, from the potential for renewal. So, too, we recognize that ecology itself rests in a view of the world that sees it as the host of possibilities. From such a view derives a spiritual dimension limited neither to philosophy nor to religion, but comprehending all in a spirituality that can encompass the whole of humanity, believers and nonbelievers. Perhaps more than any other element, this spiritual energy will bring us into forms of cooperation that will manifest and apply the unity of humanity and of humanity and Earth.

Certainly for many educators this is what inspires their preference for cooperative learning. It is palpably evident in the sense of community, unity, and possibility that we experience in our efforts as members of PEACE. It is the stuff of friendship, it is the stuff of peace, and it should as well be the stuff of curriculum.

Learning to Care: The Basis of Responsibility

In small but significant ways, PEACE has been for us, the participants, an exercise in learning to care. Our collaborative efforts have built friendships, and friendships are relationships based on caring. We are willing to risk caring for each other as we risk the struggle toward a still unfocused but mutually and strongly envisioned common future.

Working together has helped us to know each other in dimensions even beyond our professional roles. We see each other whole and human, and out of this comes caring. We see our commonalities and interrelationships, as well as our similarities and differences. We matter to each other as persons and as partners. We seek to find that our differences are usually enhancing and reinforcing diversity. We seek to recognize our own ecology of relationship, to consciously participate in keeping this relationship a viable, productive system. The seeking itself is a form of caring. We are learning something of how caring is learning.

This perhaps is one of the most telling arguments for cooperative education: that it develops the capacity to care. Caring is an active investment in and a kind of twin to hope. Both elements are essential to the abilities to be responsible, to act toward the effectuation of change, to move against injustice, to protest against and intervene in the degradation of the environment. We hope to help learners develop those abilities. We hope to help learners become *responsible,* having the capacity to respond actively and effectively, to live out a commitment to the common future.

This is a goal we embrace in PEACE. This is a goal that will inform the design of content and the methods we use in education for meeting the challenge of the new moment. When we finished our design phase, we cooperated on its application, and we will undoubtedly continue to cooperate on the revisions made ever necessary by the changing world. But we have hope that the care we offer each other will renew the energies we expend in what we know is a long and difficult struggle requiring new learnings as yet unimagined. We hope to continue to learn and imagine together.

TEACHING TOWARD THE FUTURE IN THE PRESENT

Although our work is inspired by a vision of a transformed global society, a human future of all the Earth's people and a healthy future for our shared planet, we do this work now in the daily context of our present professional positions. It is directed toward small but potentially significant projects that put our values and goals into operation in current learning environments, our communities and our classrooms. It involves efforts to develop respect for cultural differences, build relationships among the young people of our respective countries, and educate teachers in the ways of nature and help them to teach students so that they can see themselves as part of one living Earth.

Our direct and practical steps are to take the form of school "twinning," linking particular classrooms through the identification of individual teachers in each of the three countries involved in the initial stages of the project. Middle school, junior high school, and high school students can be in direct contact with each other through correspondence and audio- and videotapes, while in their respective classrooms they undertake study and consideration of the same or similar issues under the guidance of teachers seeking to introduce ecological thinking and problem solving within organic and global perspectives.

We hope that such transnational educational projects will become standard classroom practice as collaborative and cooperative ecological education develops and is extended to more and more schools in our respective countries and in the other countries we plan to involve as the project matures and expands. We have begun work to involve more people in East-West exchange, including Eastern and Western European educators as well as some others from the United States and Canada. Initial investigation into North-South exchanges and networking has also been undertaken to include schools in Asia, Latin America, and Africa.

One important aspect of these practical projects is the intention that they should, as well, involve local communities in the applications of problem solutions. While the problems to be studied are global in scope, their manifestations at the local level will be the immediate concern of the individual school projects. Students will engage with community members of all ages in seeking to resolve local problems of the environment or of human relations. They will directly confront pollution or waste disposal in their own neighborhoods, ethnic conflict or discrimination in their schools and communities.

These are but a very few and limited examples of possibilities for multigenerational, direct action in which ecological thinking and social responsibility will be applied to the actual realities in which the young are living.

Among the problems we seek to address at this stage are various ecological issues, most especially those related to the preservation of natural biosystems in local areas. The study and undertaking of problem resolution on this type of issue will require a form of environmental education that applies ecological thinking to the study and valuing of natural systems and the natural order itself, and learning to understand the Earth through understanding bioregions of various sizes—their unique characteristics, their subsystems, and their relationships to other systems and bioregions. It will require students to learn of the various life forms in their immediate environments, the types and consequences of human intervention in natural processes, and environmental changes resulting from human habitation and organized society.

Such education will also raise questions about the relationship of human society to the natural order, and make it possible for learners to consider these questions within the contexts of their own localities. It will encourage practical action to fulfill social responsibility with regard to achieving and/or maintaining an appropriate and constructive relationship between the local bioregion and the local human society.

Other issues to be addressed will be in the area of mutually enhancing human relations. We plan to stress learning about the alternative ways of expressing human universals demonstrated by diverse cultures, and the learning of respect for human dignity in respect for ethnic identity. The ethnic conflicts that characterize the current rapidly changing global order are a major concern to peace educators, for they express the violation of the very human values and human rights that are at the core of any authentically peaceful order. Our project will address ethnic differences and the study of various cultures as a humanly enriching and necessary characteristic of a world at peace. Ethnic diversity will be taught as a value complementary to biological diversity, necessary to the health of the human family and of planet Earth.

We propose to study, as well, cases of ethnic conflict, and we will attempt to facilitate action programs in which children can in some way offer aid to other children victimized by ethnic conflict. Through such specific cases students will learn the human dimensions of some of the political problems of achieving peace and will come to recognize the meaning of and the need for respect for universal human rights.

The conduct of these pioneering efforts in ecological and cooperative education will require teachers of exceptional commitment with special training in ecological thinking and the pedagogy of cooperation. Thus one of the first major projects of Stage 2 of PEACE is a teacher education program.

Individual schools and school systems are to be involved in a process of teacher education being conducted by members of PEACE. Groups of teachers introduced to ecological and cooperative education are working with project members on the development of specific teaching processes and materials. These will be tried out and revised for publication in a curriculum handbook, which will enable other teachers to attempt similar educational programs.

PEACE also involves a collaborative effort in the common training of teachers/educators, in Russia and in North America, in the use of field techniques. The training occurs in Canada and in Siberia. This common training will provide, at least for those involved, the basis for fully parallel curricular approaches in selected Russian and North American teacher education institutions.

These are some of the specific practical steps to be pursued in our efforts to bring to realization the principles and concepts we have derived during the first stage of our project. We see this as only the beginning of an ongoing, continually widening effort to bring ecological and cooperative education to many parts of the world. We continue to take inspiration and energy from our collaboration and look forward to the contributions and cooperation of other similarly concerned educators wherever they may be.

REFERENCES

Boulding, Elise. 1988. *Building a Global Civic Culture*. New York: Teachers College Press.

Diamond, Irene. 1990. "Ecofeminism." Paper presented at the biannual general conference of the International Peace Research Association, July.

Eisler, Riane. 1987. *The Chalice and the Blade*. New York: Harper & Row.

Ferguson, Marilyn. 1987. *The Aquarian Conspiracy*. Los Angeles: Tarcher.

Gorbachev, Mikhail. 1988. *Perestroika*. New York: Harper & Row.

Gromyko, Anatoly, and Martin Hellerman, eds. 1988. *Breakthrough*. New York: Walker.

Howell, Signe, and Roy Willis, eds. 1989. *Societies at Peace: Anthropological Perspectives*. London: Rutledge.

Lemkow, Anna. 1990. *The Wholeness Principle: Dynamics of Unity within Science, Religion, and Society*. Wheaton, Ill.: Quest Books, Theosophical Publishing House.

Lovelock, James. 1988. *The Ages of Gaia: A Biography of Our Living Earth*. New York: Norton.

Mendlovitz, Saul, and R. B. J. Walker. 1987. *Toward a Just World Order*. London: Butterworth.

Reardon, Betty, and Leslie Scott. 1991. "An Ecofeminist Perspective on Global Security." *International Journal of Humanities and Peace* 8, no. 3.

Sloan, Douglas. 1984. *Toward a Recovery of Wholeness: Knowledge, Education, and Human Values*. New York: Teachers College Press.

3
New Thinking: Its Application for a New Learning

Valentina Mitina

Having been a teacher and researcher for a rather long time, I have been involved professionally and socially in peace education for many decades. As the cold war came to an end and the ideas of new thinking were launched, I realized the necessity to rethink my approaches to peace education, theoretically and practically.

Under the new conditions, from 1986 in the Soviet Union and in the early nineties in the CIS countries, peace has gotten a much broader meaning; it is not only absence of war. I came gradually to understand that peace is a comprehensive concept. It means ecological and environmental security; it means global and national protection and development. New thinking was of great significance in the process of working out this notion, as it will be in trying to apply it to education.

This chapter is devoted to the speculations of Russian and Ukrainian PEACE participants on the significance of one of the twentieth century's extraordinary phenomena: new thinking, and its influence upon education. I will discuss some aspects of the educational role of new thinking primarily in my own country, Russia. We are convinced that new thinking transforms education's relationship to the tasks and realities of today.

Peace education of the nineties involves the necessary broadening of the concept of peace to include issues connected with the preservation of life on our planet and making our life more humane. The emerging new paradigm of peace education comprises such subtopics as international, ecological, and cultural education, education on human rights, and education for peace, cooperation, democracy, and social responsibility.

New political thinking has increased the possibility of changing international politics, particularly in Eastern Europe. A process has been started that offers a new chance for developing a humane world. The educational systems of all countries are facing that enormous task. The Project on Ecological and Cooperative Education (PEACE) is contributing to this international endeavor. PEACE is, on the one hand, a product of new thinking and, on the other hand, a means for realization of its main principles in education. The group of educators from Norway, the United States, and the former Soviet republics of Russia and Ukraine is trying through cooperation within the project's framework to work out new concepts for peace education in relation to the challenges of the coming new millennium. We realize that a new education must be ecological and cooperative in its scope if it is to help educate the younger generations to cope with the new problems.

There are special chapters in this book prepared by Russian participants in PEACE dealing with these two leading aspects of the project. This particular chapter focuses on showing the general connection between education and the challenges of new thinking.

THE NEED FOR NEW THINKING

New Thinking for the World Society

The conditions of the late twentieth century have stipulated humankind's need for new thinking. The term *new thinking* has now become part of the world's lexicon; it is also now a symbol in our country of the most urgent, most acute needs of the present social and historical processes, evolving toward globalism and democracy.

The challenges of humankind's situation on the threshold of the new millennium include such unprecedented global problems as the menace of nuclear suicide and providing the planet's population with energy, natural resources, food, water, and clean air. We are living under the condition of threat to the whole ecosystem; we can see that life on our planet is not guaranteed.

At the 1986 international public hearing of the World Commission on Environment and Development (WCED) in Moscow, participants stated that environmental issues stand high on the priority list of global problems; their solution, however, depends on the preservation of peace on our planet. Solving ecological problems is impossible without curbing the arms race, which absorbs tremendous intellectual and material resources, and promoting healthy life-styles and values in our young people (WCED 1987, 286). A particular feature, and the novelty, of all these global problems is that they must be solved *now*, not at some future time. Delay in solving them could have irreversible, catastrophic consequences for the very existence of the human species, for life itself on Earth.

It became urgent that peace education should include the analysis of these issues and show how scientific and technological achievements might be used for the progress of humanity and not for its destruction.

It is necessary to understand that further aggravation of global problems will affect all countries and peoples, irrespective of social systems or class. Every nation in the past has certainly encountered difficult tasks and serious dangers of diverse kinds. But formerly threats mostly confronted individual countries or groups of countries. This is the first time that all humanity has come face to face with threats of a *global* nature and immense *common* dangers.

The problems common to all humankind must now take priority: their solution is the indispensable requisite for the further existence and development of the human species. To overcome the present threats and ensure large-scale utilization of our new possibilities is one of the key tasks facing all nations and all political and social forces.

Peoples of many countries associate the introduction of new thinking in the political world with the name of former Soviet president Mikhail Gorbachev, who explained his vision of this phenomenon in *Perestroika: New Thinking for Our Country and the World* (1987). He emphasized the following features of new thinking:

- The understanding of the interrelatedness and interdependence of the contemporary world;
- The rejection of war and the use of military power, the appeal for unification and for effective actions of all progressive forces in upholding peace and social progress;
- The conviction that it is impossible to solve the complicated problems and profound conflicts of the modern world by means of armed force—we must search for political ways of settling our conflicts;
- Recognition of universal values.

It is evident that the ideas of new thinking apply to political issues. The new mode of thinking is an indispensable way to approach theoretical and practical issues of modern social realities. In this context education as a whole and education for peace in its broad perception are of substantial importance.

A Historical Background

The theoretical "layer" of new thinking has not been developed out of the blue. No single personality, scientist, or leader can perform an upheaval in social consciousness without the broad support of people.

On the one hand, new thinking is a result of the new tendencies of the world's social development; on the other, it is based on the achievements of the advanced philosophical, social, and political theories of the past. Great ideas have always been born on the crest of social activities and movements; they lead them further, and they are backed by them. Many elements of new thinking were born within the ranks of the antiwar and antinuclear movements—including the Russell-Einstein Manifesto, the Pugwash movement of scientists, and the antiwar appeals and protests by nongovernmental, trade union, youth, and women's organizations. Immense contributions to new thinking were made by the United Nations and its organizations' activities, and they had great impact in the former USSR over the past few decades.

The change in social consciousness that promoted new thinking is rooted in the efforts of educators committed to the ideas of peace, of making education an instrument for ending wars, and of creating a world outlook appropriate to ideals of peace. J. Comenius, M. Montessori, L. Tolstoy, M. Gandhi, and many others by their works and activities created the foundation for thinking and acting in terms of interconnectedness and responsibility. Many present-day educators have made valuable contributions to peace education by developing a variety of programs that promote an education in practice for peace, disarmament, mutual understanding, and ecological and cooperative learning.

New Thinking Means Rethinking Peace Education

To successfully advance the ideas of new thinking in different spheres, new social, moral, scientific, and ecological concepts are needed, because totally new conditions will determine human life today and in the future. New concepts of peace education are being developed, as are new approaches to making peace education more effective.

One main issue is to help the younger generations understand that they are the ones who will live in an interrelated, interdependent, and integral world. They are the ones who will build new relations and new forms of cooperation with peoples of other countries. They will have to realize that new relations and new ways of cooperating must promote and serve the progress and prosperity of their own country and *at the same time* that of the global community as a whole.

For this purpose profound changes in comprehensive education are needed at all levels and in different spheres. The new ideas call for changes in education as a whole, including such fundamental issues as educating the younger generations in the spirit of ecological concern, or what Robert Zuber (chapter 9) calls "ecological wisdom": the development of such qualities as care and participatory responsibility for local, national, and global problems.

This quest has been a distinctive feature of many educators in the former USSR and in Russia during recent years. The necessity of working out a new mode of thinking in developing theoretical and practical approaches for making peace education more effective is central for the present-day activities of specialists in the field. The general principles of the new-thinking concept can be used as the basis for them.

Universally Shared Values

Many of those who are working in the field of new-thinking development accentuate the need for a deeper understanding and for eliciting its humanistic inspiration. For myself, this understanding and inspiration are based on the concept of universally shared values, which constitutes the centerpiece of education for peace. Having a universal character, these values are able to unite people of different cultures and social systems in solving global problems, in providing peaceful coexistence and cooperation. These values are connected with essential realities: that all people are living in an integral, interrelated, and interdependent world; that all belong to the same species and live on the same planet; that all have a sacred right to exist, to develop, and to determine their own lives. All are in need of clean water, clean air, and a protected natural environment in which they can live together. In this way there is first of all an immense amount of common interest that unites humankind, compared to all that may divide us. Willard Jacobson maintains that these and other "big ideas" of ecology, which are universal in character, ought to be well known by those who are engaged in present-day programs of education and the improvement of the environment (see chapter 4).

While internalizing universal values, human beings are becoming aware of the possibilities for unification of the human species. We are identifying basic ideas that might become the foundation of new thinking. On the basis of universal values, humankind will learn to appreciate the enormous span of the life and history of the peoples of the world.

A leading principle of the new mode of thinking for peace education is that humanity has become aware of itself as an integral whole. Karl Marx once stated that human beings will be able to fully bring out their potential only when they become aware of themselves as a part of the global whole and conform their actions to the requirements of this idea: being one species. Today this idea is more relevant than ever for peace education in its broadened scope.

Essential Qualities to Be Cultivated

Although our world is clearly divided, full of contradictions, and composed of countries that are antagonistic to each other, the unity and interdependence of countries and peoples, and their common fate, are becoming a tangible reality. One can no longer live a secluded life, retreating into one's shell. Nothing that happens in Earth, whether nearby or far away, bypasses anyone. In one way or another, everything that happens is everybody's concern and everybody's responsibility. The fate of Earth depends in fact upon how everybody participates in one way or another in common activities.

The development of responsibility, care, concern, and participation is already included in the peace education programs in many parts of my country, at both the conceptual and the practical levels. More than sixty years ago the Soviet scientist V. I. Vernadsky generated the concept of *noosphere*. A human being, as part of the *biosphere*, the system of all life on the planet, must, at every specific level of development, take upon herself or himself some responsibility for the future fate of the biosphere. This sphere of responsibility for each person to his or her life system is called the personal noosphere of that whole system, which is the biosphere *cared for by humankind* (Sahtouris 1989).

A change is needed to accomplish this new consciousness; it may come as the result of the development in our society of the new mode of thinking. The responsibility needed will become an essential part of education as the development of human beings for a new world. The task of educators today is to prepare their students for this kind of consciousness. Students need to be trained in seeing humankind as an integral part of the Earth's biosphere. When this approach becomes education as *participation,* the basis is laid for the formation of a young person's involvement in all development of human society and the natural environmental processes in the world. Education needs to be organized in such a way that the needed qualities will develop.

Among these needed qualities is a *high level of sensibility to and care for life itself,* in the environment, in the neighborhood, on the planet as a whole—an attitude of concern for other people and for nature. In one Russian novel, the hero who lives in a distant Siberian village has just heard about the first successful heart transplantation, and he begins firing his hunter's gun into the night sky. His neighbors are bewildered: Why does a heart transplant done in a faraway, strange country concern a man in a Siberian village? When the consciousness of noosphere is developed, there are no distant and strange countries, no distant and strange problems or issues. Someone else's troubles and joy are all our own. There are thoughts and ideas, involvement and emotional coexperience, faith in the triumph of wisdom and the responsibility for life on Earth, a psychological readiness to take it upon oneself to care for and contribute to solving the most complicated problems. Betty Reardon characterizes this attitude as "the most essential active peacemaking capacity" (see chapter 2).

In the comprehensiveness of peace education, social responsibility should be one of the basic lessons learned by children. This would help to develop the sense of empowerment needed to become a responsible member of society, and it would give children an active role in solving local and global problems. Among the most important elements of this kind of activity is the development of self-awareness, awareness of others, global awareness, and skills in critical thinking and conflict resolution. One important principle has to be emphasized: if learning is seen as the way to increase our understanding of the world, ourselves, and others, then learning will be valued for its own sake and not just as a tool for reaching material goals. Effective realization of this principle means that cognition will become a means of personal, local, national, and global fulfillment.

Human beings are active beings. They develop as personalities, advancing through the process of activity for the good of human beings. Only through *action* can lasting and ingrained ways and habits of participation and cooperation develop. The changed conditions of the contemporary world compel us to work out new thinking that can overcome distrust and suspicion. The new mode of thinking helps destroy images of others as the "enemy"—images that block the mind and prevent communication. This kind of approach does not sweep away the problems and contradictions, but offers a new point of departure for overcoming them.

PEACE EDUCATION IN THE FORMER USSR AND IN RUSSIA

Traditional approaches

For more than seventy years the Soviet Union was a multinational country inhabited by more than 150 nations and ethnic groups, and highly centralized in its management.

In practically every local community there were representatives of different nationalities. International education in most of them started at this level, the community level, where the child got her or his initial knowledge about cultural diversity. The local manifestation of cross-cultural differences was thus essential subject matter for peace education. Very often Soviet educators sought to organize adolescents in activities for peace within the range of the local community. More specifically, the Clubs of International Friendship, usually based at schools and district Pioneer palaces and houses, gave extensive opportunities for peace education (see chapter 5).

In Russia, international education begins in kindergarten with issues that are well known to all the children: problems that concern groups of different nationalities living in the neighborhood. Later on it is continued at schools and out-of-school educational institutions (see chapters 5 and 8). Various holidays and festivities that acquaint children with their peers from other parts of the country are a regular part of the school program and of the activities of different community bodies (e.g., children's commissions at local governmental bodies and enterprises). For example, an all-union festival was often held in USSR communities and schools, and for it material about the various republics was prepared. National songs and dances were learned, national costumes were made, and reports on labor achievements of working people were prepared. This practice has continued in Russia today and in many other republics.

Much work is also carried on for the purpose of developing respect for the peoples of other countries. Children study history, geography, literature, and so on, and participate in related out-of-school activities.

There are various forms of international education at school. A special one is the "peace lesson," which has become a widespread feature. The peace lesson used to be the first lesson of every academic year in every Soviet school all over the country. The Committee of the Movement of Educators for Peace and Mutual Understanding recommends that the peace lesson should cover a wide range of issues, including safeguarding life on Earth, protecting nature, respect for human beings, truth and justice, morals, personal responsibility, global awareness, human communication and mutual understanding, international cooperation, and new thinking. They have issued guidelines for content and methods in the field of peace education.

During the peace lesson, students summarize their activities for peace during the previous academic year and at the same time make plans for the future. During the lesson the students are joined by schoolteachers, war veterans, peace activists, prominent citizens, and outstanding figures from factories, farms, and scientific and cultural institutions. The Day of the Lesson of Peace features rallies, manifestations, and labor actions. The opportunity is also used to collect money for the national Peace Fund.

Russian children and young people, like students from the other CIS states, are active participants in such antiwar actions as UN disarmament and peace weeks and campaigns, and in international youth actions for peace held by local chapters of such groups as Educators for Peace and Mutual Understanding, the Peace Committee, the Peace Fund, and Peace for the Children of the World. The young people themselves initiate different kinds of peace actions in which the population of the community, sometimes even the whole country, is involved.

All these activities stimulate the young people for participation in what they experience as *protecting peace*. They demonstrate that their particular skills and abilities are constructive; they take part in a common task; they are doing what they can to save the life on our planet.

So we may say that, in spite of many shortcomings, traditional peace education in our country has made its contribution to the development of the younger generation's ability to comprehend the ideas of the new thinking.

Challenges to Peace Education in the CIS Countries

The years of Soviet society's reconstruction (perestroika) and openness (glasnost) have revealed a number of serious problems in international understanding, mainly in transnational relations between peoples belonging to different nationalities living within the different republics. The animosities in Karabakh, Georgia, and in the Uzbek city of Fergana, for instance, have been ignited by political, social, and economic antagonisms, the roots of which go back to the Stalin period when national groups were ordered to move from one republic to another.

Also, elements in our traditional approach to international education proved not to be effective in the difficult conditions of our society's life. The authoritarian regime that prevailed in many spheres of social life had its negative influence. In the centralized system of education, teachers often used the same goals and methods in every district, without taking into consideration the differing cultural backgrounds of the students and teachers. We were aiming at fostering the feelings of love and friendship, but we were not aware that in some places the people of different nationalities inside a community had little or no trust in one another. Today one of the most complex and important educational tasks is conflict resolution and confidence building between children from different cultures living in the same region.

Among the important principles of peace education is that of "being an active person," a principle that has been inherent to our educational system for many decades. However, under the conditions of glasnost it has become evident that many programs for children and teenagers were not really the *activities* that we meant them to be; they were "word, not deed," bound to foster citizens' apathy instead of attitudes of participation. This, then, is another huge task for our educators today—to overcome citizens' apathy. How can we help to develop social responsibility of a truly participatory character? The danger of apathy and other drawbacks of our traditional approach to peace education are being reconsidered. Educators, as well as philosophers, are working at ways to overcome them.

According to the Russian philosopher A. Kapto (1990), international education based on new thinking should aim at the development of consciousness and the cultivation of high moral principles. The young person should be helped to understand the surrounding world and to find his or her sphere of responsibility. International education should promote new possibilities for a person to live in a truly global community. The task of international education should be to educate all people to recognize the importance and urgency of global problems and their origins, consequences, and interrelations. The task of researchers and educators is not only to proclaim the new urgent problems and give them their theoretical basis, but also to show that many already are involved in practical work in the field, and in this way to encourage others.

Soviet and Russian School Reform: Contributions to Peace Education

School and society are inseparable. Perestroika in the former USSR has initiated sweeping changes in the country's educational system. Education is considered to be one of the most effective factors of reconstruction and development of society. The generation of the twenty-first century is being educated in the present-day classrooms. According to new laws, a new educational policy was undertaken for the tasks of perestroika. This new policy was initially based on the principles of humanistic and democratic socialism, and on universally shared values. At the All Union Teachers' Congress in 1988, which was devoted to the new educational law reform, G. A. Yagodin, the chairman of the former State Committee on Public Education, stated in his report: "Education in the spirit of peace is not only an international term accepted by the majority of people; it has become for the youth a special 'branch' in education, a kind of lesson in mutual understanding and mutual activities."

The new concept of general education does not in its structure specify peace education. However, the fundamental principles of the concept constitute a solid basis for all approaches in developing theoretical and practical issues of peace education in the country. Of special significance for education are three concepts: democratization, humanization and humanitarianization.

- *Democratization* of the school urges elimination of uniformity in its administration and management, in content and teaching methods.

It urges provision for curriculum and syllabus variations, which allows the teacher to take into consideration regions' and nations' different cultures as well as students' individual abilities. Democratization also aims at converting schools into social institutions capable of overcoming their isolation from the life of the broader society. It aims at developing conditions for teaching the young openness, mutual respect and cooperation, independence, initiative, and creativity.

• *Humanization* presupposes respect for students' personalities and the development of their abilities. It points to the need to unite the teacher and student in the learning process and to make the school curriculum interesting and meaningful for the student.

• *Humanitarianization* of school education is reflected in the increase of the humanitarian aspects in the curriculum of general education, literature, art, and history. The student is helped to identify attitudes toward society, culture, and humankind as a whole.

According to the new school laws, schools and teachers are encouraged to use a flexible curriculum and syllabus. They are expected to stimulate creativity among staff and students in choosing teaching methods, in organizing the educational process, in searching for innovation, in working out their own methods, and in introducing them in their school curricula and out-of-class activities. This approach allows teachers to increase their contributions to peace education. This is supposed to be done across the curriculum by integrating peace issues into different subjects or by creating special optional courses, primarily for the upper grades of high school.

The recently published English-language textbook for the sixth grade (junior high school) illustrates the new trends. One part of the book, which is supposed to be used during the first term of the school year, is devoted to peace. The titles are suggestive: "For Peace on the Planet Earth"; "How You Can Take Part in the Peace Movement"; "In Memory of Samantha Smith, the Little Ambassador of Peace." Other texts are based on ideas of friendship ("Space Bridges—Bridges of Peace and Friendship"), poems by an English girl, Edith Segal ("Bridges" and "A Child's Wish"), and a passage from Gerald Durrell's book *My Family and Other Animals* (Khrustalyova and Bogorodiskaya 1988).

Peace and ecology-oriented texts, pictures, and problem-solving tasks are becoming integrated in the curriculum. New perspectives on peace education issues are infused into language teaching and other school subjects. Students are encouraged to express their thoughts and attitudes on global issues of the present world. They are encouraged to see that mastering the English language may give them new possibilities for cooperation.

The new concept of education for our country stresses that only through fostering democratic persons who are free and at the same time responsible is it possible to build a truly democratic society. A democratic personality should be creative, as only creative persons can become socially constructive, participatory, and caring for people, societies, and nature itself. All of these qualities can be developed. Their development is the premise for deep feelings of interconnectedness with society and nature and a personal responsibility for life.

This brief analysis of our country's school-reform principles shows that they constitute a platform for broadening and deepening the traditional vision of peace, and make education more relevant to the needs of contemporary national and global society. The principles also help to construct a new vision of peace, a peace culture based on democratic concepts and on universal values of respect for the individual and other peoples, for freedom, justice, solidarity, tolerance, and human rights.

New Initiatives

How are the proclaimed principles contributing to the reconstruction of a new peace education? How can a new peace education promote youngsters' cognitive, affective, and action-oriented abilities and skills? How are these principles introduced into school life? The process started at the end of the eighties; some examples may illustrate these good beginnings.

The topics I discuss in this section are closely related to those discussed in chapter 8 by Galina Kovalyova. We have already met with V. I. Vernadsky's concept of noosphere. In 1988, on the initiative of Soviet scientists, the international noospheric movement, "Intellect and Survival," was founded. Its goal is to build "the noospheric society," that is, a society that is developing in harmony with nature. Its participants plan to draw public attention to the fact that the resources of nature are limited and that the warming of Earth's climate threatens humanity's survival.

To build a noospheric society, it is necessary to develop a broad movement of consciousness and activism for ecologically healthy life-styles. In developing the ideas of the noospheric movement, the academician N. N. Moiseev suggested the creation of a special initiative to prepare "the system teacher." This teacher would provide a new level of general education—not only the needed knowledge but also new methods—to develop the norms of behavior needed for planet Earth to survive. "Humankind, for its survival," says N. N. Moiseev, "should feel itself to be a crew of one and the same spaceship" (Kromenkov 1989, 174).

Soviet and Russian school reform, since 1986, has underlined the necessity of developing national and historical traditions, as well as appreciation and preservation of a world culture. Schools should also contribute to the blending of two streams—national values and universal values—for mutual enrichment.

These specific goals for the new schools have helped open students' eyes to the values of other cultures' life-styles by revealing both their uniqueness and their similarities. Developing these ideas, researchers and teachers in the city of Kharkov have suggested starting a model school program they call "Dialogue of Cultures." The basic idea is to develop in students the ability to take an active part in their ongoing education.

The goals of the first- through fourth-grade curriculum are not only to help children develop knowledge and skills, but also to help them learn to see the world in its evolution. The main part of the curriculum in the fifth and sixth grades is devoted to medieval culture, in which architecture and art are integrated with the moral and spiritual values of that period. Seventh- and eighth-grade courses are based on modern culture. In grades nine and ten the curriculum presupposes the dialogue of different cultures, and their reflections in today's culture. After having studied antiquity, the Middle Ages, and the present time, and having learned how to work in the logic of different cultures and how to interconnect them, the students then return as visitors to the lower grades and give "courses of dialogue": they relate what they know and what they have experienced. While being "teachers," they discover new facets of the cultures they have studied.

This new emphasis on national and world cultural values aims at such new peace education targets as the ability to understand, appreciate, and respect other people's values, traditions, and cultures; tolerance; and the overcoming of stereotypes, suspicion, and images of others as "enemy." An integrated, multifaceted concept of peace education is still needed—one that will creatively accumulate the positive elements of the traditional approaches and at the same time be enriched by the ideas of new thinking and challenged by the conditions of contemporary national and global society.

Educators for Peace and Mutual Understanding

One of the approaches to this kind of conceptual development is put forward by the Movement of Educators for Peace and Mutual Understanding, whose main goals are the following:

- to promote new thinking;
- to promote social and political activities of the teaching community for the preservation and development of peace and life on our planet;
- to improve the education of the young at all levels, for peace and mutual understanding, global responsibility, and international cooperation.

The movement's activities include these:

• Supporting educational research on urgent world issues, on new philosophies of international relations, on safeguarding global security, and on working out ways and means of using knowledge in peace education;

• Paying special attention to the development of peace education curricula that emphasize such aspects as fostering the ability to think critically and to appreciate and internalize values of special importance to our society under the conditions of its reconstruction, as well as universally shared values that are urgently needed by the whole of humankind;

• Developing skills for constructive conflict resolution, including overcoming negative stereotypes of other people, whether living next door or in distant countries.

To further the realization of these aims under the aegis of Educators for Peace and Mutual Understanding, a research center, the Center of

Peace Pedagogy, was founded, with specialists—educators, philosophers, sociologists, psychologists, linguists, and physicians—working on a non-profit basis. The center's activities include research in the methodology and theory of peace education based on new thinking, in accordance with innovative practical recommendations. The center also studies the history of peace education, analyzes foreign experience, and collects information about similar movements and activities in other countries. All these themes are united into more than twenty research projects. Among the projects are "General Education Curriculum and Pedagogy of Peace," "Peace Education: History, Concepts, Organizations, Movements," "Peace Education as an Element of Moral and Legal Cultures," "Peace and Ecology," and "The Unity of National and International in Peace Education."

Associated groups that have formed include Mass Media and the School for New Thinking and Peace, Culture and Education for Mutual Understanding and Cooperation, Educators for Ecological Culture, Education for Human Rights in a World without Wars, Teachers for Health, and Higher Education for Peace and Social Development.

During the years since Educators for Peace and Mutual Understanding was founded (January 1988), much of the group's work has been connected with promoting various national institutions (schools, higher educational establishments, public organizations) and activities in the field of peace education. Primarily, it focuses on coordinating these kinds of activities and the exchange of innovative approaches, and helps in finding partners working in the field inside and outside the country.

On the initiative, and with the assistance, of the Committee of the Movement, several international meetings and conferences have been held, including "New Thinking and Peace Education" (Moscow, January 1989), "Education, Ecology, and Peace" (Novosibirsk, November 1989), and "Education, Culture, and Peace" (Alma-Ata, January 1991).

Much of the movement's activity focuses on the cooperation of teachers and their colleagues in other countries working in the field of peace education.

COOPERATIVE ACTIVITIES—PEACE EDUCATION IMPROVEMENT

The strategy of cooperative activities is of great help for both students and teachers in the process of developing the new peace education concept.

Such activities enhance the qualities important for peacefully working together and enrich group experiences by promoting the mutual exchange of ideas and practical ways and means for cooperative work.

Of immense importance are the new possibilities for persons to get to know each other across national borders, which in itself is a means of peace education. Our peace teachers are supposed to work at two levels of cooperation: inside the country and with other countries. The first level of cooperation involves improving the effectiveness of child-adult and teacher-teacher cooperation in educating our youth to meet the tasks of contemporary national society and the modern world as a whole. It is of great importance to develop individual participatory responsibility and to train persons to contribute to solving local, national, and global problems. Cooperation at the second level, cooperation between countries, means the joint search for knowledge, skills, and practices that are relevant for different countries, even globally.

UN International Cooperation

Regarding the second, external level, it is important to acknowledge and appreciate the activities carried on by the UN and its specialized agencies, especially UNESCO. They support and in many cases guide quite a number of international cooperative programs of peace education.

Educators in Russia have been engaged in many of these international programs—in particular in working out UNESCO's "Recommendation Concerning Education for International Understanding, Cooperation, and Peace" and "Education Relating to Human Rights and Fundamental Freedoms" (1974). One of UNESCO's international initiatives in which we have taken part is the ASP, the UNESCO Associated Schools Project, which works for ecological and global cooperation in a practical way. Our school authorities have from the start (1953) been active in the promotion of these schools. For several decades UNESCO has been committed to a wide and impressive range of activities that have contributed to international cooperation and better understanding between nations.

Cooperation among Countries

To make educational activities more effective, new paradigms based on the new mode of thinking are needed. These problems are widely discussed by concerned educators in many countries, and some interesting approaches have been found for solving them. One is the cooperation of Norwegian, Russian, Ukrainian, and American researchers in the common undertaking that has produced this book, the Project on Ecological and Cooperative Education (PEACE), with its orientation toward new ways of thinking and acting.

Another example of this kind of mutual undertaking at the international level is the cooperative research and practical work of American and Russian classroom teachers under the aegis of the nonprofit organization Educators for Social Responsibility (USA), the Academy of Pedagogical Sciences, and Educators for Peace and Mutual Understanding.

The common projects are themselves approaches to using new-thinking principles to find solutions to common issues, such as how to teach adequately about each other's countries; how to overcome students' negative stereotypes (psychological, social, political); and how to teach about human rights, critical thinking, democracy, and social responsibility.

In August 1988, the project of the American and Russian classroom teachers held its first joint two-week summer institute, the main topic of which was "Teaching New Ways of Thinking." The words of a Russian participant might have been taken as a motto: "Old thinking means trying to teach each other; new thinking means trying to understand each other."

One of the summer institute working papers stated: "New ways of thinking in education is a new approach based on the priority of human values, global concerns, and multiple perspectives. As we learn new ways of thinking, we grow in our ability to understand, accept and tolerate various perspectives and to generate more alternatives" (Education for Social Responsibility 1989). One of the Russian participants offered the following recommendations to teachers in the participating countries attempting to improve their students' knowledge—and willingness to learn—about each other:

1. Use resources from both countries whenever possible
2. Encourage critical thinking to help students understand different points of view and distinguish between fact and opinion
3. Analyze and assess similarities and differences between the countries as to typical views on foreign policy issues and use this in the resource materials

4. Develop definitions and understandings of such concepts as foreign policy, national security, global security, and international human rights

5. Deepen the understanding of the interdependence and necessity for cooperation among all nations

6. Recognize and understand some of the historical circumstances that have shaped the foreign policies of the two countries

7. Encourage a questioning attitude in students to help them clarify and assess the foreign policies of the two countries

8. Identify some of the barriers to the development of new ways of thinking about the foreign policy of the two countries and devise ways to overcome those barriers

9. Teach about human rights in the context of each country's political and economic systems

10. Identify and explore ways to overcome intellectual barriers to new information about each other

Through educational collaboration during the following years and at institutes in Leningrad (1989), Flint, Michigan (1990), and Baranovichi (1991), participants were searching for answers to urgent educational problems, such as these:

- How can we teach new ways of thinking?
- What role should critical thinking play in such teaching?
- What changes, based on new ways of thinking, are needed to teach democracy and social responsibility in our schools?
- How should resolution of ethnic conflicts be taught?
- In what ways can teachers promote these changes?

While searching for answers, participants worked out some innovative approaches for teaching based on the new thinking. They broadened their knowledge, skills, and awareness, and experienced changes in their personal values and attitudes. Said one of the Russian participants, "My ways of thinking certainly have changed in this institute. Some of my stereotyped ideas about American people and the United States have been overturned. I also learned a lot about the methods of teaching new thinking. This has all been most interesting, and I will share it with everyone I can in my own country."

This example of (at the time) American-Soviet educators' cooperation illustrates one of many approaches resulting from the changing relationships between the two countries. As Betty Reardon says, "Such projects challenge—through a new moment—the educational systems in these two countries—and in all other countries as well" (see chapter 2).

CONCLUDING WORDS

Teachers of the world are involved in the task of developing their own abilities and those of their students to become fully participatory citizens in an increasingly interdependent international community. Educators are aware of the unique moment of history that awaits their expertise and empowerment. By the realization of new-thinking ideas for new learning on the basis of such projects as international teachers institutes and the project PEACE, teachers can take several further steps toward understanding the values and skills they need for developing a peaceful, democratic, ecological, and cooperative future.

REFERENCES

Bateson, Gregory. 1972. *Steps to an Ecology of Mind*. New York: Ballantine.

Educating for New Ways of Thinking. 1989. A U.S.-Soviet Institute. Cambridge, Mass.: Educators for Social Responsibility

Gorbachev, Mikhail. 1987. *Perestroika: New Thinking for Our Country and the World*. New York: Harper.

Kapto, A. 1990. *Filosofia mira: istoki, tendentsii, perspektivy* (Philosophy of peace: sources, tendencies, perspectives). Moscow: Politizdat.

Khrustalyova, L., and V. Bogorodiskaya. 1988. *English Text-book, Grade 6*. Moscow: Prosvesseniye.

Kromenkov, N. A. 1989. *Obrazovaniye, Celoveceskii Faktor, Obssestvenyi Progess* (Education, human factor, social progress). Moscow: Pedagogika.

Reardon, Betty A. 1988. *Comprehensive Peace Education: Educating for Global Responsibility*. New York: Teachers College Press, Columbia University.

Sahtouris, Elisbet. 1989. *Gaia: The Human Journey from Chaos to Cosmos*. New York: Pocket Books.

Yagodin, G. A. "Cerez Gumanizatsiyu i Demokratizatsiyu k Novomu Kacestyn Obrazovaniya" (Humanization and democratization as the basis for reaching the higher level of quality of education). *Hcitelkaya Gazeta* (Teachers Newspaper), 22 December 1989.

World Commission on Environment and Development. 1987. *Our Common Future.* New York: Oxford University Press.

4

"Big Ideas" of Ecology That Every Peace Educator Should Know

Willard J. Jacobson

VITAL QUESTIONS FOR OUR GENERATION

How can nuclear war be prevented?

How can we stabilize human population growth?

How can we obtain the food, clothing, and shelter needed by everyone?

How can all children, young people, and adults obtain the education needed to achieve their full potential?

How can we obtain clean and usable water?

How can we obtain the clean atmosphere needed for healthy living

How can the spread of deserts be prevented?

How can the spread of communicable diseases, such as AIDS, be prevented?

How can we generate the electricity that we need and want without endangering the environment?

How can we save our forests? Grasslands? Rivers? Lakes?

How can we safely dispose of our wastes? Toxins? Radioactive materials?

How can and should we prevent the extinction of plant and animal species? How can we maintain diversity in our ecosystems?

Is planet Earth warming? If so, what can and should we do about it?

Is the ozone layer thinning? If so, what may be the effects of this? How can it be prevented?

How can we achieve sustainable development without critically damaging the environment?

Problems! There are many environmental problems facing humankind. This list is drawn, in part, from the report of the World Commission on

Environment and Development, *Our Common Future* (1987), and from the materials and reports of the International Environmental Conference convened in Rio de Janeiro in 1992.

In this chapter I discuss how humankind is related to other organisms on the planet and list some of the critical problems that threaten our peace and well-being. In the process I will define the science of ecology and note some of the characteristics that make it especially useful to peace educators.

Of special importance are eleven "big ideas" of ecology that can be used to identify interrelations among organisms and the environments in which they live. Eleven examples are given of how these can be used to raise key questions that may have been overlooked, to clarify critical issues that still may be obscure, and to raise the level of participation in the study and resolution of problems.

Our Species and the Biosphere

We are *sapiens,* the thinking species. However, our species is also the only member of the genus *Homo.* Members of a species, such as *Homo sapiens,* usually have similar body structures and usually can join with others of the species to reproduce. In general, members of *Homo sapiens,* regardless of race or ethnic background, can join with others of the species in reproduction.

Being one among literally millions of species, we differ in many ways from other species. But like most other species we need food, water, oxygen, and many materials needed for the growth of body tissue. Species often compete for the essentials. Those that fail in this competition often become extinct, as the fossil records show. It has been suggested that, if there should ever be a large-scale nuclear war, *Homo sapiens* might join many other species in the deathly quiet of mass extinction.

Species are engaged in slow evolutionary change. The agent of change generally is *natural selection.* For example, in a section of what became an industrial area of Britain, tree bark used to be light-colored, and most of a species of moths that often rested on the bark of the trees also were light-colored. When the area became industrialized, the tree bark became darkened. Light-colored moths were much more conspicuous against the dark background and were much more likely to be detected and eaten by birds. The proportion of dark-colored moths increased. This is one of the few cases in which the process of natural selection has been observed. Usually evolution through natural selection takes place over very long periods of time. But all species, including *Homo sapiens,* are involved in the process. As change takes place, the nature of the genetic material that is passed from generation to generation is also changed.

Cultural evolution is probably almost unique to *Homo sapiens.* It involves changes in the tools, technology, and ideas that we use. Compared to genetic evolution, cultural evolution is quite rapid. For example, people from Asia probably began to cross the Bering strait to North America twenty to thirty thousand years ago. Within a relatively short time, languages evolved that were strikingly different from other Indian languages. Almost all of the Indians had some form of agriculture. Some of the new inhabitants who migrated to Central America developed a calendar that many believe is superior to the ones in general use today.

In *New Lives for Old,* anthropologist Margaret Mead reported on her return to the South Pacific islands where she had lived and studied before World War II. During the war, strange new technologies were introduced into these South Sea isles. Upon her return to the islands after the war, Margaret Mead was amazed at how the islanders had accommodated themselves to and even used the new technologies. Certainly, compared to genetic evolution, cultural evolution can be very rapid.

The scientist V. I. Vernadsky developed the concept of the *noosphere* as a human being's share of responsibility for the future of the biosphere. To take one's share of responsibility requires a new mode of thinking. Valentina Mitina describes some of the qualities that are needed to prepare young people to bear their noosphere—to take on their share of responsibility for the biosphere (see chapter 3). As a result of its potential intelligence, humankind can help protect the biosphere and raise the quality of life.

Major Aims

One of the major aims of education for social responsibility in democratic societies is to enable citizens and future citizens to more effectively deal with the problems that we face. Students can learn intellectual approaches and procedures with which they can study and deal with problems. Faced with a problem, they need not come to the investigations completely empty-handed. For example, they should have at their command certain questions, such as those at the end of this chapter, with which they can begin their analyses.

One "big idea" in ecology is the concept of systems; the appropriate system for analysis may range from a small system within the body of an organism to the global system. It is important that we identify appropriate systems for study and action. Students who have had some basic education in ecology should know that one of the questions to be asked is, "In what system should we begin our study and analysis of the problem?" Then, after study and analysis of the problem, we can stand back and reflect critically upon what has or has not been done. "What have we learned from our study of this problem that we can use as we approach this and other problems in the future?" This reflection upon our experience is one of the ways we learn from what has or has not been done. It is one of the ways we "learn how to learn."

In all societies, the resolution of many problems requires the cooperation of many. This is especially true of environmental problems. Even the most heinous autocrat cannot prevent littering and the desecration of the environment. Wastes are tossed into reservoirs of drinking water; insects and human wastes contaminate food supplies. Cooperative action by citizens who become knowledgeable about the environment and learn how to care for it may be the most effective approach to environmental enhancement. For example, in the United States and other agricultural countries, one of the most successful conservation efforts has been soil conservation programs; you seldom see fields on hillsides that are not strip-cropped and contour-plowed. Through intensive soil conservation education programs on farms and in schools, those who till the soil came to know the importance of soil conservation practices.

Farmers who have become sensitized to the need to protect the topsoil have said that it is painful to them to see unprotected topsoil, knowing that most of the topsoil can be washed away in one heavy rainstorm. We are dependent upon the environments in which we live for almost all that is necessary for life. We have the responsibility to insure that all that is necessary is available to everyone, not just today, but forever.

Probably for the first time, one species, and one generation of that species, can take steps that will make it difficult if not impossible for other organisms and other generations of humankind to live and thrive. A catastrophe such as a nuclear war might make it difficult for life to continue in many regions, if not the entire planet. Surely, our generation has responsibilities to future generations. One is that the environment be left in such a condition that the generations to come can live and thrive.

Science of Ecology

To help meet our responsibility to future generations, to other inhabitants of the planet, and to ourselves, we can turn to a science in which some of these problems have been studied—the science of ecology. Ecology has been defined as the study of organisms in their environment. Others have defined ecology as environmental biology. Certainly, a major dimension of ecology is the study of the environment and the interrelations within it. Ecology is both a holistic and a reductionistic science. It is holistic in that it involves the study of interrelationships within systems and in the system—the whole being seen as greater than the sum of its parts.

In its holistic dimension, ecology discovers and studies relationships such as those between slash-and-burn agriculture and the apparent warming of the Earth's atmosphere. But it also does reductionistic studies of smaller systems. For example, much has been learned from carefully controlled experiments that study the effects of introducing foreign organisms into ecosystems. It is reported that reductionistic studies are underway to find the possible effects of introducing organisms that break up oil spills. Because ecology is both holistic and reductionistic, it can contribute to a better understanding of the environment.

In project PEACE, we are not engaged in ecological research. Instead, we are primarily interested in the broad interrelationships found in large ecosystems. As Betty Reardon (chapter 2) has stated, "For this project the ecological approach emphasizes relationships and interlinkages. It is a way of thinking that is grounded in holism, in the consideration of an issue, a topic, or a problem, in the broadest possible context—where possible, with the largest system of which . . . [it] is a part."

Certainly, ecology is related to the achievement of peace. Susan Ahearn (chapter 6) suggests that for creating "landscapes of peace" a "more holistic ecology education is the key to the process." For many, the lack of some of the essentials for life can be a source of conflict; it is difficult, for instance, to sit idly by and watch one's child or grandchild starve. Conversely, it is certainly a matter of justice to make certain that everyone has access to the environment and the essential products of the environment. Without justice, there may be only the peace of the absence of war, a peace that is tenuous and often threatened by conflicts.

Ecology also can be seen as an application of intelligence to the environmental problems that may or may not be the consequences of our actions. Robert Zuber, in chapter 9, calls attention to the importance of ecological wisdom.

The study of ecology can reduce the chances that critical factors will be overlooked. Before changes, and especially radical changes, are made in the environment, attempts should be made to ascertain what may be the likely consequences of these changes. It may seem highly desirable to build a new irrigation system to grow more food, but before the irrigation system is built, ecological questions should be asked: What will happen to the regions that, as a result, will have less water? What will happen to the level of the groundwater table—will the wells go dry? Of course the possible consequences of not doing anything should also be explored. We can use the science of ecology to predict possible consequences, or comparative "risks," of proposed actions and thus possibly make more intelligent decisions.

Risk analysis is thus an important and useful process in environmental decision making. An ecological approach, with its emphasis on interrelationships, is especially helpful in gaining the insights and perspectives that can make risk analysis more effective. The following are among the questions that can be asked during the analysis of risk:

- Who will be affected by the implementation of a proposal, such as the proposal to increase the amount of water used for irrigation?
- Will the effects of the proposal be much greater on some than on others?
- To what extent should this disparity of impact influence a decision? The proposal to spray insecticide on a marsh may have little impact many kilometers away, but it may have a much greater impact on people and other species living in and around the marsh.)
- Is there urgency in the call for action? (Even if the local school is in a budget crisis, the outbreak of an infectious disease in the school requires that action be taken immediately.)
- Will the results of a proposed action be worth the cost? (It is very expensive to enlarge a city's water system, but in a city that seems to have a water crisis every year, many citizens may argue that it must be done.)
- What are the risks of not taking action? (Often risks are assessed for

proposed actions while possible serious risks in not doing anything are ignored.)

The "Big Ideas" of Ecology

What should be studied and learned of ecology by those who are engaged in peace education? Should peace educators be prepared to engage in discussions and decision making with regard to the environment as well as issues of conflict and security?

I suggest that those who are engaged in the struggle for peace and the improvement of the environment should gain an operational understanding of some of the most basic concepts in the science of ecology. The "big ideas" of ecology can help us gain a more profound understanding of the environment and the critical environmental problems we face. An understanding and use of these ideas may also reduce conflict and increase the likelihood that we can achieve peace. The big ideas in ecology, like those in other sciences, are based upon the work of many, and they may change as others continue to study and investigate. The broad generalizations of science, including the big ideas, belong to everyone who strives to understand their meaning and uses them in their work.

In all sciences it is assumed that these broad generalizations are universal in their application. For example, consider the notion, which I will discuss later in this chapter, that most matter in planet Earth is involved in cycles such that, in general, matter is neither created nor destroyed. Ecologists and other scientists who study phenomena in systems like planet Earth assume that such statements hold throughout the planet. Their colleagues, the astronomers who study phenomena in the universe beyond planet Earth, assume that these generalizations hold throughout the universe. As investigations continue, however, the generalizations may need to be changed—into *revised* statements that are assumed to be universally applicable.

THE "BIG IDEAS" OF ECOLOGY—ELEVEN CONCEPTS

The following are some of the big ideas of ecology that can help us better understand the environments in which we live and deal more intelligently with the environmental problems we face. Each section gives examples of how the big idea can be used in observation and investigation.

Systems

A system is composed of all the elements that should be considered when we study a phenomenon, deal with a problem, or strive to achieve a purpose. In what may be the most important photograph ever taken (figure 4.1), we can see planet Earth as viewed from space—as part of the planetary system in which we live. By all reports, every astronaut who has viewed Earth from space has been awestruck. Many problems that have seemed so important, such as bitter fights over national boundaries, take on a different perspective when viewed from outer space. The perspective of the *planetary system* can give us new and useful insights.

In ecology, a variety of systems, both large and small, are considered. The system that deals with all life on the planet is called the *biosphere*. When we deal with the problems of increased carbon dioxide in the atmosphere and global warming, we are dealing with the *planetary system* and concerned about the effects of the global warming on the biosphere. When we consider both living organisms and their physical environment, we are considering an *ecosystem*. A pond may be an ecosystem, and we might be concerned about the water in the pond, the pond bottom, and all the plants and animals in or around the pond. When we study only the living organisms in a system, the system we are dealing with is a *community*.

A tropical rain forest and a prairie grassland are both ecosystems, and each ecosystem has a community of interrelated living organisms that live in the ecosystem. All the individuals of one species in a community constitute a *population*. All the human beings living in a system constitute a population of human beings.

Sometimes, we deal with *internal* systems, such as digestive and circulatory systems, within organisms. The *cell* is a basic system in tissue. There are single-celled organisms, such as the amoeba, in which all the complicated functions of life take place in a single cell. More often, living organisms are composed of large numbers of highly interrelated cells that perform all the functions needed for life. Information is transmitted from a cell to the next generation by the transfer of genetic material from the parent cell to the offspring.

Fig. 4.1. The Earth, a planetary system.

Is there a similar information transfer on the planetary scale? Can we gain new insights into information transfer on a planetary scale by considering how it is done in a cell? The system may be *local*, as when we consider community waste disposal, or *global*, as when we study the spread of diseases such as AIDS. When dealing with some health problems, the appropriate systems may be *cellular* and *subcellular* systems. Often we shift systems to see from different frames of reference. For example, in the study of AIDS it is necessary to study the immune system within the human body, but it is also essential to study how such a disease is transmitted from human being to human being and from a population on one continent to populations on other continents.

Humans without *cultural and social systems* cannot survive in most environments in the planetary system. For instance, the human child is utterly dependent upon others for the care it needs and remains dependent for a long period. Humans probably are unique in the extent of their need for cultural and social systems.

In *agriculture* we often deal with both small and large systems. Throughout most past eras, agriculture was carried on by a *family system*. Most of the work in the field and with animals that were a part of the system was done by the adults in the family, women and men. At critical times everyone, including children and grandparents, was pressed into service to save the crops and find stray animals. Sometimes the need for help on the farm limited children's schooling. Many have asked whether limiting children's education is too high a price to pay for their help in doing all that must be done by the family system.

One of the strengths of the family system is that it can call upon all members of the system in times of emergency. Both young and old gain experience in working with each other. Another strength is that the family knows its land and may have a primordial understanding of what is really important for the welfare of the family. However, there are times when family systems need to cooperate. For example, when grain is ripe, it must be harvested quickly before rain and hail, rats and birds destroy much of the crop. Even on farms in India, where there are many who seek work, mechanical threshing machines are brought in to separate grain from chaff before much of the grain is lost. In the North American Midwest much of the harvesting is done by large combines. The people who operate fleets of combines start harvesting when the grain begins to ripen in the South. They follow the ripening grain until the harvest is finished on the plains of Canada. This can be viewed as family systems cooperating in larger systems to do what needs to be done.

Cooperation

Cooperation in a larger system is needed to carry out agricultural research and education to increase production and protect against plant and animal diseases. Some of the most basic agricultural research that has led to remarkable increases in wheat production was carried out in Mexico. Rice production has been increased by research carried out in the Philippines. The education that is necessary to improve agriculture often is carried out in agricultural extension systems associated with large universities. In a sense, this is research and education in a global system.

Cooperatives are institutions in which individuals, families, and other social systems work together to achieve what they cannot achieve separately. Producer cooperatives make the production, collection, and marketing of farm products more efficient. For example, milk must be cooled so that it will not spoil, must be transported to city markets, and then be transferred to those who need it. The single farmer finds it difficult to do all of this. Similarly, through consumer cooperatives, people work together to determine their needs and shop for and buy the goods that can meet these needs. Through consumer cooperatives, consumers can gain the advantages of purchasing on a larger scale to get lower prices.

In North America, the large farmers are best able to make use of modern agricultural technology. In both India and North America, those who cannot use the new technology leave their farms and move to the cities. In the United States in the fifteen years from 1954 to 1969, ten million people moved from rural to urban areas—one of the great migrations. There have been similar migrations in many lands, but there has been very little exploration of the possible consequences of such huge migrations, nor has there been much planning to deal with the problems such migrations have given rise to.

Study and action in planetary, or global, systems is of special importance. Problems in the atmosphere and the hydrosphere often can be studied only in large, often planetary, systems. National boundaries are of little consequence when dealing with global problems. Such United Nations agencies as UNEP, UNESCO, FAO, and WHO have been active in the study of environmental problems. The conference on environmental problems held in the summer of 1992 in Rio de Janeiro was one of the largest international conferences ever held—almost all nations participated. The conference provided an unprecedented opportunity for the sharing of ideas and experiences and for discussion of planetary problems.

But data must be gathered around the world. New technologies, such as earth satellites, must be utilized if we are to learn more about some planetary problems. While the technologies to study some of these problems are available, usually they are very expensive. For example, the testing of nuclear weapons may release radioactive materials into the atmosphere that may eventually spread around the Earth. The study of the spread of radioactive materials obviously must be done on a planetary scale. Because many environmental problems transcend national boundary lines, it has been difficult to harness the resources needed to tackle some of the global problems. Who should support research into planetary problems? Who should pay for the steps that must be taken to save our forests? To deal with some of the intractable global problems, we certainly need new thinking and much better global organization. Many of us need to extend our vision so that we can think in broader terms.

The concept of a system is important in ecology. One of the important steps in the study of the environment and environmental problems is to determine the system(s) in which investigations should take place. Some problems, such as the AIDS epidemic, are spreading from continent to continent and must be viewed globally. However, part of the solution for AIDS may come from laboratories where the disease is being investigated in cellular systems. There is a certain amount of wisdom in the phrase attributed to René Dubos: *Think globally; act locally*. In the future, we also shall have to "think locally; act globally." The big idea about systems from ecology, is that we should become aware of the system in which we are thinking and acting and be prepared to shift from system to system as the need arises.

Cycles

Most matter in planet Earth is involved in cycles, such that, in general, matter is neither created nor destroyed. Instead, the matter is naturally recycled and used over and over again. It is especially important to recognize that most organic materials needed for life are involved in natural cycles. Thus, most, perhaps all, of the materials that are needed to sustain life are not destroyed but remain in the cycles.

Most materials can be used only when they are in certain *phases of these cycles*. People struggle to get essential resources that are in the phases of these cycles when they can be used. This can lead to sharp conflict.

The following are examples of natural cycles:

> Water cycle
> Oxygen and carbon dioxide cycle
> Nitrogen cycle
> Producer-consumer-decomposer cycle

Water is abundant on planet Earth: some suggest that our planetary home should be called the "water planet"; over three-fourths of the earth's surface is covered with water. But much of the water is being seriously contaminated. The Aral Sea has become much smaller because rivers that previously flowed into it are now being diverted in large irrigation projects. In the past, the Aral Sea was an important source of seafood. Now its fishing industry is almost gone, and those who depended on the sea for livelihood have had to go elsewhere. Similarly, the once-pristine Mediterranean has become seriously contaminated by runoff from neighboring watersheds, sewage from adjacent cities, wastes from factories, and and wastes from the vessels that ply the sea. It has been thought that the oceans and seas are so vast that a little garbage and a little waste can't possibly hurt them. They have been hurt!

The water that we seek and use usually is in certain phases of the water cycle. Generally, we use water after it has fallen as rain and before it flows into the ocean. A wide range of demands are made upon water while it is in this phase of the water cycle. In large regions of Earth, water is needed for irrigation to grow food and fiber. Large quantities of water are also needed, for a wide range of uses, by people living in cities. If a nation upstream uses almost all the available water for its own irrigation projects, the people downstream may be driven to radical action to ensure that everyone, including themselves, has the water they need.

Many human practices interfere with the natural flow of resources through their cycles. Great amounts of material may be held for long periods of time in phases of the cycles where it is inaccessible. Other materials may be released into the environment sooner than would occur naturally. For example, in the oxygen and carbon dioxide cycle, large amounts of carbon are locked in the big trees and other plants in the tropical rain forest. But if the trees and other plants are cut down and burned, a tremendous amount of carbon dioxide is released into the atmosphere. This can have a profound impact upon the environment. Carbon dioxide is a good absorber of infrared heat radiation. Incoming solar radiation penetrates the atmosphere and is absorbed by the Earth's surface, and some of this energy is radiated back into the atmosphere as longer-wave infrared radiation. This reradiated infrared heat radiation is absorbed by the carbon dioxide in the atmosphere. An increase of carbon dioxide in the atmosphere might lead to an increase in the amount of heat energy absorbed in the atmosphere, and this might be a cause of "global warming." Global warming is an example of how changes in a natural cycle can have a profound effect upon the environment. Is global warming taking place? An ecological approach to this question can lead to a somewhat different perspective on the problem than that of "common sense."

Common sense often leads us to not take any action until we have strong evidence that a phenomenon such as global warming is taking place. But by then it may be too late to take effective action. Risk analysis can be a more effective way than common sense to study the problems. In some cases, it may be critical to take action while there is still time to act.

Risk Analysis

Risk analysis entails weighing the risks of various courses of action. Which is the greater risk—waiting to take action until we are quite certain that global warming is taking place? Or taking the actions, such as reducing the amount of forest burning, that might reduce global warming if it is taking place? Weighing the risks of various courses of action or inaction before we know for certain that a phenomenon is taking place *may keep our options open.* If we begin to reduce the amount of carbon dioxide in the atmosphere, we retain the option of doing something to deal with the problem if global warming is actually taking place. If it is not, the reduction of carbon dioxide in the atmosphere probably involves little risk.

The Producer-Consumer-Decomposer Cycle

The producer-consumer-decomposer cycle makes food available to organisms in a system.

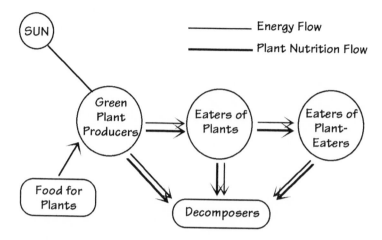

Fig. 4.2. Energy flow in the producer-consumer-decomposer cycle

Green plants are the great producers; they take carbon dioxide, water, and nutrients from the soil, pond, or ocean and use energy from the sun to manufacture food for almost all living matter. In this process the oxygen that is needed by both plants and animals ("consumers") is released. Among the great sources of oxygen in the atmosphere are the tropical rain forests. Destruction of the great rain forests will, therefore, remove a major source of oxygen. A reduction in the amount of available oxygen might be calamitous for many organisms throughout planet Earth.

Living organisms consume the food manufactured by green plants to use it for energy and the growth of tissue. But organisms do not live forever. When they die, small organisms called "decomposers" break down the tissues, and the nutrients that are released can be used again by another generation of producers to make food. Sometimes organic materials are withdrawn from the local cycle. In developing countries, organic material in the form of dung is used as fuel to heat homes and to cook foods. These organic materials are then lost from the local cycle, and, unless other fertilizers are added, the fertility of the soil will inevitably be reduced. Likewise in modern agriculture, food and fiber products are withdrawn from the local cycle and often distributed throughout the world. The fertility of the soil is depleted, and fertilizers must be added to the soil if it is to continue to be fertile.

Most materials on planet Earth are involved in cycles. It is interesting to note that almost all of the chemical elements that make up living tissue, from nitrogen to oxygen to carbon, are involved in natural cycles. Hence, it is important to recognize these cycles and to be concerned if changing conditions threaten their normal operation. If some phase of a cycle breaks down, as when decomposers are destroyed by chemicals, the consequences for all organisms in the cycle may be very serious.

Balance and Change

Balance

In some phenomena there must be a balance between what "comes in" and what "goes out." The concept of balance in the environment is essentially the basic conservation law: the amount of matter and energy in a system remains the same. In many systems there must be a balance between the matter and energy entering a system and that leaving. In the case of planet Earth, the amount of energy entering the Earth system must be about equaled by radiant energy leaving the system. Otherwise, there would be either a rapid increase in the mean temperature of Earth or a cooling such as those that have led to glacial ice ages.

But if the amount of matter and energy in a system remains the same, how can we run out of energy? The amount of energy remains about the same, but as it is used the energy is converted into less usable forms— often heat. Water behind a dam on a hillside has potential energy, but as the water flows down the hill this potential energy is converted into a less usable form. There is energy in coal and oil, but when they are burned, the energy is changed into heat and is in a less usable form.

Often there is a balance among various populations that live in an environment. When some population, such as the human population, grows rapidly, a delicate balance may be weakened, and the well-being of other populations may be threatened. The primeval tropical rain forest contains large varieties of plant and animal life. But when the trees are cut down in slash-and-burn, many populations of plants and animals cannot survive. Again, delicate balances may be threatened.

In every large city, great effort must be expended to maintain a balance in the city ecosystems. New York City, for example, is one of the most densely populated cities in the world. Almost none of the necessities for life are produced there. Almost all of the food eaten by New York City residents comes from elsewhere; a survey of the food products in stores and bazaars will show that the foods come from all over the world. Again, to maintain a balance, the paper and plastic in which the food is brought to the city must be disposed of; the garbage from New York City is placed in large landfills where some of the garbage will eventually decompose, or it is dumped into the Atlantic Ocean.

Ecologically, it would be desirable to find ways to return the potential fertilizer to the soils and farms. It would be helpful to use less, and biodegradable, packaging materials. Then these and other materials could be composted into fertilizer and returned to the soil on the farms from whence they came.

There are cities, such as Milwaukee, where city wastes are composted to form fertilizers and then sold to gardeners and other tillers of the soil. It has been suggested that eventually it will be possible to mine the huge garbage dumps of the cities for composted materials that can be used as fertilizer to enhance the growth of plant materials that we use as food or fiber. From an ecological perspective it would be desirable not to dispose of wastes by ocean dumping. The effects upon fish and other ocean life is not completely clear. In any case, it is desirable to eventually return the organic wastes to the soil.

Much of the energy used in the city comes from the burning of oil and other hydrocarbons, which store solar energy that was collected by plants several hundred million years ago. The wastes from burning hydrocarbons are discharged into the atmosphere. But hydrocarbons formed hundreds of millions of years ago also release waste materials such as carbon dioxide and soot that will affect our atmosphere, rivers, lakes, and oceans. As more and more people in countries throughout the world move to cities, serious problems of waste management and disposal arise. Some of our most noxious wastes are discharged into the atmosphere.

In many great cities, like Los Angeles, temperature inversions trap pollutants near the surface of the ground. Chemicals from automobile exhausts can cause eyes to water and increase the incidence of respiratory ailments such as pneumonia, emphysema, and the common cold. The concept of balance is one of the big ideas of ecology that can help us to view and understand in a useful way many of the environmental problems that we face.

Change

The concept of balance has been deeply embedded in ecology for a long time. It has sometimes been called the "balance of nature." Now this concept is being questioned. It is suggested that *change* is a *more basic* concept. Nature, that is, is not likely to be in a state of equilibrium. Instead, nature is more likely to be in a state of turmoil and change. Reflect, for instance, on the environmental effects of fire, or on how a very aggressive wolf pack leader may destroy its territory's balance in the predator-prey relationship between wolves and deer.

Studies of ocean sediments indicate that there have been great fluctuations in temperature during the last several million years. Thus, it may be change and not equilibrium that is the constant. In these systems characterized by change, the question is not, *should* humans intervene, but rather *how* they should intervene. In this view, it is not sufficient to say that "nature knows best."

A big idea in ecology is being questioned. Is balance the natural state or is it change and turmoil? It is important in the sciences, including the science of ecology, that big ideas be questioned, debated, and eventually subjected to empirical tests. Readers of this book should have the opportunity to watch how a challenge to a big idea is made and, perhaps, eventually resolved. In the second edition of this book, will we emphasize balance or change?

Succession

Plants in their natural settings are involved in natural succession. Natural succession may start from solid rock, desert sand, open water, or volcanic ash. An example of succession may start with lichens on barren rock and pass through stages of algae, mosses, grasses, shrubs, trees, and the final *climax condition*. Natural stages of succession lead to a climax condition, which will persist until conditions change.

The various stages in which plants and animals exist may be considered as transitions toward an eventual climax condition. The nature of the climax condition will often depend upon the climate and especially the amount of rainfall. All environments, ranging from the city sidewalk to the tropical rain forest, are in some stage of succession.

An abandoned hard-surface road in Norway will pass through various stages of succession until it reaches a climax condition, which may be a coniferous forest. The climax condition in the northeastern United States is a hardwood forest. In northern Russia and northern North America the climax is the plants of the Arctic tundra. The environmental factors within the climax condition are balanced so that the climax condition will persist until there is a radical upset in the environment.

Usually, the climax environment will support only a small human population. Those who live in climax conditions will usually get the food and fiber that they need by hunting, fishing, and food gathering.

There have been few cultures in which all of the necessities of human life have been obtained from the climax environment. At one time it was thought that some of the North American Indians depended almost entirely on food and fiber from the climax ecosystem. More recent research seems to indicate that almost all of the North American Indians engaged in agriculture.

Agriculture is an intervention in natural succession so that plants such as wheat, rice, maize, and grasses can grow. However, if a cultivated field is abandoned, succession will resume and eventually the climax condition will be reached. The awful destruction that accompanies modern warfare may result in the destruction of almost all plants and animals, leaving the battlefield almost completely barren. Much of the vegetation in certain areas of Vietnam was denuded with chemicals such as Agent Orange. It has been estimated that millions of land mines have been left in Afghanistan; the land mines must be removed before there can be safe access to the denuded battlefield. But succession probably will begin, and the battlefield will pass through the natural stages of succession. The wreckage left by the armies of Tamerlane and Genghis Khan six to eight hundred years ago can still be seen. Under desert conditions, succession takes place very slowly.

Population Growth Patterns

Almost all populations have an intrinsic capacity for growth. Observe the common dandelion! After it has flowered, each dandelion plant will have a large number of seeds, each attached to a gossamer tuft that can be carried great distances. If all the dandelion seeds produced by all the dandelion flowers were to successfully propagate, the entire Earth would soon be completely covered with dandelions, and many other species would be relegated to extinction.

The same holds for almost all other species. Each population has the intrinsic capacity for growth; if this growth is unchecked, other species will be overwhelmed. Most checks to population growth are natural. Most dandelion seeds will land on surfaces where they cannot survive.

Eventually, there are checks to the growth of all populations. Otherwise, one population would overwhelm all others. The introduction of a species into an environment where there are few natural checks can lead to explosive population growth. This happened when rabbits were introduced into Australia, where many of the natural checks to rabbit population growth were absent.

What happens to populations that undergo very rapid population growth? Figure 4.3a shows a population that has grown very fast but has stabilized and the total population remains the same. Many would argue that, since there are no large fluctuations of dramatic growth or deadly kill-offs, this is a desirable pattern of population stabilization.

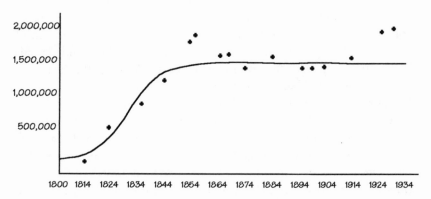

Fig. 4.3a. A population that has grown fast and is stabilized.

Figure 4.3b shows a sharp decline in population. In many populations such rapid declines have led to extinction. Actually, this has been the fate of most species that have inhabited this planet. There are those who suggest that this might be the fate of humans if we should become engaged in a large-scale nuclear war.

Largely because of developments in public health and food supply that reduce the death rate of children, humankind is experiencing very rapid population growth. Starting a relatively short time ago, public health measures such as the provision of relatively sanitary water supplies and the development of means of controlling communicable diseases through inoculation and vaccination reduced death rates among the young, and more survive to the age when they can reproduce. Not long ago in many countries most children would die before the age of five. It

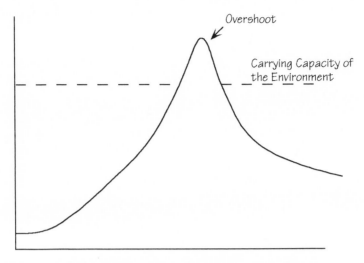

Fig. 4.3b. A pattern of rapid population growth and decline.

has been estimated that throughout most of the time humankind has been in existence, the human population may have doubled every one thousand years. Recently the human population has been doubling about every forty years. Figure 4.4 shows the recent rapid human population growth that has taken place in the last few hundred years.

What will be the future pattern of human population growth? Will it be the stabilized model in which the population stabilizes around a certain level, with no sudden rapid growths or deadly kill-offs? Or will it be the kill-off model in which humankind, after a very short sojourn on this planet, joins most of other species on this planet in extinction? Or will the human population follow a sawtoothed pattern characterized by sharp rises and falls?

Tolerance

Organisms can live only under conditions within certain ranges. Conditions may be too hot or too cold, too wet or too dry, for human survival without our cultural products; the range of tolerances for the human animal is very narrow. But human beings, with their cultures, use clothing and shelter to make it possible for them to exist almost anywhere on Earth and in the nearly complete vacuum of outer space. Some of the limiting factors for various populations are temperature, available water,

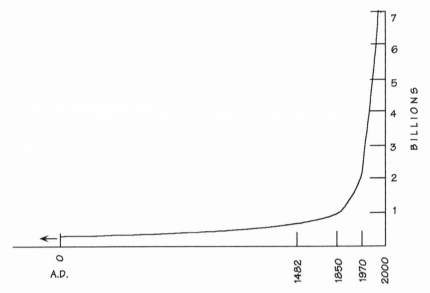

Fig. 4.4. Generalized world population growth curve

and fertile soil. Some organisms that share the biosphere with us, such as the panda, require very special conditions, and if these conditions are modified even slightly, their survival is threatened. Some plants and animals, such as some insects, are able to survive under a wide range of environmental conditions.

We can envisage conditions in our biosphere changing so that tolerance levels are exceeded. A planetary increase of the average temperature or, conversely, the advent of another ice age could make it difficult for humans to survive. One of the environmental factors that might go beyond human tolerance levels is high levels of radioactivity. It has been suggested that one of the organisms that might survive nuclear war is the cockroach. As a result of rapid natural selection, some insects that are comparatively resistant to radiation might be naturally selected, that trait being transmitted to the generations that follow; thus, they might survive.

While the species *Homo sapiens* has existed on the planet for only about four million years, the cockroach has survived for several hundred million years. Are we, with our large brain and unequaled culture, who can create the weapons that may destroy us, less likely to survive a nuclear holocaust than the omnipresent cockroach that squeezes into the cracks of our homes?

There are intricate interrelationships in our environment. Certainly, it is important that, through education, everyone becomes aware that these interrelationships exist. It is especially important that we become aware of them in the ecosystems in which we live. Certainly, it is important that these sensitive interrelationships be monitored and investigated by those who have achieved some expertise in the matter. It is important that citizens, young and old, keep actively informed about environmental factors that affect us all and can be of critical significance to everyone.

Food Chains and Food Webs

There are important interrelationships among organisms, their foods, and their environments. *Food chains* show the direct interrelationships between different organisms and what they eat. They demonstrate the flow of matter and energy within an ecosystem. Human beings are usually plant eaters or eaters of plant eaters. Like most other organisms, we are more efficient users of energy from plants.

Food webs can be more intricate, showing the interrelationships among food chains. In a food web, many specific organisms rely on other specific organisms to sustain life.

The interrelations between organisms in ecosystems can be very intricate and sensitive. Small changes can lead to unforeseen consequences. The caribou that live in Alaska and Northern Canada migrate north and south with the seasons, and the plants of the tundra that they eat can recover when the herds migrate to other grazing grounds. However, nonmigratory reindeer have been introduced there, and the plants of the tundra are now sometimes overgrazed.

The food webs in which humans live also can be profoundly affected by what occurs in a section of a food web. The failure of the Irish potato crop led to a constant threat of starvation and eventually the migration of millions of people from Ireland to North America. In this case, a potato blight, which might seem inconsequential, led to death for some and the migration of millions from home and community. More recently, repeated droughts and protracted warfare, in which food deprivation is seen as a way to attack the enemy, have led to serious starvation in East Africa. Often when there is famine, as in East Africa, it is the children, the next generation, that suffer the most. Because of the sensitivity of interrelations among organisms in food webs, many ecologists urge that great care be taken before new organisms are introduced into ecosystems. The starling, for example, was introduced into North America reportedly because of someone's desire that all the birds mentioned in Shakespeare's plays be represented in North American fauna. But the introduced bird competed well with the birds that were already in North America. Some ornithologists believe that populations of birds, such as the bluebird, have been threatened by the rapid spread of the starlings. Unfortunately, there apparently was no attempt made to investigate the possible effects of the introduction of this new bird into North America.

The introduction of chemicals and other new materials into ecosystems also can have unforeseen effects. There have been cases in which poisonous insecticides have been sprayed directly upon workers in the fields. These chemicals can also have serious detrimental effects on organisms that are not directly sprayed. Too often, the possible effects of spraying have not been considered. Materials like insecticides may be concentrated as they move up food chains and webs. At the bottom of a food chain, an insecticide is quite dispersed and relatively harmless. As small animals eat the treated plants, and larger animals eat the small animals, the insecticide becomes concentrated. Insecticide becomes very concentrated in large birds of prey. The shells of the eggs laid by these birds become very thin, and, too often, the shells will crack before they can hatch. Small changes in food webs, such as the introduction of insecticides to protect crops from insects, may have their intended benefits but may also have unforeseen harmful effects.

The introduction of harmful organisms and materials in biological and chemical warfare certainly could have dire consequences. In World War I, changes in the atmosphere, such as wind direction changes and temperature inversions, had unforeseen consequences. Chemical warfare was not used in World War II, but the horrifying consequences of chemical warfare were again brought to our attention when Iraq used chemical weapons against Iran and against their own Kurdish population.

Food Pyramids

Food pyramids are based upon the food production of green plants. Photosynthesis is a process in which green plants use solar energy to combine carbon dioxide and water and other nutrients to make food. Green plants can utilize only a very small percentage of the incoming energy from the sun to manufacture the food that is used by almost all living organisms. Some of the food that is manufactured enters food chains or webs.

The farther the food is along the chain or web, the smaller is the percentage of the original solar energy that is consumed. Humans get some of the energy by eating cereals such as rice, wheat, and corn. However, humans are omnivorous and also eat meat and other animal products. Food pyramids show the relationships between the nature and type of consumption and food production by green plants. The food pyramid in figure 4.5 depicts how energy is converted at different levels.

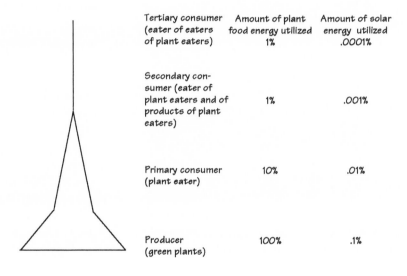

	Amount of plant food energy utilized	Amount of solar energy utilized
Tertiary consumer (eater of eaters of plant eaters)	1%	.0001%
Secondary consumer (eater of plant eaters and of products of plant eaters)	1%	.001%
Primary consumer (plant eater)	10%	.01%
Producer (green plants)	100%	.1%

Fig. 4.5. Energy conversion in the food pyramid.

The energy conversion in the food pyramid roughly follows a "10 percent law." Green plants convert about 0.1 percent of the solar energy that reaches them. At the next pyramid level, primary consumers who eat green plant products utilize about 10 percent of the energy made available by green plants and 0.01 percent of the solar energy. Meat-eating secondary consumers utilize 1 percent of the energy made available by plants and 0.001 percent of the solar energy. Tertiary consumers, such as some birds of prey, utilize only 0.1 percent of the plant food energy and 0.0001 percent of the solar energy. Obviously, the lower on the pyramid the food is consumed, the more efficient the process.

From the standpoint of the pyramid, it is inefficient to depend on meat and other animal products for food. If everyone ate primarily plants and very little meat and other animal products, there would be more food available for everyone. Even now there is serious undernourishment among some and heartbreaking starvation among others. Many children go to bed hungry at night, and the lack of adequate nutrition can have long-range effects on children's mental and physical development. True, there are serious problems of transportation and distribution of food, and these problems can and should be conquered. But more food will have to be made available. One of the ways to make more food available for people is to eat more plant food and have less plant food converted into meat and other secondary foods.

The human population is now over five billion, and our population will probably double in about forty years. Where will the food for more than ten billion people come from? As people gain in economic resources, they often eat more meat. But as the human population grows, we may have to forgo the luxury of being secondary consumers.

Radiation

The release of large amounts of radiation from radioactive materials can have very harmful effects that can persist over long periods of time. We have also seen the effects of radiation from the testing of nuclear weapons, nuclear accidents such as at Chernobyl, and the release of radioactive materials in weapons manufacture, as at Hanford. The release of radioactive materials can cause great harm over long periods of time. In part because radiation and radioactivity have not been major factors in warfare in the past, it is important that we become aware that modern warfare is different, and no one can be completely certain of the nature of the dangers.

The decay and persistence of radioactive materials is measured in *half-life*, the length of time required for half of the radioactive material to have decayed. One of the products of a nuclear explosion probably would be radioactive strontium, which has a half-life of twenty-eight years. Strontium is taken into the body in milk and other food products. Strontium, like calcium, enters the bones, and to have increased radioactive materials incorporated into the structure of the bones is a very serious matter. One of the factors that contributed to the 1963 test ban was the recognition of the harmful effects upon mothers and small children of radioactive strontium. Another product of nuclear explosions, plutonium, has a half-life of twenty-four thousand years. Contamination of the environment with radioactive materials that have a long half-life means that some of the environment may remain radioactive and uninhabitable for a very long time. After a nuclear war, large areas of Earth's surface probably would be uninhabitable. If a great deal of radioactive material of long half-life were released in your area, "home" certainly would be a place you could never go back to.

High levels of radiation may affect plants and animals for very long periods of time. One of the effects may be an increase in the rate of mutation in exposed organisms. A *mutation* is a change in the nuclear material that is passed from generation to generation. For example, in 1791 a short-legged sheep was the offspring of two sheep with legs of normal length. A change had taken place in the nuclear material in the cells of this animal, and this was transmitted from generation to generation to generation. An organism that has inherited such a genetic mutation is a *mutant*.

It is believed that some mutations are the result of a bombardment of living cells with radiation. Most mutations are deleterious. If the level of radiation is raised, will there be more mutants? What will be the effect on the populations exposed to high levels of radiation? Most importantly, these mutations may be carried from generation to generation, possibly forever. In many ways the environment is very resilient, as can be attested to by anyone who has tramped over some of the battlefields of northern Europe. Where the holes have been filled and the fields leveled, farming can begin again. But nuclear war is different. The effects of radiation will persist for a long time.

Nuclear War

A nuclear war would be radically different from any war that has ever been fought. It is critically important that all citizens become aware of some of these profound differences. In 1815, the Indonesian volcano Tambora erupted violently and blew huge quantities of dust and other materials into the atmosphere. Soon the erupted materials were spread around the Earth, and there were colorful sunrises and sunsets reported from many regions. More importantly, the amount of solar energy reaching the Earth's surface was reduced. In New England, where ordinarily the frost-free period is long enough to grow such crops as corn, there were killing frosts in late June and early August.

If there were to be a nuclear war and the explosion of many nuclear bombs, there would be much more soot, soil, and dust blasted into the atmosphere than from the eruption of a large volcano. However, our experiences with volcanic eruptions give some indication of the kinds of effects that might ensue from the explosion of a number of nuclear bombs.

The effects of huge quantities of soot, dust, soil, and debris being blasted into the atmosphere has been called "nuclear winter." As a result of nuclear explosions, large fires would start, and the soot released would be especially effective in blocking incoming sunlight. Subfreezing temperatures might persist for several months. The primary food producers, the green plants, would not receive enough solar energy for sufficient photosynthesis to take place. The possible effects of nuclear winter cannot be predicted with assurance. There are some who believe that nuclear winter might kill life on our planet, while other scientists believe that life would survive. All agree that nuclear winter would be catastrophic and must be avoided. The nature and magnitude of these effects is part of the uncertainty inherent in ecology.

Nuclear war would affect us greatly in ways that cannot be predicted with any degree of certainty. The events that would take place in nuclear war would be unprecedented. There really are no experts on what the world would be like after a nuclear war.

Uncertainty

Inherent in ecology is the concept of *uncertainty*. We seek interrelationships within systems, but some may be elusive. DDT was a very useful insecticide. It could be used to eradicate the anopheles mosquito and prevent the dreaded disease malaria; some regions that had been virtually uninhabitable became livable. No longer did children need be feverish, shake, and eventually die because of this dreaded killer.

But there were unforeseen interrelationships. The DDT became concentrated in the tissue of birds that ate fish and other animals in which the chemical had become concentrated. The eggshells of these birds were very thin and broke before the offspring could hatch, and some birds high in food chains faced extinction. This factor was not foreseen when DDT was first used as a very effective insecticide.

Some factors and situations are *unprecedented,* and there is no way that we can foresee whether the unprecedented will occur. There has never been an exchange of nuclear warheads in a nuclear war. What would happen if all the drinking water in the reservoirs that serve our cities were to be irradiated and anyone who drank the water would become violently ill? While we may know a great deal about some systems, other systems simply have not been studied extensively. Because we have limited global government, and studies of the planetary system are very expensive, we do not know as much about the global system as we know about smaller systems that are more accessible. The experiences we have had with earth satellites and other relatively new technologies have given us a taste of the kind of information that can be gathered. Still, many of our statements about systems that have not been studied extensively are fraught with uncertainty.

THE BIG IDEAS OF ECOLOGY REPRISED

The study of ecology can involve study and investigations in the laboratory and the field. The professional ecologist acquires years of experience and well-honed skills. Most of what we know about various ecosystems and the difficulties that may plague us in ecosystems we owe to the professional ecologist.

All of us need to understand and use knowledge and insights available to us in the science of ecology. To do this, it is very helpful to have as profound an understanding as possible of the major concepts, or big ideas, of ecology. An understanding of these ideas can help us be more effective as we critically participate in the study, discussion, and investigation of serious environmental problems. We can learn and help as we raise such questions as the following:

1. In what *systems* are the problems being studied and analyzed? Are these the most appropriate systems? Could something be gained by considering other systems as well?

2. Why is *cooperation* in smaller and larger systems of special importance to carry out the research and education that are necessary to protect life on the planet?

3. Are the matter and energy involved in problems parts of *cycles*? In what parts of the cycles are the matter and energy? What is happening to the matter and energy in these phases of the cycles?

4. What is the nature of the *balance and change* among various factors in the ecosystems being considered? What is threatening the balance? How can the balance be maintained? What are the possible consequences of upsetting the balance?

5. What stages of *succession* are the organisms in an ecosystem involved in? What is affecting natural succession? What are the possible consequences of impinging upon natural succession?

6. How has the size of the *human population* changed over time? How is the size of the human population likely to change in the future? What effect is this likely to have upon the human population and the environment in which it lives?

7. What are the ranges of *tolerance* of various organisms in our ecosystems? What would happen if conditions were to go beyond tolerance levels?

8. What would happen to *food chains* and *food webs* if foreign organisms or chemicals were introduced?

9. If poisonous chemicals are introduced to the lower level of the *food pyramid*, what happens to the higher levels?

10. What would be the effects of the release of large quantities of *radiation* into the environment? How could this be prevented? What would be the consequences to the environment of a nuclear war? How can nuclear war be prevented?

11. What can be said about the degree of certainty of the information that we are using in dealing with the environment? How could the certainty be increased?

What are our societal responsibilities? What responsibilities do we have for those who have less than enough? What responsibilities do we have for the generations to come? Tomorrow and tomorrow and always. Our children, grandchildren, and great-grandchildren and generations into the future have a stake in what we do to and with the environment. Our greatest gift to those to come after may be a safe, beautiful, and bounteous environment. For this we yearn.

A deeper and more profound understanding of the big ideas of ecology may help us achieve that which we long for.

REFERENCES

Global Education Associates (G.E.A.). 1989. *Breakthrough* 10, no. 4 and 11, no. 1 (Summer/Fall). Special combined issue entitled "Ecological Security in an Interdependent World," edited by Patricia M. Mische and Melissa Merkling.

Gromyko, Anatoly, and Martin Hellman, eds. 1988. *Breakthrough: Emerging New Thinking.* New York: Walker.

Jacobson, Willard J. 1979. *Population Education—A Knowledge Base.* New York: Teachers College Press.

Odum, Eugene P. 1971. *Fundamentals of Ecology.* 3d ed. Philadelphia: Saunders.

Schell, Jonathan. 1982. *The Fate of the Earth.* New York: Avon Books.

World Commission on Environment and Development (Gro Harlem Brundtland, Chairman). 1987. *Our Common Future.* New York: Oxford University Press.

Yablokov, A. V. 1986. *Population Biology: Progress and Problems of Studies on Natural Populations.* Translated from the Russian by Pyotr Aleinikov. Moscow: MIR Publishers.

5
Social Responsibility and Ecological Culture through Ecological Education

Sergei Polozov

In 1988 I accepted an invitation to take part in project PEACE, for I realized only too clearly that ecological problems as such could not be solved unless a number of social and educational problems were solved also. It was obvious that an attempt to direct the attention of educators to certain aspects of ecological education can facilitate the solution of important social and pedagogical problems. Ecological security and social responsibility are closely linked and interconnected with vital processes, both natural and social.

It is not for me to judge how important my contribution to PEACE may be, but I gained a great deal by participating; working together with my excellent colleagues has given me many new insights. I feel satisfied as a result of our working together and forming new friendships.

In this paper I describe the most acute problems for Russian educators. This could help the Western educational public to understand some painful educational processes that were characteristic of the former Soviet system and also continue to some extent in the new national states. Some points that I will review are urgent for Western society as well. My aim is to lay out for the readers problems demanding immediate decisions from the school teachers of my country. The association Educators for Ecological Culture was created in 1990 and is the first public association of educators in ecology in Russia. In the last few years a number of other ecological organizations and associations have sprung up.

During the first three years of our work on PEACE, the world has undergone great changes. Radical changes have taken place in the former Soviet Union; the changes were so rapid that I did not know what territory would be called the "Soviet Union" during the coming months or years. The events of August 1991 became a turning point for the country in all spheres of activity; the political changes constantly affected the educational system and the cultural level of society as a whole. It is hardly possible to analyze the tendencies of these changes; I hope that they will be positive, and I'm working to help them become realized.

ECOLOGICAL SECURITY

For many years the attention of politicians and peoples of all countries has been concentrated primarily on the process of disarmament and ensuring international military security. By the end of the eighties the first really constructive steps were taken that might give some grounds for an optimistic view of the future. We have to think about disarmament and international security as only a *part* (however, an important one) of the general process of creating healthy international relations in various spheres of life in the world community. Ecological security and nature protection rank among the most important of these spheres. The indissoluble connection between armed conflicts and ecological threat was clearly demonstrated by the events in the Persian Gulf. Nature protection is today one of the most important fields of peoples' activity and requires immediate joint efforts of all states. It is difficult to conceive of any meeting between political or public leaders that pays no attention to cooperation in nature protection—this concern is the most important recent trend in international affairs. In fact, any effort by any person in the sphere of solving ecological problems on any scale is to be looked upon as socially meaningful activity.

THE BASIS OF ECOLOGICAL EDUCATION

Nature Protection—Social Responsibility

I am confident that young people's interest in nature protection problems counts as one of the most important means of developing social responsibility. Why? It is evident that an ordinary human being looks upon even urgent political problems as something abstract, as not really relevant to her or his own life. Even more remote is the possibility that ordinary persons can have any real influence on the course of political life in their country or in international affairs.

The questions of improving the ecological situation seem much more tangible. For a great many persons in a number of regions of the former USSR and in the new independent states, improving the ecological situation is becoming a major goal. They know that the attainment of nature protection is closely connected with their own immediate physical survival, and this gives them a real reason to start working for the future and the fate of their community, their fellow citizens, and the whole of humankind.

Coming into contact with a problem in our everyday lives, in our native lands, near our homes—and not just through a TV screen—makes the problem concrete, real, and tangible. To experience this—together with others—is in fact to take the first step toward the solution of the problem. It is a practical step toward a real and socially meaningful activity.

Humanism and Anthropocentrism

Today it is evident that systems of upbringing and education, even in states with the most different social and political organizations, are to a considerable extent oriented toward introducing human values to the growing generation. We want our children to be:

- Healthy—to have at least a minimum standard of physical culture
- Educated—possessing a certain amount of knowledge
- Intelligent—able to use knowledge independently, draw conclusions, and accept adequate decisions
- Practical—able to enact relevant decisions and consistently seek improvements
- Approachable—ready for and capable of friendly communication with other people
- Well-bred—having at least a minimum standard of behavior
- Humane—capable of compassion.

The above qualities are not listed according to relative importance. By listing humaneness as the last point, I want to stress its significance for personality formation. Ecological education plays a very important role in the development of a humane personality. Love of animals and the ability to apprehend the beauty of surrounding nature are qualities which from time immemorial have been considered obligatory for a truly humane and cultivated person.

A humane attitude toward animals is traditionally perceived as pity for animals, our "junior siblings in mind." This tradition is extremely strong and is based on the notion that humans are the crowning glory of nature. This tradition also has (regrettably) an objective reason: animals in today's world are first of all to be pitied.

Generally such emotions—and this kind of approach to solving ecological tasks—is fully in line with an anthropocentric outlook. Really, this is the way we often teach our children: "You are a human being. You are the strongest and the mightiest. And if you want to become a good human being, you must direct your power over nature along the path of humanism."

To develop this kind of outlook in youngsters is generally the dearest wish of most educators dealing with the problems of ecological education. This is the aim of official nature-protecting propaganda in our country, perhaps in ninety-nine cases out of a hundred. (But even this kind of "humanism" is sometimes neglected, nowadays.)

The overwhelming majority of existing textbooks, curricula, and programs on natural history at all levels of the educational system of my country are based on an anthropocentric outlook. Eva Nordland (chapter 1) introduces Bateson's criticism of this traditional anthropocentric school of thinking. In an anthropocentric paradigm, humanism is the pity of the strong toward the weak. We are used to accepting such "pity" as a general moral principle, but we cannot any longer accept the attitude as a way to relate to nature. Something different is required from us as we pass over into the twenty-first century.

As our understanding of life's biological essence is deepening, as we come to know more of the laws governing the functioning of natural systems at all levels of their organization, we are simply bound to fully realize the *universal quality of everything living in the common arena of life*. True humanism lies in the notion that a human being is no special creature having an exceptional right to give or to take away another's life at will. The acceptance of this thesis means to develop ecological culture at the level necessary for humankind today. We might call this attitude *biocentrism*—or the thesis that a human being is an equal among equals in nature. Several thousand years have passed since biocentrism was declared as a thesis. This idea has still not become widely accepted, either in society as a whole or among educators in general.

The educational system of my country has not made a single step from anthropocentrism to biocentrism. It has not even gained an understanding of the necessity to take this step.

Ecological Culture

Culture in general is first of all a conscious rejection of force toward weaker beings, in any sphere or at any level of relations, from the interpersonal to the international. I think that demonstrations of force against weaker beings do not belong to the nature of human beings who have developed confidence and self esteem.

We might call the temptation to use "threat gestures" a sort of atavism inherited from a purely biological past; but historically that would not be correct. For the overwhelming majority of animal species, to demonstrate threat is an extreme manifestation of aggression that becomes a violent conflict only in rare cases. For human beings to threaten to use force is a sign that they are not spiritually mature—that is, that they possess a low level of culture.

Avoidance of the use of force toward nature is the only road for an ecologically mature social community; we must start to decrease violence to a minimum level. Policies of violence lead—through their ecologically negative consequences—to a complete liquidation of all economic and other activities. An ecologically mature culture, supported by material resources and intellectual possibilities, gives a society the opportunity to rise to a qualitatively new stage. It means to prevent the use of violence, among "ourselves" and among "others," and the ecologically threatening effects of violence on nature as a whole, including humankind.

The whole discussion concerning a desirable level of ecological cultural development in the disastrous ecological situation of today's world inevitably leads us back to prosaic and tangible problems. It is not appropriate, even for "a true gentleman," to waste one's time wondering whether one's necktie is elegantly enough tied when *the house is ablaze*. The important attitude is this: to save the children—and then to save the most valuable other things.

Ecological culture today means, first of all, to cultivate in people the ability to accept many (sometimes extremely difficult) limitations regulating behavior and activities in the natural environment. As Eva Nordland points out in chapter 1, at this moment in history humans can no longer choose whatever life-style they please. It is necessary to declare ethical norms guiding our relations with nature; we also have a strong need for juridical norms of nature-protecting legislation allowing society to regulate behavior that violates ethical norms. Thus, the development of ecological culture in the process of ecological education is intimately connected with *ecological ethics* as well as *ecological legislation* and *ecological crime*. These issues must be given the closest attention by educators, lawyers, and sociologists. Because of the unity of the biosphere and the general interrelation of the planet's ecosystem as a whole, social consequences of both ecological ethics and ecological crime acquire a universal, global character.

Even though the knowledge we have about these matters is overwhelmingly clear to many of us, we have to admit that not everyone agrees. It is probably in the sphere of the development of ecological ethics and of preventing ecological crime that international contacts among specialists could have the greatest strategic effect both in the field of environment protection proper and in social consolidation of world community efforts.

The basis for cooperation is global-scale ethical norms for relations between human beings and nature. Susan Ahearn (chapter 6) and Betty Reardon (chapter 2) elaborate on these points. In this connection UNESCO initiatives are highly welcomed concerning the creation of an international scientific committee on "Ethics and World Community," with the special aim of elaborating the concept of ecological and cultural security.

The notion of ecological culture is closely connected with developing the sense of social responsibility in the full meaning of the word: responsibility for one's own deeds and for society as a whole, responsibility toward future generations and, in the end, toward life itself.

Ecological World Outlook

Betty Reardon, Eva Nordland, and Valentina Mitina discuss problems about different aspects of new thinking in their works. In spite of sometimes complete ecological ignorance in some strata of society, we must not restrict our perspectives in the sphere of ecological education only to developing new ecological thinking. New ecological thinking is the ability to comprehend and analyze integrally the processes going on in the natural environment, taking into account the current political situation and economic conditions.

It is also necessary to strive for the formation of *an ecological world outlook*, meaning the priority of the ecological approach as the fundamental principle and methodological basis for all material and spiritual activities of individuals and society. It is evident that the creation of an ecological outlook is a very complex goal. As I see it, it is possible only as a realization of a triad: (a) mastering basic ecological knowledge, (b) on this basis forming strong personal convictions, and (c) acquiring practical experience in ecologically healthy activities. This task is difficult, even considering the glorious didactic traditions of, for instance, biology and geography. The realization of the task requires entirely new efforts. I cannot here go into the didactics that are needed for the immense task of forming an ecological outlook and developing an ecological culture. But I will devote some attention to its initial stage, which I consider a key one: creating in youngsters an interest and involvement in nature protection.

It is essential that children's and teenagers' participation in ecological projects have both an *emotional* basis (e.g., connected with aesthetic education) and a *rational* basis. In any group of children we will find some with a well-developed interest in nature and living organisms. As a rule, the younger the children, the larger the percentage of these.

It is a very important point in education to encourage especially these young people's participation in nature protection. Many teenagers are indifferent to their natural surroundings. But even these youngsters may get involved through purposeful activities initiated by interested peers or by adults with authority. Also, "difficult" teenagers, even delinquents, may participate actively in nature protection.

In my practice we do not exclude using material incentives for involving youngsters in ecologically useful activities. This may include rewarding them with tickets for popular entertainments. This method does not guarantee positive results; it may lead to only formal participation without any real interest in the work. Irrespective of the form of children's union, it is the personalities of the adult leaders that matter most. The results depend to a great extent on the leaders' ability to involve the young people in the common cause and also on the adults' enthusiasm and other personal qualities. After the project is established—its forms of organization developed, traditions created, and children of different ages taking part in it—then the mechanism of succession begins to operate: Older children encourage younger ones and are even able to instruct them.

Ecological Information

An indispensable condition of ecological culture formation is to attain a certain amount of knowledge about the present ecological situation, the processes going on in nature, and how society affects the ecological balance. It is necessary for every person to know about these effects. Since 1950, Earth's human population has increased by one hundred percent, but increases in food production ceased in 1984; a layer of fertile soil one centimeter thick is formed naturally over three hundred years, but humans destroy it in three years; fresh water makes up only 3 percent of total hydrosphere resources, and 75 percent of fresh water exists as ice at the poles and 20 percent as underground water; most of the oxygen we inhale is produced by tropical forests that are being destroyed today at a catastrophic rate. Early in this century one animal species a year vanished from the Earth, but today it is one species a day; most of these species have not even been described by zoologists. The number of emigrants from ecologically unfavorable zones has exceeded the number of political emigrants; destruction of the ozone layer and the greenhouse effect have probably led to disastrous global changes in climate.

It may seem that today, having an avalanche of ecological information of all kinds through mass media, it should not be difficult for people to get to know all these facts and more—but this is not so. Important facts about the unfavorable ecological situation are—sometimes—deliberately concealed from the general population. Some facts are held back, some are given in inexact wording, some are simply distorted. Thus, to attain objective ecological information, even if it is not secret, is possible only under certain public pressure and by the influence of mass media on the public institutions.

For example, before the August coup attempt in 1991, at the Congress of People's Deputies it was declared that 20 percent of the Soviet population lived in ecologically disastrous zones and 40 percent more in ecologically unfavorable environments; in some regions today the length of human life is accordingly shortened. We learned that 21 percent of officially checked sausage products in the USSR in 1987 had contained poisonous chemicals in concentrations dangerous to human health, 42 percent of the milk products for babies (!) and 30 percent of all food products in St. Petersburg (Leningrad) also proved dangerous to health. These figures from the Ministry of Health were not secret, but when the information was made public, only eighteen copies were circulated.

Of course, not everything is hopeless. In 1990, *The State of the Natural Environment in the Soviet Union* was published—our country's first-ever inter-departmental report on the environment. It is an attempt (though an imperfect one) to estimate objectively the ecological situation in the country.

It is natural that differences in the democratization level in different countries result in disparities in the difficulty of obtaining true ecological information by the public. But the problem exists virtually everywhere. This leads us to an important conclusion: youngsters need the ecologist/teacher to help them critically analyze the information they received. They need to *learn* to make determined efforts and prepare themselves to understand the fact that there can be, and often are, certain forces in a society interested in hiding or distorting ecological information.

Apart from learning the facts, everyone needs a certain amount of knowledge of modern ecology's theoretical basis and the legal, social, and political aspects of interrelations between humans and nature.

"Blind Enthusiasm"

The core of ecological education is a personal belief in the necessity of struggle for ecological security. Only a personal conviction can turn theoretical knowledge into fertile practical activity in the field of nature protection. Only conviction can provide the ethical norms for practical interrelations between humans and nature. The process of forming personal convictions has been intensively studied for decades, taking into account the influence on the individual of the schooling process itself, the mass media, advertising, the closest environment, family, and so on.

One of the paradoxes born of the modern ecological situation is that a civilization based on the progress of science and engineering may be helpless when it comes to creating a well-founded program for removing the threat of ecological crisis. The cause of this is the unpredictable character of anthropogenic changes in the natural environment. The real ecological consequences of human activity are always greater, more varied, and deeper than our evaluations and forecasts of these consequences.

With due respect for the prognostic significance of ecological modeling and forecasting, we have to admit that at the modern level of methodological development of science a comprehensive, adequate evaluation of the consequences of humankind's conscious or unconscious influence on nature is highly problematic. Certainly, this does not mean giving up the search for scientifically motivated ways of forecasting the influences of civilization on nature and of preventing ecological crisis on Earth. We have every reason to believe that considerable success may be achieved in this sphere in the near future. But today, bearing in mind the variety of regional peculiarities of ecological problems and, frequently, the lack of scientifically founded programs, we are to prepare our youngsters for efforts that do not always lead to success. We must avoid the cultivation of a "blind faith in victory."

Struggle for ecological security is such a long, laborious, and unpaved process into the unknown that those taking this road must be ready to work in some cases only on "blind" enthusiasm—that is, on the basis of deep personal conviction.

PRACTICE IN ECOLOGICAL EDUCATION

Activities for Children and Youth

The most difficult and important problem in the field is to find forms of cooperation between children and teenagers that will make youngsters enthusiastic and ensure their wholehearted participation in nonformal nature protection. I can't possibly name all the forms of young people's participation in nature protection that have existed for decades in my country, but at least I shall mention some of them. Most important are those that unite youngsters as small groups in local communities (villages, settlements, districts) where such factors as family ties, cultural traditions, social and economic characteristics, parents' occupations, and life and work conditions affect the character of interrelations between humans and nature.

Nature-protecting Activities

The following are some forms of children's participation in practical nature-protecting activities in my country.

- *Nature-lovers' clubs* unite children and teenagers of different ages and their parents. The clubs are led by either local museum employees, schoolteachers, or parents. These clubs carry out the following activities: protection of and control over rare natural species, planting greenery in new districts of towns and cities, and organizing flower exhibitions.

• *Young naturalists' stations* in towns and districts (e.g., zoological, botanical, ecological circles) are the oldest form of nature study and nature protection organized for children and teenagers. In 1988 the seventieth anniversary of the Young Naturalists movement was celebrated in the USSR. This movement numbers about thirty million school children in 1991.

• *Green patrols and school forestries* are children's and teenagers' unions engaged in planting trees, caring for young forests, regulated collection of medical herbs, creating seed funds for forestries, and so on. These unions also carry out usage control of forests and other nature resources.

• *Gardening centers* are organized in town districts for creating parks and lawns in towns, growing flowers for kindergartens and other public institutions in the district, and organizing exhibitions and fairs for collecting money for peace and nature protection funds (zoo funds, nature protection societies, etc.).

• *Blue patrols* are specialized unions for study and protection of water systems and their flora and fauna in a given region. They have the functions of public control over water usage and water pollution.

• *Ecological routes* are created by Young Naturalists organizations for ecological information and the education of the population; special routes cover typical and exotic ecosystems of different levels of man-made modification. These routes introduce common and protected species.

• *Microreserves* are small, guarded territories set up on the initiative of children's groups and public organizations at collective and state farms and forestries. Besides protecting nature in the given regions, young people study the juridical background of different-scale protected areas such as reserves.

• *Children's expeditions* are organized during school vacations to various parts of the country with the aims of nature study, discovering the character of man-made nature modifications, and helping reserves and forestries.

• *Nature study-oriented activities* for children and teenagers include children's apiaries and microfarms (in cattle-breeding and agricultural districts).

In all cases children are given some initial vocational instruction and some knowledge of interrelations between nature and national economy. Youngsters are, through these activities, brought up in the spirit of caring about living species and being responsible with regard to natural resources. All these forms of activity are aimed at developing children's civil consciousness through their participation in ecological and nature protection projects. Of course, there are many more such activities as well. The problems connected with nature protection are usually discussed in the specialized children's monthly *Young Naturalist*, which has been issued since 1928.

Formal and Nonformal Education

In organizing the process of youngsters' ecological training, it is important to create a harmonious combination of formal (curricular) and nonformal approaches. The benefit of formal methods (involving lessons on definite subjects and other forms of activity determined by the curriculum) is that they reach a considerable contingent of children and teenagers and generally have access to better equipment than extracurricular events. But, being compulsory, this kind of activity is less effective for pupils who are not especially interested in ecology problems.

Extracurricular work, though it never draws in as many youngsters, has great efficacy because it unites interested allies. Experience shows that such alliances between a competent leader and children of different age groups are sometimes able to solve ecological tasks on a nearly professional level. Moreover, their successes frequently have great influence on public opinion and are effective means of developing public interest in nature protection problems. The enthusiasm of such groups catalyzes an extremely important process of ecological education. Adults educate youngsters, and youngsters educate adults. We cannot underestimate this process. For many adults it is their children's example that proves a decisive stimulus for joining ecological culture activities and developing increased social responsibility.

Thus, formal approaches in ecological education are extensive, guaranteeing at least a minimum level of ecological knowledge in the general population. Nonformal approaches are intensive, considerably advancing true ecological culture. But the interdependence of these two approaches, and consequently the necessity of their correlated development, is evident.

Ecological Opposition

Economic, social, and political spheres of the state bureaucracy and other ecologically conservative forces have engaged in actions *against* ecologically progressive work. The causes of this antagonism are sometimes rather complex and must be analyzed by considering general and specific ecological, economic, social, and political interests.

As a rule, ecological education does not provoke any counteractions from an "ecological opposition," but in their practical nature-protection activities, learners face bureaucratic despotism, unfounded prohibition, and concealment and distortion of information. Youngsters may perceive this as social confrontation, especially when things become emotional. Such confrontations are undesirable because our goal in working to solve ecology problems must be to consolidate public forces, at both a national and an international level. It is important to demonstrate clearly and conclusively that nature protection opponents embody a low level of ecological culture, no matter what interests they might be guided by or what arguments they might give for their position.

It is also necessary to analyze the essence of ecological conflicts and discuss plans and tactics for their solutions. We must give special attention to legal aspects of confrontations concerning ecological issues, and also focus on legislative and moral responsibility for blatant examples of ecological crimes.

A good way to prepare youngsters for these confrontations over extremely complex and sometimes ambiguous problems is to use *role playing*—have them play out the roles of "experts in confrontation." For example, an analysis of ecological crime suggests that we should study the *motives* that make people break nature-protecting laws. It becomes necessary to demonstrate that crimes are sometimes committed because of elementary ecological and legal illiteracy; other crimes are committed for direct profit. Some such crimes are committed if an economic manager passively follows the deep-rooted immoral practice of organizing business without regard for long-term effects on nature, being aware of the imperfections of legal and economic control. This kind of crime is the most dangerous, and, widespread as it is, it is connected with the way the economic system is organized in our country.

Personal Responsibility

The ecological crisis is deepened when the political system is not open to the idea of personal responsibility. It was extremely characteristic of the totalitarian party-bureaucratic system in the Soviet Union during the last decades that in most cases it was difficult or simply impossible to determine the personal guilt of bureaucrats in committing ecological or other crimes.

When the personal guilt of an official is obvious and can be proved, the state seems to have been incapable of administering adequate punishment. This situation did not change much in the Gorbachev era from 1986 to 1991. Since the breakdown of the Soviet Union, our society's continuous attempts at democratization and ecological glasnost, including our attention to ecological problems, arouse some hope. Considerable improvements have undoubtedly taken place in this field; however, they have not changed the situation as a whole. That is why it is extremely important that the new generations learn to see the roles and possibilities of the public and mass media in taking personal responsibility for crimes committed.

The most important basis for a new situation is *strict ecological legislation,* including all-around nature-protecting laws, actual *control* over their realization, and *financially stimulating mechanisms* for rational nature utilization, first of all in the sphere of economic activity. Without observance of such regulations, all educational and other measures will remain ineffective. Awareness of this fact is an additional burden on those who have taken up the difficult task of eliminating ecological illiteracy. This is exactly the meaning of "going ahead in spite of everything"!

A GLOBAL LEVEL: ECOLOGICAL PROCESSES
AND INTERNATIONAL INTEGRATION

Ecology Is Global

One feature of present world community development is the rise of material and spiritual processes at the global level. To solve the problems facing humankind, we must integrate material and intellectual resources on the same scale. These processes are not yet universal; but they are vital enough to have penetrated into science, politics, and communication. In my country such processes are also penetrating the thinking of ordinary people—more at the private level than in the bureaucracy. In some cases the new thinking has raised the effectiveness of international cooperation to an entirely new level. We are mentally ready for *acting together.*

Parallel to this new development are tendencies of growing hostility among social groups, both nationally and internationally. In Russia, for example, this is connected with how glasnost, the new openness, has revealed various economic and social problems. For many decades information about broad-scale social injustice and destructive policies has been concealed. The new knowledge is accompanied by intensified antagonism, especially in the economic sphere. Tendencies of estrangement undermine the integrating efforts needed to solve national and international problems, the most important being to ensure world ecological security.

Educators for Ecological Culture (SAEEC)

Understanding the immense importance of every kind of effort to solve this most urgent problem, and fully aware of the acute necessity to consolidate efforts around matters common to all, educators in 1989 put forward an initiative for creating the association Educators for Ecological Culture (SAEEC). This association is organized in the committee framework used by Educators for Peace and Mutual Understanding. Strategic directions of SAEEC's activities include the elimination of ecological illiteracy, the development of ecological culture in all layers of society, and the consolidation of the efforts of all public forces, intra- and interstate, in solving ecological problems. For several decades in Russia we have had, as I have shown, broad practical experience with the ecological education of youngsters, but it has never been organized nationally. At present, many educators are still unacquainted with it.

It is no less important to exchange experiences in this sphere, so SAEEC is planned as a kind of center that will coordinate efforts in the field of ecological education. The association unites school teachers, college tutors, Young Naturalists leaders, and members of the Academy of Pedagogical Science and the Ministry of Education. Until 1991, it also included the State Committee of Education of the USSR.

As a public organization SAEEC is uniting the efforts of all those interested in contacts and exchanges of experience in matters of ecological education and training, including preschool tutors and counselors, school teachers of all specialties, college tutors in general and special education, managers of every kind of out-of-school or nonformal ecological union, and, finally, parents concerned with the ecological education of their own children.

More specifically, the SAEEC's activity has the following orientations:

1. SAEEC Goals
   - To instill the new ecological thinking, ecological outlook, and ecological culture in the broad mass of educators and learners
   - To develop the social, political, and professional activity of educators in nature protection interests
   - To improve the younger generations' education and training in the spirit of peace and ecological security
   - To consolidate all public forces, intra- and interstate, with the aim of solving ecological problems
2. SAEEC Tasks
   - To contribute to the activation of educators' scientific comprehension of today's global ecological problems
   - To contribute to the consolidation and coordination of activities of various parts of the public education system and public organizations in educating children and youngsters in the spirit of a humane
     attitude to nature
   - To contribute to summing up and teaching the advanced experience, new ideas, and initiatives in the sphere of ecological education
   - To improve special training of educators at all levels in the sphere of ecological education
   - To contribute to many-sided activities of educational and public organizations in the ecological education of youngsters, turning them toward practical activities in nature protection and the struggle for ecological security
   - To contribute to the organization of scientific research, working out methods and practical guides to help practitioners in the sphere of youngsters' ecological education
   - To take part in international educators' activities on ecological

matters, develop cooperation with educators in other countries and work out the theory and practice of ecological education

3. Content of SAEEC Activities
- Collecting information about forms, methods, and directions of ecological education in this country and abroad
- Summing up and spreading the experience of practical work involving youngsters in nature-protecting activities
- Involving all educators, scientists, and parents in practical work in the sphere of ecological education
- Purposeful development of new and modified forms and meth ods of ecological education
- Analyzing proposals for improving existing textbooks, curricula, and programs, taking into account the importance and urgency of raising people's ecological culture
- Setting up contacts with international organizations dealing with problems of ecological education, taking part in mutual projects, and getting acquainted with international experience in this sphere

Promise of Ecological Education

Nature protection is a sphere of activity that gives people unlimited opportunities for realizing the potentials of their personalities. People of very different intellectual and cultural abilities may get involved in the broad field of nature protection if they wish to do something for people living near them, for nature, and for themselves.

Every interested teenager can find ways to participate. Tasks may have various degrees of complexity and a rich emotional appeal, and offer broad opportunities for intellectual efforts, decision making, practical participation in the realization of these decisions, and estimation of the social effect of the results attained. All of this provides an opportunity for a youngster to find a healthy life program combining harmoniously a realization of initiatives for society's welfare, satisfaction with work, a definite position in society, some material prosperity—and the attainment of an ideal of "success in life."

Nature protection activity inevitably includes a person in social interactions on various scales. Comparing different levels of specific nature protection tasks, a young man or woman gets practical knowledge of the importance of the main principle of social life: the principles of integrity and mutual assistance. The basis for this knowledge is laid in the family and in the local community.

More abstract goals, such as to unite efforts on national, international, and global levels (e.g., coordinating tree-planting projects) are understood later and with greater difficulty. The complexity of these problems makes evident the importance of multiscale international contacts. Every step here is of great value; at one end are discussions by state leaders on strategic directions of the struggle for ecological security; at the other end is the work of children's groups and their exchanges of experiences.

In this connection I would like to point out that the problem of developing ecological culture is especially hard to solve in countries with relatively low living standards. Attitudes focused on improving one's living standard are a serious obstacle to attaining ecological culture for people in all countries, but especially in countries with low living standards including even starvation.

Barbarous consumption of natural resources in the pursuit of quick profits had reached a fantastic scale in the former Soviet Union and in the CIS countries up to 1991. The struggle to get foreign currency at any price has aggravated exploitative trends in the use of natural resources and has repeatedly increased the pressure by human beings on unique ecosystems.

A rising income from the exploitation of ecosystems means extraction of natural resources in brutal ways. The critical situation in the country has, as never before, aggravated this brutality, rationalized through false claims of economic necessity, and so has become an obstacle in developing citizens' responsibility toward nature.

In our work for an ecological culture it becomes vital to focus on the concept of *ecological crime*: the use of natural resources without consideration for the long-term effects on nature as a whole. To appeal to the conscience and consciousness of the starving and destitute is, to put it bluntly, an impossible task for an educator. But to start projects for an ecological and cooperative education is a necessity. The complex and multifaceted task of ecological education must be taken on in various countries for all age groups of learners according to the different educational systems and taking into account the material basis of education, the population's living standards, and the peculiarities of the ecological situation in the country, all against the background of prevailing ideologies. We have to acknowledge the necessary "disparities" in the quality of youngsters' ecological training in different countries.

At the same time we must keep in mind the global character of ecological processes and the necessity to react to them on the same global scale, and so demand that ecological literacy be raised to the highest possible level in every nation. At the same time we have to keep in mind that the rate of transformation of the natural ecosystems affected by human beings is so high that we cannot tolerate a low level of ecological education in any country.

Regional Programs of Ecological Training

The only possible way to build a safe basis for universal ecological education is to create regional programs for international cooperation—that is, educational systems in neighboring countries that are especially dependent on each other ecologically. When the disparities in ecological cultures between neighboring countries are great, the need for material and intellectual support between countries is easier to acknowledge and thus easier to get started. Neighboring countries stand a better chance to put pressure on each other and also to make it clear that mutual support is in the interests of all. This type of mutual support may make it possible to more quickly raise the level of ecological education in each society, to the benefit of all societies.

What about material expenditures? Should economically developed countries pay the costs, with a clear understanding that "saving" in this sphere today will demand far greater expenditures tomorrow? Given the aggravated ecological situation, it can prove fatal to "wait and see." It will hardly be possible to improve the situation in the future without present radical reform of ecological education and the formation of an ecological outlook.

In this connection the creation of an *international fund for ecological security*, proposed by the Soviet Union under Gorbachev in 1990, could help to solve a number of problems. The source of this fund, according to the proposal, would be the sums released by economically advanced states during the process of disarmament. Another important point in the proposal is to increase the proportion of ecological programs within the UN structure.

CONCLUDING WORDS

Encouraging young people's participation in the sphere of ecological problems and nature protection tasks is one of the more profitable ways of helping them develop an active position in life. One of the positive aspects of this effort is that the attainment of the aim is realized through working in an optimistic and humane life program.

To be active in projects for ecological and cooperative education means to develop social responsibility and the ability to care for human beings and nature. A person may not decide to devote her or his whole life to nature protection, but work in an ecological project constitutes an important step in developing a personality engaged in the welfare of society and humane values. At the same time, involving youngsters in nature protection and cooperation is an extremely significant step toward the formation of an ecological outlook in the population as a whole, and thus in developing an ecological culture.

NOTE

I'd like to thank my American coauthors and Soviet colleagues, my students, schoolteachers, and pupils for their help in this work. I am especially grateful to the editors of this book—Eva Nordland, who initiated our joint efforts and contributed to it so much, and Betty Reardon, whose efforts toward the publication of this book have been invaluable.

REFERENCES

Global Education Associates. Breakthrough 10, no. 4 and 11, no. 1 (Summer/Fall). Special combined issue entitled "Ecological Security in an Interdependent World," edited by Patricia M. Mische and Melissa Merkling.

Kapto, A. 1990. *Filosofia mira: istoki, tendentsii, perspektivy* (Philosophy of peace: sources, tendencies, perspectives). Moscow.

Naess, Arne. 1988. *Ecology, Community, and Lifestyle: Outline of an Ecosophy.* New York: Cambridge University Press.

Reardon, Betty A. 1988. *Comprehensive Peace Education: Educating for Global Responsibility.* New York: Teachers College Press, Columbia University.

Shaposhnikov, V. 1984. *Problems of Common Security*. Moscow: Progress.

Solowejchik. S. L. 1989. *Vospitanie po Ivanovu*. (Upbringing on Ivanov's ideas). Moscow: Pedagogika.

Vernadsky, V. I. 1977. *Nauchnaya misl kak planetarnoe javlenie*. (Scientific thought as planetary phenomenon). Moscow: Nauka.

World Commission on Environment and Development. 1987. *Our Common Future*. New York: Oxford University Press.

World Council for Curriculum and Instruction. "Caring for the Earth: An Educational Imperative." 1990. [Special Issue]. *The Forum* 4, no. 1 (June).

6
Educational Planning for
an Ecological Future

Susan Ahearn

A GLIMPSE OF THE ECOLOGICAL SOCIETY

According to the report *Our Common Future,* by the World Commission on Environment and Development (1987), *sustainable development* is a process of social change in which policies and practices are established to meet human needs, both material (physical necessities) and nonmaterial (e.g., access to a clean environment, political and spiritual freedom, meaningful work, and good health). Social change, within this context, must not occur at the expense of the resource base upon which societies are dependent.

In moving toward a sustainable society, *social justice* will be a common goal. Decisions will have to be made based upon ecological considerations and the needs of those affected by the decisions, as determined by a broad, participating citizenry. Human fecundity is to be reduced, and human populations will have to become compatible with the productive capacity of the regional ecosystems.

Technologies will be assessed on the basis of their risk to humans and the environment, and the citizenry will become active participants in selecting which technologies they want. Finally, the process of moving to more ecological societies will allow for the development of an economy that offers a stable system of production and exchange that is inseparable from the region's ecology.

The *interconnectedness of ecology and economy* (both terms come from the Greek word *oikos,* meaning "household") will become manifested in a dynamic equilibrium in the ecological, sustainable society. Public discussions must ensue in that context, to insure that the moves being planned are *sustainable in biological, physical, and sociopolitical aspects.* This requires

121

that societies undergo substantive change that undercuts current beliefs and social practices that justify overconsumption and environmental destruction. The current social systems cannot remain in their present forms. Since unsustainable social practices could contribute to the collapse of the ecological systems, the move toward sustainability requires a concern for more natural systems.

SOCIAL PROCESSES BUILDING ECOLOGICAL SOCIETIES

Teachers Learning to be Transformative Intellectuals

The task of building more ecological societies requires that the concept of security be based upon environmental integrity, justice, dignity, and nonviolence. Educators are beginning to question the educational structures and assumptions of our outmoded paradigms. This can only mean that a radical shift will occur, with education becoming based upon the interdisciplinary nature of learning, questioning the fundamental categories of all disciplines, and seeking to make societies more democratic.

An example of this process can be found in the People's Education Movement in South Africa. This movement is aimed at involving broad numbers of people in the struggle for the shift of power to the majority of South Africans. It is a shift from restrictive response to a serious questioning about the nature of education and the explicit links between educational, political, economic, and cultural reproduction (Abrahams 1990). Through this movement, people are becoming organized and mobilized to develop a nonracist, democratic South Africa in which all sectors of the people become organized to take control of their education and their lives, establishing strong working alliances and developing cooperative work and active participation. This is the antithesis of the authoritarian and individualistic values that dominate school practices there and in so many nations of the world.

The Move toward Self-Determination and Decentralization

A variety of innovative, localized approaches to building ecologically based communities can offer inspiration to educators in planning a more appropriate education for their students. These examples involve political, economic, environmental, and educational components. Each is participation- centered, includes multiple generations, and is locally focused within a global context.

The first approach is that of Colegio de villa de Leyva in Colombia. This is a "green school," designed to help local peasants achieve environmental literacy and be empowered to make decisions in their communities, based on the equilibrium and solidarity of natural systems. Experts interact with nonexperts (who may have indigenous knowledge of the land) for the purpose of bettering their communities. The lesson here is that we are all learners, colleagues, co-participants, stakeholders in the process of building a sustainable future.

Another example comes from the experience of the indigenous peoples of northern Russia—the Chukchi, the Itelmens, and the Evenki—who live in the Koryak Autonomous Area. These northern ethnic groups are sharing their ideas for development of their national futures and socio-economic futures with native peoples of North America (Mohawks of New York, and Innu and Inuit of Canada). In a 1990 congress, indigenous peoples shared stories of the problems and potentials of developing technologies for processing traditional goods, development of northern occupations, the struggles of living in isolated regions, and sustaining cultures based on traditional foundations. The inspiration contained in this example is the realization that although we may be focusing on local, regional concerns, the same or similar concerns exist in other places, where people are struggling to develop viable, ecological ways.

Several tribal groups of the Canadian North are collaborating with government resource management agencies in managing fisheries and wildlife to insure that natives have access to resources for subsistence. The natives and the government are sharing in decision making, based upon indigenous knowledge (i.e., knowledge of a place accrued over generations of occupancy) and scientific knowledge. Despite past animosities, the two groups are learning to work well together, realizing their mutual aim of maintaining resources. The lesson from this example is that there may be potential partners for creating new opportunities for learning that previously had never been considered.

A third inspiration comes from the concept of the community land trust. Throughout North America there has arisen a model of land tenure based on the equitable distribution and rational use of resources by local members. Land is held as a common trust for present and future generations, and humans are viewed as tenants upon the land rather than as owners.

In British Columbia, the Linnaean Farm represents a typical effort in western Canada to integrate human activity into the natural community. This land trust includes a 316-acre farm on Cortes Island, two ecological reserves, a bird sanctuary, a school, an ecological gardening program, a permaculture program (harvesting and sustaining the fruit crops of trees), and a holistic forestry management plan.

Students move beyond the school walls to participate, with other children and adults, in activities that contribute to the well-being of the natural community. The lesson here is that the locus of learning begins in our *oikos,* our local household, which encompasses our local built and natural community. If we become successful scholars of the local natural community, we can develop sustainable, ecological pathways to the future.

Decisions made by those most affected by the outcomes may be the best decisions. It will be the aggregate of local or regional efforts that ultimately will create a healthy, viable planet.

PRAXIS AND ECOLOGICAL EDUCATION

In the context of educational planning for more ecological societies, it is imperative that educators discern how educational institutions are located within, and dependent upon, various cultural systems, such as economics, culture, and politics, as well as on natural systems, such as communities and ecosystems. The cultural systems are human constructs embedded in natural systems (e.g., in the ecosystem that encompasses humans as well as the other living organisms within a physical environment, or a region that is bound by uniformity of climate, soils, and plant and animal life).

Curriculum development becomes *praxis* (practice contemplated) when educators move from discernment to questioning the power domination occurring in cultural or social systems and to devising curricula based on the questions raised during this process. Praxis is not a means for regimenting teachers into set routines, but a way of extending the communal power of the learning community (Freire 1979).

Traditional educational practices have given priority to efficiency and order, which subsequently and unconsciously, perhaps, has reinforced an oppressive bondage to the status quo. Teachers are asked to "deliver" a curriculum to students, who later must regurgitate the information in paper-and-pencil tests if they are to survive the schooling process.

More and more, teachers find themselves in the straitjacket of time constraints, classroom housekeeping duties, and little opportunity to teach creatively, as they prepare students for the public examinations at the end of each course. In contrast, Paulo Freire's process of "conscientization," developed to engage people in determining their own goals and to change the processes of learning, offers educators a way to question the authority that disallows development of their dignity and their value and each person's role as "cocreator" and "subject" in the process of becoming fully human.

Through dialogue, teachers can question the decisions that determine the direction of education. The main idea is to break away from the domination of external forces to personal empowerment by organizing the learning community to regain control over legitimate education. In this context, *legitimate* refers to education within and about the human and nonhuman local community and the threats to its stability and integrity. In dialogue, questions arise relating to authority and responsibility, and the dialogue informs the teaching practices and topics covered. This in turn informs the dialogue. This praxis gives rise to models and strategies for developing an ecological society.

Here are a set of sample questions, derived from dialogue and praxis, which may be helpful in developing legitimate curricula:

1. What does it mean to be a student, a school, a group of learners within the Ussuri Valley of the Russian Far East, or the Great Smoky Mountains of the United States? What distinguishes the learning opportunities available here from those in other regions? How am I (how are we) unique as an ecosystem, a community? (*Self-identity*)

2. Who are the other members, human and nonhuman, of this region? How might we become acquainted with them and begin to accept responsibility for our mutual well-being? (*Getting acquainted; Becoming intimate with members of local region*)

3. How do I (we) feel toward the other inhabitants of this region (human and nonhuman)? (*Affirmation of feelings*)

4. What conflicts or violence exists within this region, including violence toward the Earth that ultimately threatens human survival? (*Violence as unacceptable*)

5. How can we change our relationships (to nature and among humans) from one of domination to one of partnership? What are appropriate behaviors with respect to the capacity of this ecosystem to sustain the community? (*Learning to get along*)

6. What skills can we learn in order to live with more care in our natural communities, and how can we solve problems here more peacefully? (*Conflict management*)

7. What things can be done to benefit members of this natural community (e.g., restoration of degraded vegetation or allowing an area to remain undisturbed)? (*Environmental peacemaking*)

8. How are the human members of my community alike, and what are our common needs? What are the needs of the other living things in the region? (*Meeting basic needs of everyone*)

9. How are these needs met presently, and how will they be met in the future? What natural resources are involved, and who controls access to them? How can a more equitable distribution take place? (*Justice and sharing*)

10. What resources in this region are limited, what is extracted, and what renewable resources (e.g., forests, soil, wildlife) must be replenished? Which resources should be left undisturbed, and for how long? Which resources may be used, and for how long? Who determines use, and who benefits from the extractions? (*Sustaining and replenishing*)

11. How does life (human and nonhuman) in this region interrelate with other regions? How are we independent? (*Diversity*)

12. What fears do we have, and what knowledge and actions are needed to overcome them? What is the potential for catastrophe emanating from within this region? (*Empowerment*)

13. What are the names of those things in this region that contribute to war and violence against people and the Earth? (*Eliminating war and violence*)

14. How do we want our *oikos* to look in the future? What needs healing? What can we do to assist each other in behaving responsibly (e.g., assuming responsibility for the condition of public spaces of our communities)? What will contribute to a sense of enchantment and a desire to participate fully in the work of sustaining life in this region? (*Social responsibility*)

AN ECOLOGICAL FRAMEWORK FOR EDUCATION

The Theoretical and Philosophical Basis

Educators who are serious about participating in the transformation to a new world order, based on the aggregate of locally sustainable communities and regions, must be having second thoughts about the ability of conventional education practices and settings. After asking the hard questions within the process of dialogue and praxis, the responses must be attached to a framework for legitimate education.

The framework presented here contains four areas of concern:

1. The importance of the local landscape (natural region) to developing individual identity and place of meaning

2. The importance of space and how it is perceived (e.g., sacred space or profane space), and its relationship to socially responsible behaviors

3. An understanding that there are varying views of the world, some being more ecological than others; knowledge of one's own worldview as a way to develop an ecological worldview

4. Primal human values and the educational legacy of indigenous peoples, including different modes of educational experience

This framework is elucidated below.

The Ecoregion as a Meaningful Landscape

Many writers from diverse disciplines stress the importance of the physical environment in supporting a child's emotional well-being and sense of identity. Many authors attempt to focus on the question of "place," that is, the unity of an individual's experience in a geographical setting over a period of residency numbering in years, as playing a part in emotional well-being. The most useful writing on this topic comes from Searles. In *The Contribution of the Non-human to Normal Development and Schizophrenia* (1959), Searles professes that one role of the landscape in the development of a normal ego is that of "shock absorber" upon which children project various aspects of themselves to integrate them into a sense of self. From his work with schizophrenic patients, Searles concludes:

> The considerable percentage of these persons who as children have had the experience of numerous changes in residence, have been deprived thereby of what is, in normal living, an important source of security for the child—the security of dwelling, year after year, in familiar surroundings. (Searles 1959, 82–83)

This suggests that we must, for the benefit of our emotional well-being, become committed to dwelling in one place over time, becoming rooted and intimate in our knowledge of our surroundings. Indeed, many people feel that the modern mobility of North Americans has contributed to becoming a wasteful, throwaway society, incapable of acting responsibly toward our "place." People "trash" a place, then move on, out of sight of the devastation, which is then out of mind of the culprits. In addition, absenteeism on the part of multinational corporations, government agencies, groups, and individuals creates the ability to lay waste to places that are far away from the sources of decisions.

As educators, invested with the responsibility of creating meaningful learning experiences for children, we must integrate into our planning an understanding of the development of children (ontogeny) into fully integrated adults, willing to think for themselves and to accept responsibility for the growth of others. It is known that children move through several emotional phases in their development and that the success of the sequence depends on appropriate nurturance. Educators can take advantage of this knowledge as they seek to develop environmentally appropriate behaviors. The task is to both anticipate and respond at the appropriate times. This capacity must be developed if we are to prevent subsequent generations from becoming what Shepherd (1982) calls being "ontogenetically stuck" or "psychologically amputated."

During normal emotional development in the first few months of life, the child develops an *autonomy*, or subjective oneness, and this is followed by a strong desire to focus on the mother's face and body. By the age of three to seven years, the child is making an inventory of things and their parts. By eight to twelve years, the child focuses on the "place" or locus of meaning in her or his life and develops an interest in natural history. By the thirteenth to fifteenth year, there is a strong need for independence within a dependent relationship, such as a mentor could provide. By the age of sixteen to nineteen, the young person is able to focus on ecological and sociological relationships and begins questioning cosmology. By twenty years of age, the adult emerges as a separate self with potential for continued individuation. To anticipate and respond to this ontogenetic process, educators now are learning to assist young people in developing a sense of "belongingness" in the natural community within the context of the natural phases of human development.

It is generally understood that an individual's identity grows from the interplay between autonomy and symbiosis, between the Self and the Other, allowing for a person to develop a model of relatedness to the world. On this basis, educators are recognizing that they must incorporate increasing numbers of environmental immersion experiences into the curriculum. Given the context of the ontogenetic sequence, the role of the teacher during immersion experiences is to remain open and attentive to the children's readiness for building meaning.

Meaning refers to meaning between the Self and the Other, the relationship between the two, the way in which the biological and physical environment can be classified, the understanding of why things happen as they do, and the ability to live in the present with a concern for the future, to develop intimate associations of space (i.e., location as the source of knowledge and memory; holding images of the location even when not receiving stimuli from them). This relationship between person and place can be charged with personal and social significance, featuring symbols that inspire correct living and reflecting the moral character of the present generation and previous ones. This relationship to a landscape exists among most aboriginal groups.

Western Apaches of Arizona tell stories in which are embedded specific landscape features—mountains, old trees, textured rocks. Their claim that the land makes the people live right is understood in the context of stories told "in location." Their morality stories tell of ancestors who made choices—right ones and wrong ones—and faced the consequences of their actions. The stories remind the young of appropriate behavior for dwelling in that specific region. The rocks, mountains, and trees where the events occurred serve as continuous mnemonic devices through each generation for proper moral conduct. Although the storyteller dies away, the landscape objects remain. When an Apache says that a rock stalks her every day, it means that the rock reminds her of some faulty behavior she exhibited, which was observed by others and pointed out through the medium of storytelling in order that the behavior might not be repeated.

As educators expand the locus of learning to include the broader community, both natural and cultural, models of socially responsible behavior (as well as examples of irresponsible acts) can be derived from the landscape as events unfold in specific places. Stories of successful relationships between humans and their landscapes can be embedded within the natural features—retold and recorded as the process of transforming degraded lands and disharmonious customs continues to unfold. As Eliade states in *The Sacred and the Profane* (1959), "If the world is to be lived in, it must be founded" (p. 83).

As the move toward building more ecologically viable societies progresses, a recurring theme appears: that the Earth is divided into natural regions, defined by natural characteristics rather than human politics or conflicts. An understanding of the ephemeral nature of political boundaries as determinants of human activity has been stated eloquently by astronauts such as Mohammed Ahmad Faris of Syria ("From space I saw Earth—indescribably beautiful with the scars of national boundaries gone") and Russell Schweikart ("There are no frames, no boundaries" [Kelly 1988, 144]). Their observations are inspirational for rethinking the boundaries of our geopolitical maps. If students are taught only the boundaries between one group and another (usually as a result of conflicts) rather than between regions of significantly different life forms (interdependent on the health of the whole system), of course they will fail to understand appropriate methods for protecting those life forms.

These natural regions of Earth can be called "ecoregions," since they are areas of distinctive recurring patterns of *vegetation* and *soil,* controlled by *climate.* The ecoregions of Earth form a complex arrangement or structured pattern based on these three elements. It is important for educators to focus on the scale of ecoregion that is familiar to their students for outdoor immersion experiences, restoration work, and concept formation. Sergei Polozov (chapter 5) points out that the area near a person's home can be the site for socially meaningful behavior that is real and concrete. Essential to this idea is the sense of belongingness, which may be a key to unlocking the motivation to engage in environmental action in the local community, the familiar environment.

The largest scale of ecoregion, the *ecoprovince,* generally encompasses an area of several thousand square miles and can be determined by the climax phase of succession of trees or grasses. In Russia, this sort of ecoregion may be represented by the steppe or taiga. In the United States, the Northwestern Atlantic Coastal Plain is the ecoprovince. This scale, however, is too large to be intimately familiar to most students in elementary and secondary schools.

Within the ecoprovince are several smaller regions, identifiable by distinctive physiographic features such as mountains, valleys, and rivers. Life within one of these smaller-scale ecoregions is quite distinctive. Sustainable cultural patterns arise from the capacity of the humans there to live within the resource limitations at this scale of the landscape.

In the United States, for example, within my home ecoregion, I perceive coastal Massachusetts, Connecticut, Rhode Island, and all of Long Island, New York, as the Long Island Sound Ecoregion within the Atlantic Coastal Plain Ecoprovince. Human life and culture in this area focuses on Long Island Sound. The people have been, and still are to some degree (despite its pollution), dependent on the quality of the sound's waters and the web of life there and the producer-consumer-decomposer cycle that makes seafood available to the humans of the region. Upper-elementary-aged children may be familiar with distant parts of this scale of ecoregion, but still this scale is far too large for an intimacy to be present.

A smaller scale of ecoregion, with which students may be intimate, is the *ecosection*. Within my home region, this can be represented by the individual watersheds of Long Island. Aboriginal peoples, centuries before, distributed themselves into territories with varying styles of culture and subsistence. On Long Island, different peoples occupied different watersheds in order to collect the rich harvests of shellfish and other estuarine organisms. Activities in the eastern Peconic River watershed, for example, a pine barrens area with acid, sandy, nutrient-poor soils, gave rise to cultural patterns that were not duplicated in the peoples of the western Long Island watersheds, which were characterized by grasslands and richer soils.

The smallest scale of ecoregion, the *ecosite*, may be just at the back door of some students and be very familiar to them on a day-to-day basis. The concept of the ecoregion, especially on the watershed scale, offers a tangible unit of landscape, familiar to most students, around which to organize for investigating environmental and social issues, and within which students can interact with neighbors, friends, and others in restoration projects or community service. The watershed offers a positive idea of what a *boundary* is. The *ecoregional boundary* defines *the space within which each person must become socially and environmentally responsible.*

The boundary is like a semipermeable membrane rather than a border, because it allows the flow of things through it. It distinguishes what is more related to the Other from what is more related to the Self, but the identity of both is preserved.

The ecoregional border offers new reference points and a new understanding of the importance of good behavior of each neighbor toward the land. The highest ridge above a stream may be the dividing point between two watersheds. Water does not flow according to human desires in most watersheds, but follows the natural contours of the land, flowing downward by the force of gravity, into a valley. The ridgetop boundary, the divide, may distinguish who is directly responsible for what ends up in the water from who is merely a neighbor.

Since each ecoregion has ecological parameters and characteristics, the culture that arises in it might be

1. distinctive and appropriate to the landscape;
2. developed by the inhabitants, based on an intimate understanding of what processes are occurring there, working through dialogue and praxis; and
3. developed within the natural, common rhythm, focusing on appropriate behaviors and specific mnemonic devices identified on the landscape from real events in the lives of the people.

Basic (i.e., legitimate) education includes these three elements.

Having determined the ecoregion that will be meaningful to their students, educators may wish to cooperate in collecting widely scattered information about the chosen ecoregion. This information could be compiled into a resource directory, an inventory, or a descriptive listing of the region from which to select material for curriculum development. The source material might be organized in a variety of ways.

One way would be to use the "big ideas of ecology," described by Willard Jacobson in chapter 4. For example, information on cultural *systems* would include information on the ecoregion's economy, transportation, agriculture, health, politics, and so forth. Ecological systems would encompass all information on the floral or faunal communities. *Cycles* could include population cycles, nutrient recycling, the water cycle, economic cycles, and seasonal cycles. *Balance* might include the extraction of minerals or renewable resources and the replenishment or restoration efforts occurring or required. What *successional stages* are present within the ecoregion, and what is their relationship to cultural history and the nature preservation efforts? *Population* growth patterns can be studied in the region, as they relate to housing concerns, food distribution, and water availability and quality. *Tolerance* relates to fisheries and water quality or stress on parts of the infrastructure, such as transportation systems. Food *chains, webs,* and *pyramids* can be studied as they relate to protection of habitats, including human habitats. *Radiation* relates to local energy sources, including solar income (available for plant growth) and weapons development. In even the smallest unit of a landscape, there will be many *uncertainties*—for instance, in water supply or quality, food availability, or energy.

In the learning process, the emphasis may fluctuate between a person's learning the ecoregion and relating that understanding to larger spatial contexts (the ecoregion beyond and the global context). Local learning in the familiar setting becomes memorable and personal because at this scale a person can receive positive feedback from neighbors and relatives and positive recognition within the community, as defined by the ecoregion.

The Canadian experience of working on the development of a sustainable society is one example of a nation's beginning to be redirected toward a more ecological future. Documents such as *The Green Plan* (Environment Canada 1991) suggest the ecoregion (bioregion) as an organizing unit. *The Newfoundland and Labrador Conservation Strategy* (1991) is based on the ecoregional concept, and Nova Scotia's "theme regions," as described and elucidated for purposes of provincial environmental education, essentially correspond to the ecoregion concept (Davis and Smith 1988).

The ecoregion, as a major theme in conservation today, is an important construct for meaningful education and developing social responsibility in learners. It is a natural laboratory, a living museum, a stage upon which the individual's identity becomes formed and relationships to nature become defined. Relevant meaningful learning begins when teachers determine what is already familiar to the learner and proceed from there into the unknown. The local environment should be more familiar to students than distant environments, therefore more meaningful and an appropriate place from which to educate for an ecologically viable future.

Distant environments offer students the opportunity to compare and contrast, collaborate, and identify the common interconnections between regions. Like the *matrioshka*, the progressively smaller Russian dolls nested within one another, so the ecoregions of Earth constitute an interlocking, interdependent set of patterns and processes, each giving rise to unique human cultural patterns and life forms.

The Importance of Sacred versus Profane Space

The framework for an education derived from the ecoregion construct rests upon the assumption that the environmental crisis is a crisis of relationship. *Anthropocentric societies* fail to prepare their citizens to understand that humans are a part of nature, and subject to its laws, just like other animals.

Sergei Polozov has pointed out that in the CIS countries the overwhelming majority of textbooks, curricula, and programs on natural history are based on an anthropocentric outlook—the view that humans are stewards over all of the rest of nature. Although we in the United States are exposed to sophisticated natural history television programs, which have assisted in modifying this view somewhat, the underlying crisis still exists in which most humans are unable to perceive their natural relationship to other living beings. And even more frightening is the fact that few people understand their dependence, as humans, on ecological systems and other species for survival. This crisis of relationship manifests itself in various ways. Children are educated in buildings that keep the rest of the natural world at arm's length; they fail to develop a knowledge of the natural systems that support their lives in their own local areas and as part of a global system. The land and community of life around them is rarely a subject of direct discovery within most conventional educational systems. In light of this, it is important to investigate the land as space, and how, throughout history, it has played a role in the development of socially responsible behaviors.

According to Eliade (1959), the taking of possession of a space (e.g., erecting a fence, a sign, a symbol) is ritual behavior that serves to consecrate the space, setting it apart as a sacred territory. The concept of sacred space, as elucidated throughout history, offers a peek into the designation of special lands and humans' responsibility toward various spaces.

Eliade discusses the implications contained in the designation of sacred space:

> Sacred space makes it possible to obtain a fixed point and hence to acquire orientation in the chaos of homogeneity, to "found the world'," and to live in a real sense. The profane experience, on the contrary, maintains the homogeneity and hence the relativity of space. No true orientation is now possible, for the fixed point no longer enjoys a unique ontological status; it appears and

disappears in accordance with the needs of the day. Properly speaking, there is no longer any world, there are only fragments of a shattered universe, an amorphous mass consisting of an infinite number of more or less neutral places in which man moves, governed and driven by the obligations of an existence incorporated into an industrial society. (Eliade 1959, 23)

According to our understanding of sacred space, then, there must be numerous examples of sacred space within contemporary society, one example being the nature preserves and parks of any given region. These areas usually are well marked with boundary markers and signs that indicate the appropriate behaviors for visitors to the preserve or park.

Behaviors governing access to these kinds of lands can serve as a starting point for educators in defining what kind of basic socially responsible behaviors in the ecoregion might be developed. These behaviors can become a starting point for an inquiry into environmental studies and the consequences of inappropriate behavior in the region. This suggests a substantive approach: looking for the effects of specific behavior, such as the direct and indirect consequences of trampling vegetation, the impact of soil compaction of local floral species, and the effects of over-consumption of material products.

Educators may engage in ecological thinking (circular rather than linear thinking), as Betty Reardon puts it (chapter 2), by formulating questions that guide groups and individuals in making life-affirming decisions in day-to-day life; for instance, the choice to apply pesticides in the garden may be preceded by basic observations and discoveries in the garden and neighborhood.

Several large natural areas of the world have been designated as *biosphere reserves,* due to their assemblage of natural features found nowhere else on the planet. Some of these preserves are being managed using a model known as the "multiple use module" (MUM). In such a module there is an inviolate core area of sensitive species and habitat, surrounded by areas of progressively diminishing human use. To describe this model of the landscape using the language of Eliade, the core is the most sacred of areas, and the profane begins at the outer edges of the preserve. This area is governed in terms of appropriate behaviors.

The ecological framework rests on the assumption that all lands and waters within an ecoregion can be evaluated and designated as either sacred or profane. Sacred spaces would consist of the areas that are essential to supporting the lives of the people—places such as the towns' water supplies, natural areas large enough to support an assemblage of the regions' native *biota* and the ecological processes needed to support them, areas of food production, areas from which building materials are derived, and so on.

Citizens of the region would learn appropriate behaviors regarding the protection of these areas to insure the health of the community and the replenishing of resources removed and the recycling of waste products within the ecoregion itself. Ritual behavior would insure that such learning was passed on to newcomers and the younger generation—for instance, through community participation in the start of the harvest, including an understanding of the spiritual dimensions and intimacy of relationships among all members of the ecosystem. Anatoly Golovatenko (chapter 7) recognizes the significance of the spiritual to the development of the individual. Both ecological and spiritual ideals can bind communities together in serving the common good within a space of personal and ecological significance, the ecoregion.

Worldview Theory

In the struggle to develop an intimate understanding of the local landscape, there is a need for developing a perspective that is more one of partnership than one of domination. This perspective, or view of reality, is known as a "worldview": a set of cognitive presuppositions about the world around us. Assumptions about reality differ dramatically among individuals as well as groups; basic assumptions depend upon and are influenced by perceptions of reality. Within someone's worldview there may be variations that may be compatible with the development of an ecological life-style and that may be guided in the right direction with appropriate molding experiences.

Michael Kearney's (1984) theory presents a model that simplifies the complex concept of worldview. Built upon empirical anthropological research, Kearney's theory is both a theoretical framework and a macro-structure for shaping norms and values. Kearney's theory is a description of seven cognitive categories called "universals": the Self, the Other, Relationship (between Self and Other), Classification (of the Other), Causality, Space, and Time. People differ in their worldviews because they differ with respect to one or more of the universals. The content of the universals develops from hierarchical assumptions.

Variations in the categories of *Self* and *Other* may range from the extreme in which the Self is so separate from the Other as to be completely alienated or psychotic, to the other extreme in which the Self and the Other are so intimately connected that they are thought to be one and the same. This latter assumption may be found among many non-Western groups, Eastern mystics, and some indigenous peoples. Most individuals in industrialized societies tend to fall somewhere in between these extremes but closer to the former than to the latter.

The sense of Self and Other depends on the *Relationship* between the two. This relationship is determined by cultural experiences. It can be thought of as a continuum of dominance or harmony. People in some cultures see the relationship between Self and Other as sympathetic with nature, a set of relations, companionship and appreciation. Others view nature as an object of domination. The way people view relationship to the Other generally determines how they behave.

There are several methods of *classifying* the Other that have significance for educators. What is real or unreal relates to what is concrete or abstract, depending on the maturity and experience of the learner. What a teacher may present as reality may be simple unreality for a student. It may be that it is a variation in a student's classification universal, rather than a misconception, and this may be at the root of many difficulties in conceptual learning.

Causality is another part of the worldview model, involving why things occur. Phenomena may be explained differently by different groups of people based on worldview variations—such as the affinity of the Self for the Other, or a view that things have their own consciousness and are alive, that things have a will, that things exist for humans, or that things have their own power.

Space relates to the ability to form an awareness of constancy or change in processes and locations. Landscapes that are inhabited differ dramatically and are known to affect the cognition of space of its inhabitants.

Colin Turnbull's study of tropical forest pygmies demonstrates how the dense forest experience made it difficult for the pygmies to identify and comprehend things seen at a distance. When the pygmies moved into an open area of the land, they thought that cattle they saw at a distance were ants. Spatial dimensions, such as the directions of wind changes or water flow, are difficult for many urban dwellers to determine.

According to Kearney's anthropological studies, individuals tend to live within a past, present, or future orientation of time. The category of *Time* refers to concern with the immediacy of events. People in the dominant cultures of most industrialized nations have a strong future individualistic orientation that is useful for achieving success in business and scholarly endeavors. The orientation is based on delayed gratification.

Other groups of people experience the future as seemingly unreal, not tangible. To them the immediacy of the present is more important. Societies with an orientation to the past use the past as a model for the future and a source for societal renewal. Time may be thought of as oscillating (e.g., between the present and some other time), or linear (e.g., beginning in the past and moving along into the future).

These seven universals offer a basis for understanding differences in individuals as well as societies. In the attempt to develop educational programming for an ecological future, it is appropriate to consider the worldview variations that are or are not congruent with an ecological lifestyle. Effecting change will involve a reorientation of inquiries into history as a basis for generating broad and deep knowledge of ourselves and our places of habitation. John Titchell, in his book *Ceremonial Time* (1984) describes the process he underwent, in his small New England town, of delving deep into its history. Using town records, local myths, the stories of neighbors with good memories, and a knowledge of local natural history, he searched for an appropriate ecological life-style on one small piece of land.

Primal Human Experience

With every cultural group, there is a set of ideas concerning how the world was created, how it works, and the relationship of humans to the nonhumans. Within the diversity of ideas is the educational legacy of indigenous peoples, who have given rise to different modes of learning and building relationships between themselves and the nonhuman Other. In particular, it is important to focus on two aspects of this legacy: the immersion experience, and the oral tradition of storytelling.

In T. C. McLuhan's book *Touch the Earth*, (1971) there is a passage from the autobiography of a native author in which the latter reflects on his experience of learning. He complains that he went to the white man's schools and learned to read from schoolbooks, newspapers, and the Bible. Eventually he found that these were not enough; civilized people depend too much on printed pages. He turned away from his school training to what he called "the Great Spirit's book"—the creation—which can be read by studying nature.

A common practice in native education is described here:

> You don't ask questions when you grow up. You watch and listen and wait, and the answer will come to you. It's yours then, not like learning in school. (Tedlock and Tedlock 1975, xxi)

The immersion of native peoples in the forests, deserts, prairies, and mountains of the world gave rise to a rich legacy of stories. They lived in the presence of these stories, which to them were (and are) sacred, just as to the Christians, Jews, and Muslims the, New Testament, Torah, and Koran are sacred. The stories focus on one's place in the natural world and what knowledge is needed to walk through it safely. The stories are used even today to shape behavior, convey information, and bind the people together. Typical of the native story is the use of personal language to build a relationship between the characters of the story, who are mirrored in the landscape (Ahearn 1991).

The Substantive Areas of Study

The areas of study within this framework are encompassed within the seven ideas of Kearney's worldview theory.

The category of *Self* can focus on developing the understanding of the individual as a participant co-creator of the new society, intimately connected to, dependent upon, and influential toward the well-being of the non-Self (Other).

The category of *Other* develops the understandings of the biological and physical attributes of the ecoregion, at varying scales (cellular to ecosystem), then of the planet, from ecoregion to ecoregion.

Relationships include not only the affirmation of feelings of the Self for the Other but the inappropriateness of violence of all forms, and the empowering skills needed to overcome negative behaviors, at varying scales.

Classification encompasses the ways in which we can organize the

Other and its diversity, locally and on progressively larger scales. It refers to an understanding of "belongingness" to groups, communities, societies, nations, ethnic groups, and humankind, as Anatoly Golovatenko (chapter 7) suggests. But it also refers to the varying scales of the community of life, from the ecosite scale to the larger ecoprovince.

Causality includes the study of succession and other ecological phenomena and how the humans of the ecoregion can interact in more sustainable ways. It also includes a study of the economics of the ecoregional community, its comprehensive dimensions, and the "Earth deficit," which is the abuse of air, water, soil, vegetation, and wildlife, and provides a way to understand "progress" compatible with the life system of the planet. It also includes studying, developing, and engaging in simpler, more efficient, less expansive methods for the production and exchange of energy and products, which means focusing on local economic self-reliance, achieving a balance between specialization and diversity where individuals cultivate a broad range of capabilities within themselves (from individual to family to community to nation-state).

Important Elements to Include in a Learning Cycle

Immersion Experiences

Immersion experiences, such as extended time spent in natural areas, away from human bustle, are an important part of this framework. It is known that immersion experiences can dramatically alter attitudes toward nature and shift the perception of the human from one who controls to one who must bend (Sherl 1989). Immersion experiences in wilderness are known to force some learners to become introspective in an attempt to come to grips with their powerlessness over unpredictable encounters with wild animals, storms, and the like. This relinquishing of control over nature in a person's perception is known to be the first step toward facilitating self-control, learning restraint, and curbing destructive behaviors toward nature.

This kind of learning setting challenges the person to become more alert, more aware, and more fully human. It is a setting encouraging participation and cooperation with others. Throughout history, wild areas have offered the opportunity for transcendent experiences, in which the Self and Others are perceived as continuous, or one.

Significant Adults/Mentors for Youth

It often has been said that the most important factor in helping youth develop empowering attitudes in coping with horrors, environmental crises, and social injustices is the presence of significant adults struggling for a better world. This need for children to personally know adults who are involved in activism suggests that the old practice of mentorship be incorporated into learning experiences. Role models could be identified and matched up with small groups of children in an elementary school or with one teenager. These adults might be selected on the basis of their commitment to the future ecological society as well as on the basis of their interest in young people. Students could learn about the mentor's perspectives, skills, and interests relating to building sustainability. At some point, the children would work on a community project with the mentor. This kind of service orientation has already been established in several schools; students are doing meaningful projects in their communities, away from the classroom.

Local Studies in a Global Context

Educators with a concern for an ecological society can begin to recognize the challenges within their own regions and experiment with methods to promote cooperation with educators in distant regions who share their concerns. Efforts to strengthen education can be based on the assumption that there are common issues and methods for teaching students about the environment in the environment. There usually are counterpart groups in other regions that would benefit from collaborative exchanges.

Exchanges might include (1) living and working in another region, developing new skills for use in the home ecoregion; (2) study tours oriented toward practical ecological studies or projects; and (3) internships in which organizations in different regions host each other in order to develop specific skills for use in the home region.

An approach to understanding global issues in a regional context is the study of environmental dependency between regions based on the migratory species shared in common. For example, a common migratory bird of both North and South America is the southern redstart (*Setophaga ruticilla*), a small warbler of brilliant orange-red found high in the treetops.

The bird overwinters in Central and South America and the Caribbean Islands. Like so many other birds, it is continuously in motion, catching insects for food, and is an integral part of the North American forests from May to September. Extending from Newfoundland on the Atlantic Ocean to British Columbia on the Pacific and south to Florida and other states on the Gulf of Mexico, this tiny traveler has one of the most extensive ranges of the North American passerine species.

In Latin America the destruction of tropical forests threatens the redstart's survival during September to May, suggesting a possible scenario in which the redstart fails to appear on its nesting grounds in North America. Meanwhile, overdevelopment in North America contributes to the shrinking forest cover that is its habitat from May to September. Each year a smaller population flies southward to the overwintering grounds. Attempts to protect the birds by establishing sanctuaries or restoring habitats in one part of the range are doomed to failure if complementary efforts do not take place in the other part of the range. Children in North America, engaging in studies of their southern neighbors, need to learn not only social histories but natural histories and ecological processes of the life they share in common.

Communications technologies can also bring students closer together around common problems and solutions. Students in the North can select an ecological problem with which they are concerned, and children of the South can share in providing information, ideas, and results of environmental action; and vice versa.

The similarities between the interests of Northern and Southern Hemisphere peoples need to be emphasized to personalize the ecological interdependencies of both. A tangible object such as a local bird, which is an indicator of the health or degradation of the local environment and the entire ecosystem, can illustrate this.

Structuring Interactions in a Learning Cycle

Leadership Styles

The teaching methods employed in the process of educating for an ecological society can convey as strong a message to the learner as does the content. If we are educating for participation of a broad citizenry, then we must allow students to be active participants in educational programming.

Participative leadership includes the dissemination of power for completion of a task among all members of the class. The teacher participates as well as facilitates. This approach is essential in field investigations where natural phenomena are being studied. Directive leadership includes conventional techniques such as the transmission of a body of knowledge. This strategy may be reserved for situations in which the teacher can focus attention on points related to experiences that students already have in common.

Permissive leadership invites the learner to formulate a task and determine effective ways of accomplishing it. This approach is most appropriate after students have studied the basics of a topic and can pursue aspects of it that interest them. During activities in which the permissive leadership style is being used, students might be required to demonstrate some level of competency in social interactions and safety practices.

The assumption here is that the teacher has some control over or choice of the physical environment of the learning activity. The learning setting will determine which combination of leadership styles to use, which will subsequently affect students' interactions and their ability to perform certain kinds of tasks.

Expanding the Concept of School Using the Living-System Metaphor

The concept of a *living system* offers a viable metaphor for an ecological education. Inherent in this metaphor is the interactive dialogue among system members, who are living and being continuously renewed without damage to their structural integrity. Since living systems are self-regulating, self-organizing, autonomous, and self-referential structures, they are able to transform themselves. This character of living systems relates to the phenomena of open exchange, such as interactions between the system and its structural boundaries. The living-system metaphor leads us to an understanding of *mutual and reciprocal causality* as contrasted with linear cause-and-effect relationships.

The concepts of mutual and reciprocal causality are significant for planning ecology education. Rather than studying smaller and smaller parts, students need experiences in interactive dialogue between various systems. For example, the learner and the curriculum can be seen as a living system; the children and teachers, as subsystems of the school; the school, as a subsystem of the learning community, which includes both the built and the natural environment. Curriculum can be constructed so that learners are able to live it, own it, and have peer dialogue about it. Learning includes reconnecting human/environment relationships, as the natural world is seen as part of the human's habitat. Development of the identity of the human as an ecological Self is a step in the process of building an ecological society. We need to reclaim responsibility for our "place," our habitat, for perceiving, exploring, and understanding its importance to human survival.

The required transformation begins with looking at the universal needs of children—their natural ontogenesis, or individual development, which has not changed throughout the thousands of years of the existence of *Homo sapiens*. Fulfilling those needs requires some experience with the wild places of the planet, not just the places constructed by humans.

The concept of a school already is being redefined in many places. As technical areas become more specialized, requiring equipment unavailable to schools, science educators are taking their students into the communities to expose them to these learning settings. Gradually educators recognize their limitations and the value of an expanded concept of a school as rooted in the larger learning community of the ecoregion, other regions, and the planet, which is a total system.

School site development projects can transform the immediate environment of the school, just outside the door. Asphalt jungle and grassy monoculture, found on school grounds throughout the world, can become diversity-rich places for discovery, inquiry, and artistic expression. The new science of habitat restoration, *restoration ecology*, applied to the school grounds can enrich the learning experiences of teachers, students, and the community. Many of these techniques are known to personnel in local natural resource management agencies, and through collaborative relationships the aims of both groups can be met.

For example, school grounds, converted to natural tall-grass prairie with very tall grasses and flowering coneflowers, can contribute to the natural diversity of the ecoregion. Patches of prairie are excellent habitat for pollinating insects such as butterflies and skippers. Patches of plants that may be considered weeds by most are perhaps the local flora most needing nurturance. Outdoor learning sites, known as "ecostations," can be constructed or manipulated to allow for natural history studies and science investigations. Not only is direct observation pedagogically sound, but it demonstrates how science can be an important tool in restoration of degraded sites.

Educators already play an important role as visitors to many parks and preserves in North America (Ahearn 1988). This role must be expanded, since nature protection in local communities is important to sustaining the ecosystem processes that allow for life to continue. Teachers can begin to establish cooperative and collaborative relationships with the conservation professionals in their local regions, who have jurisdiction over natural areas that are living museums, natural laboratories, outdoor classrooms for the study of science and culture.

Although pristine natural areas do not exist everywhere, there always are wastelands nearby that are highly disturbed by humans and nutrient poor, requiring restoration to health and diversity. Other areas may require detoxification of the agricultural chemicals in the soil through a sequence of plantings. Projects such as restoring an empty lot to native grasses are labor intensive. They require people, commitment, and time—three resources available in abundance in the typical school. The challenge to educators is to develop the capacity for envisioning educational potential in practical work such as restoration of habitat. Learning to operationalize that vision into a plan of action will draw upon the best that each group has to offer.

IMMEDIATE RESPONSIBILITIES

For ecological societies to emerge, certain elements are essential. The first is that the public, not just the governments, must be provided with up-to-date technical information on the basis of which to make decisions in support of ecological development. This requires channels of communication and information flow between and within institutions, organizations, and individuals of each nation. Next, the latest science—restoration ecology—must be given additional financial support in order to get on with the massive tasks of preserving biological diversity in each nation. Current technologies are insufficient to prevent further erosion of vital life-support systems of the planet. This requires acceleration of basic research into the development and implementation of resource management technologies. The findings need to be communicated to the public and to the governments, who must redirect the vast amounts of monies used on weapons overproduction into these areas of research and education.

Finally, an international communication forum needs to be developed so that environmental management efforts can be discussed among ecoregions and new collaborative arrangements can be designed. The approach needed is for governments and scientific, nongovernmental, and citizen-action coalitions of the planet to come together in a collegial atmosphere to communicate up-to-date measures in a move toward building ecological societies. As these tasks unfold, societal support for ecological approaches to development and education will increase. The challenge to educators is to address the issue of how to avoid ecosystem collapse. The old worldview that has brought the societies of the planet to this threshold will ultimately be replaced by a more functional and life-supporting one.

Educators can examine their own views through reflection, dialogue, and action relating to meaningful schools, learning about primal human experiences (historical and contemporary), understanding variations in worldviews, and developing ways to affirm their life-supporting components. Curriculum planning with colleagues will naturally follow.

Educators are the key component in the move toward building ecological societies. Not only are they shareholders as citizens, but they are essential in creating or selecting the appropriate milieux for learning. As the ones who design the learning setting and are responsible for developing skills in learners, they share in the responsibility for leading the societal transformation. Conscious planning of the learning milieux, the body of knowledge to be understood, and the process of education can demonstrate to students the shifts that are necessary; school content and methods must justify the kind of world we are trying to build.

As the world wrestles with issues of war and peace, governments are in a position to select either the path of militarism or common security based on the equitable process of public participation.

Stepping into the Unknown

> I set out into the unknown and nobody on Earth could tell me what I would encounter. There were no textbooks. This is the first time ever. But I knew for certain that it had to be done. It was clear that I had to be very careful.
>
> —Aleksei Leonov, Cosmonaut, USSR

In former days, during my nature rambles, I often would decide to leave the well-trodden path of the mesophytic forest of southern Ohio, where I grew up, to traipse cross-country to see a rare wood warbler that might have migrated into my woods from its overwintering grounds in Colombia. The "waves of warblers" appeared every May and challenged my skills of observation and patience and my sense of adventure. I never knew where the crisp song or flash of yellow would lead me as I followed the tiny birds throughout the hemlock hollows. The steep cliffs were a constant danger to the careless.

If I was stealthy and attentive to my surroundings and to the behavior of the birds, their chip notes would lead me to their nests. Some years there were no nests to be found, and the search became the goal itself. Other years, the reward was the discovery of nest and hatchlings, the opportunity to set up a bird blind and observe feeding behavior for days. The elegant tiny birds, destined to fly to South America by the end of summer, inspired me to undertake this annual adventure in the bush. Had I followed the well-trodden path through the woods, I would have seen only the common species, tolerant of human disturbances. To leave the trail was to risk getting lost, injured, wet, and cold, but it held a more worthy goal.

Like Leonov's historic space adventure and my nature ramble, there is nothing to be gained on the well-trod path into the future. As for the unknown, there are no models, guidebooks, footpaths, or experts, although it appears that a more ecological education is the key to the process. Positive exchanges between the Russian and American people are creating opportunities for redirecting educational, scientific, technological, economic, and indigenous skills in service of the planet and the natural communities, which are interrelated.

REFERENCES

Abrahams, Mark. 1990. "A Changing South Africa: A Challenge for People's Education and Radical Pedagogy." Unpublished paper, Memorial University, St. John's, Newfoundland.

Ahearn, Susan Kains. 1991. "Education and Biodiversity." Ph.D. diss. Columbia University, New York.

———. 1991. "Native Metaphors for Scientifically Explained Phenomena." Forthcoming.

Anderson, Ann G. 1990. "Living Systems in Mathematics Education." Ph.D. diss. University of Alberta, Edmonton, Alberta, Canada.

Davis, Derek S., and Dale Smith. 1988. "Analyzing Nova Scotia's Natural History: A

Production of a Resource Book for Land-Use Planning and Environmental Education." In *Landscape Ecology and Management*, edited by Michael R. Moss. Montreal: Polyscience.

Eliade, Mircea. 1959. *The Sacred and the Profane*. New York: Harcourt Brace Jovanovich.

Environment Canada. 1991. *The Green Plan: A National Challenge*. Quebec: Hull.

Freire, Paolo. 1970. *Pedagogy of the Oppressed*. New York: Herder and Herder.

Goudie, R. Ian. 1990. "Toward a Conservation Strategy for Newfoundland and Labrador: Consideration of Ecoregions." Unpublished paper to guide technical discussions, St. John's, Newfoundland.

Kearney, Michael. 1984. *Worldview*. Novato, Calif.: Chandler & Sharp.

Kelly, Kevin W., ed. 1988. *The Home Planet*. Moscow: MIR Publishers; New York: Addison-Wesley.

McLuhan, T. C. 1971. *Touch the Earth*. New York: Promontory Press.

Mitchell, John H. 1984. *Ceremonial Time*. New York: Warner Books.

Noss, R. S. and Harris, L. D. 1986. "Nodes, Networks, and MUMs: Preserving Diversity at All Scales." *Environmental Management* 10:299–309.

Searles, H. 1959. *The Non-human Environment in Normal Development and Schizophrenia*. New York: International Universities Press.

Shepherd, Paul. 1982. *Nature and Madness*. San Francisco: Sierra Club Books.

Sherl, Lea M. 1975. "Self in Wilderness: Understanding the Psychological Benefits of Individual-Wilderness Interaction through Self-Control." *Leisure Sciences* 11: 123–35.

Tedlock, Dennis, and Barbara Tedlock, eds. 1975. *Teachings from the American Earth*. New York: Liveright.

Turnbull, Colin M. The Human Cycle. New York: Simon and Schuster, 1983.

7

Education for Democracy, Social Responsibility, and Creative Activity in Russia Today

Anatoly Golovatenko

WHAT IS SOCIAL RESPONSIBILITY?

Our first task is to determine what social responsibility is in general. Does it belong to an individual only, or also to a group, a community, a society? What are the characteristics of social responsibility in a teenager as an individual? Is the content of the concept of social responsibility something eternal, or is it changeable? How do concrete economic, political, and cultural conditions influence the formation of social responsibility?

It is impossible to exhaustively answer all these questions, but let's make an attempt, starting with social conditions. There are both common and special features of a responsible individual in various social and political systems. Each society makes its own demands upon an individual; each society at the same time is shaped by the needs and requirements of its members.

It would be mistaken to speak about the individual "in general"; the issue concerns society. But it is possible to define several traits that, in my opinion, are typical of each responsible individual living under economic, social, political, and cultural conditions of any sort.

Belongingness as Part of Responsibility

A responsible person understands that he or she is a member of various groups, collectives, and communities and also belongs to a society, a nation, an ethnic group, humankind. A responsible person regards his or her *interconnection* with others as a precondition for normal human life, not as a means to success or an obstacle that hinders the way to personal achievement. A responsible person does not consider other people as "means" only, that is, merely as instruments of personal success. He or she tries not only to use another's aid, but also to contribute to the aspirations and desires of others. Hence, responsibility cannot be combined with a utilitarian approach to social surroundings. Responsibility also means *reciprocity*.

Tolerance

A responsible individual acts according to her or his own convictions, but simultaneously takes it into account that others as a rule have different opinions and views. Accordingly, responsibility is the ability to combine loyalty to one's own principles with readiness for compromises. It is clear, though, that not just any conviction can be combined with toleration; the opinions of a responsible individual must be consistent with universal human values.

Respect for Tradition

A responsible individual is a supporter of traditional moral values and universal human rights. Responsibility is, accordingly, connected with conservatism, but it does not rule out the possibility of modifying one's surroundings. Responsibility is not a passive attitude to life; but any activity of a responsible individual is limited by ethical and legal norms. Such limitations are not regarded by a responsible individual as restrictions by an external force; they represent self-restriction.

It is impossible to list all the conservative and reform components existing in the consciousness of a responsible individual. The way to combine the two components depends on concrete social conditions. For instance, American society needs reforms as much as Russia does; indeed, any society does. But the depth and intensity of these needed reforms are greater in Russia than in the United States. Hence, the relation between the conservative and the reformist attitude needed in various countries— and in the mentality of their inhabitants—has to be different.

We must take this difference into consideration when we speak about how to use traditions (both national and universal) and innovations in education.

Freedom From—Freedom To

The concept of social responsibility is connected with the concepts of freedom and liberty. A responsible individual is free, meaning not only *free from* something, but also *free for* something—free to think and act in a constructive way.

Persons who possess the first form of freedom, freedom from, believe themselves to be independent of society. This independence is, of course, very relative, but all the same real. Any democratic society can provide freedom of this kind. This is an important result of social development, but it is neither a result, nor an aim, of *personal* development. A person acquires freedom from violence, from lawlessness, from tyranny; he or she enjoys this freedom.

This sort of freedom is connected with a responsibility that may be called "external" or "minimal" responsibility. Its origin is the society's laws, not the conscience or consciousness of an individual. When society demands that an individual act according to some rules, the individual possessing external responsibility is ready to observe such rules. Hence, this form of responsibility can be called "passive responsibility." It is not connected with any creative activity. The first and minimal level of responsibility can guarantee, to a certain extent, the conservation of humankind's social and cultural achievements. It can prevent society from destruction but cannot promote social or individual development. So, there is an interconnection between freedom *from* something, *negative* freedom, and social responsibility.

Positive freedom may be called "constructive freedom" and is connected with the ability to take into consideration the achievements of previous generations and contemporaries. Positive freedom is also connected with the ability not to be prejudiced against those who have different opinions; it is connected with the ability to adopt all ideas that can help in the search for solutions to problems ahead.

In other words, being socially responsible means to be ready to transform reality, in the sense of improving reality according to universal values. A responsible person is active, but his or her activity combines a readiness for conservation with a readiness for alteration.

Ability to Compromise

Responsibility does not exist in the abstract. It would be wrong to think that some sort of "global" responsibility is the most important. In this way the famous slogan "Think globally and act locally" may be misleading. It is necessary to think and act both globally and locally and to think and act in the framework of one's abilities and possibilities, taking all the opportunities there are.

It would be wrong, generally, to think that responsible thinking is always about global problems only. A responsible person cannot ignore global problems, but also cannot give them absolute priority. In certain situations there can even be contradictions between local and global interests, between an individual and a group, between a group and a nation, between a nation and humankind, and so on.

We speak about the priority of universal values and common interests of the whole of humankind, and this is a correct approach; but, at the same time, a responsible person cannot ignore the interests of an individual or a small group for the sake of abstract universal interests.

As a rule it is impossible to find a solution that is perfect in the sense that it is good enough for everyone; the aim of a responsible individual is not a "maximally good solution," but an "optimal" one—one that is good or tolerably good for everyone.

In other words, social responsibility is also the ability to give up an idea for the sake of reality. No idea can be regarded as absolute or "the most important one." The twentieth century has exhibited the fatal flaw of attempting to put into practice such global ideas as those of socialism, typical of European Marxists and Russian Bolsheviks, and nationalism, the basis of German Nazism. A similar danger is potentially connected with every global idea.

For instance, there is not only the "red" or "brown" danger, but also a "green" danger. It is difficult to predict all the consequences of "green maximalism." If we regard ecological ideas as the most important ideas always and everywhere, we might arrive at an "ecological dictatorship." To prevent this, we need precisely social responsibility. A responsible person has to take into account not only general, global principles, but also concrete situations.

It is impossible, for example, to liquidate in one moment or in a short time all the industrial factories injurious to the health of people and to natural surroundings; it is impossible (now and even in the near future) to do away with all the negative results of people's productive activity—without at the same time doing harm to society and individuals. In such situations a responsible person has to choose "the lesser evil."

Hence, we must reject maximalist ideas in all spheres, including ecology, and act carefully and cautiously to find a "middle way," a compromise between the ecological ideal and real-life situations, bearing in mind the different interests of different groups and persons.

The ability to compromise is also a very important feature of the responsible individual. He or she is a "compromiser," and tries to combine different ideas and to find peaceful agreement between people.

Human Beings as "Owners"

Given our assumption that each responsible individual has to see not only global problems, but also local and concrete ones, we can draw another conclusion: each responsible individual has to keep in mind not only humankind, but also individuals, and to pay attention, first of all, to the person.

Individuals are at the center of the phenomenon called "responsibility." Further, when speaking about special traits of our country and its influence on the formation of social responsibility, I shall dwell on this question: What is personal or individual responsibility, and what is collective responsibility? To be responsible, an individual needs to live in a society characterized by some definite social conditions.

In addition to freedom *from* and freedom *for,* there is one more significant precondition: a responsible person has a right to *private property.* I would like to emphasize that private property is not only a phenomenon of the material world, but also a reflection of a way of thinking that has certain characteristic elements. The first element is the ability to define some sphere or room for individual activity, a spiritual equivalent of something that belongs to *somebody,* relatively separated from other things belonging to other people. The second element is a readiness to bear the responsibility for results of the said activity.

I want to point out the difference between the universal right I have to personal property and the capitalist's right to own land or natural resources that ordinary families live on. The actual possession of various material things—a piece of land, a workplace, and so on—is not in itself vital for the formation of responsibility, but the *potential* possession, the *right* to be an owner, is. A person can be responsible only if he or she owns something. A person who owns nothing, whether in the material sphere (in the world of things and material phenomena), in the spiritual sphere (in the world of thoughts and emotions), or in religious life, will never be able to understand the deep meaning of "responsibility." Such a person is not *personal* enough; he or she does not have *individuality* in the philosophical meaning of the term.

To many people, this idea seems obsolete or bourgeois. I do not agree; we must take into account the close connection between the material and the spiritual life.

It is relevant to remember here some historic facts. The rise of private property is connected in time with the beginnings of the notion of human personality. Private property became the basis for a person's self-awareness.

It is no mere chance that words connected with personality and property often have the same roots: *privacy* and *private property; personality* and *personal* in English: *propre* and *propriété* in French; *Meinung* and *mein* and *Eigenheit* and *Eigentum,* in German. Similar concurrences are typical in Russian, too. This linguistic regularity was one of the fundamental ideas of Destutt de Tracy (1754–1836, France) and Max Stirner (1806–56, Germany).

There is a close and deep-rooted connection between individuality and property, and this is reflected in language, law, philosophy, and even the religions of various nations. This connection makes clear the relationship between property and individuality. It would be naïve to hope that responsibility could be formed without a basis in personal property combined with the negative freedom that belongs to a relatively high level of legal development.

Even more important than this right itself is *the readiness to be a proprietor,* and the experience of taking care of material possessions. The readiness may be the result of each person's experience over time, as a child and as a young person, of taking care of "what *belongs to me.*" Social responsibility has in this way its origin in individual activity, as a precondition for normal personal development. The readiness to be an owner is in this way an important step toward personal responsibility for one's own activity. The experience of being an owner helps us to realize that if

I have something, something depends on me. When an individual realizes this connection, he or she moves forward in responsibility.

An additional comment is needed. Each person has in her or his possession not only material things, but also abilities, skills, intellectual resources, knowledge, and the like. This sort of "possession" is natural for everybody, even if we seldom consider our intellectual and spiritual power to be "aspects of ownership." I do not intend here to go deeper into this complicated problem. I would, however, like to stress the importance of *the feeling of possession.* We have some spiritual abilities (gifts from God, increased by ourselves). This feeling can prompt us to manage or utilize our gifts in a better way, that is, to become more responsible. So the feeling of possessing spiritual "things" also leads to development of our capacities.

That is why education for social responsibility is connected theoretically, and must be connected practically, with the formation of respect for intellectual (spiritual) and material private property. The problem of influence exercised by private property on human mentality, and the influence of this mentality on social behavior, was especially important in former Soviet society up until 1991; for seven decades we have lost so many opportunities.

Responsibility Is Dependent on the Social System

I have outlined six general features of a responsible individual; they are important but cannot be regarded as exhaustive. There will always be a variety of social systems in the world, and various ways to form social responsibility.

The former Soviet society was a very special one. It is well known that social and economic conditions in the USSR were—and still are in Russia of today—very different from those in the West. Analysis of socioeconomic history, both Russian and Soviet, is, of course, a complicated problem that cannot be treated here. However, in our society, as there has been a lack of democratic experience, there has also been a general lack of tradition of showing respect for the person. For centuries the basis of Russian historical development was the idea that an individual does not need personal rights; the concept of the community was more important than the concept of personality. When our society was relatively homogeneous (till the eighteenth century), a community was expected to guarantee the interests and requirements of an individual; a similar situation existed in medieval Europe.

Most Western countries have chosen a line of development that is different from that of Russian and Soviet society. Mechanisms for coordinating various individual wills did not seem to be necessary in our society. Each person felt, as a rule, responsibility to his or her community, and was taught to submit voluntarily to a collective will.

Today the situation has changed; step by step, social life has become more complex and complicated; the old ideas are not accepted any more. Compared to the West, here development has been slow and has contributed to conservation of old political forms and social interrelations. Gradually religion became the basis for personal responsibility.

Apart from religion there were no reasons to be responsible; the social component of responsibility was lost. Against this background, social relations based on mutual responsibility between individuals never struck deep roots in Russia or in other republics in the former USSR up to 1991.

Gradually, religious foundations were razed almost to the ground. Total compulsion instead of responsibility became the general principle of social organization in Soviet society. The forms and aims of this compulsion differed during various periods of our history, but the issue of social responsibility was never on the authorities' agenda for school and culture. The Russian (Soviet) people have known only one type of responsibility: the legal responsibility of a citizen to the state. Even the term *responsibility* itself is connected in the Russian/Soviet mentality with official propaganda that spoke about "a high feeling of responsibility for the state and the Communist party." Legal responsibility has been based on our system of laws, which throughout the Communist period of our society has been at variance with universal legal principles, such as those embodied in the UN Charter for Human Rights.

In my opinion, it is possible to genuinely realize the ideal of the "fully responsible" individual only under the conditions of democracy and in a rule-of-law state. So, what we need in our society is to be guaranteed the external safeguard of responsibility, and accordingly the right of "freedom from" as a premise for internal responsibility.

Only if an individual—and any group of individuals—can be influential in political, economic, and social life, can citizens be expected to act as responsible persons. In an undemocratic society the majority of the population display a passive responsibility. This means they are ready to observe laws and moral rules that are enforced.

SOCIAL RESPONSIBILITY IN A CHANGING COUNTRY

Under Gorbachev, between 1985 and 1991, the Soviet Union became a rapidly changing society, moving toward general democratization and the creation of a rule-of-law state.

Theory of the Rule-of-Law State

The theory of the rule-of-law state (*Rechtsstaat*, in German) was developed in the eighteenth and nineteenth centuries by philosophers like Kant, Mohl, and Welcker in Germany, Locke in England, Montesquieu in France, Jefferson in the United States, and Chicherin, Kistyakovsky, and Novgorodtsev in Russia. Step by step the general principles of the legal state were realized by politicians in the countries of Western Europe and North America, and were put into practice, embodied in constitutions and other laws. Russia has never before had a rule-of-law state. The attempt to form such a state in March–October 1917 failed.

By Marxist standards of law, the socialist state in our country was never legal. Marx and Engels declared that the only possible form of socialist state is the dictatorship of the proletariat. Engels in his "Critique of the Gotha Program" disagreed with the leaders of the Social Democratic party of Germany, who believed that socialist laws could replace "bourgeois" laws and be more just than other laws. In Engels's opinion, law belongs to the phenomena of capitalist society; the working class merely can and must use bourgeois law in a transition period toward communism. According to Marx's theory, the proletariat would enjoy bourgeois rights (today we call them "universal" rights), as long as a state existed, and then laws would be replaced by ethical norms. For this reason, Marxists did not pay special attention to legal issues. The issue of human rights seemed also to be of minor importance to them.

Rule-of-Law State in the USSR and Russia

Practice has shown that many of Marx's ideas, including Marxist ideas about law, are illusions. The domination of Marxist theory in the former Soviet Union and other "socialist" countries led to the rejection of the best achievements of humankind in the sphere of law. After the October revolution in 1917, law was regarded only as one of the means of promoting the class struggle.

During the years of Stalin's dictatorship, laws became an instrument of repression used to strengthen the power of the Communist party. During Khrushchev's and Brezhnev's governments, the state continued to be a power standing above the principles of universal law. This situation alienated law from the people and led to a common lack of human rights.

There is a difference between principles of law and laws in force. The *principles of law* are general; they do not depend on the will of any person, group, party, class, or state. These principles are connected with the nature of human beings. The *laws in force* are products of human activity in legal and political spheres. A concrete law can be in accordance with the principles of law or contradict these principles. A *rule-of-law state* is a state where there is harmony (at least as an ideal) between the principles of law and the laws in force. Citizens in this state are responsible persons (as an ideal). When there is no notion about this harmony as an ideal, there can be no social responsibility.

There are three important features of any rule-of-law state:
a. The supreme authority belongs to the law and not to the state.
b. Everybody enjoys universal human rights.
c. There is a division between the legislative, executive, and judicial authorities.

A rule-of-law state is a state subordinated to law. The state itself may neither change nor abolish principles of law. Rights and freedoms are not a gift from the state, granted by the state to society or to an individual; the state cannot take these rights away from anybody.

But the essential task before us in Russia today is to take the difficult road toward becoming a legal state. Like any other state, Russia must be transformed and improved to reach this goal.

EDUCATION FOR LAW CONSCIOUSNESS

The School and the Law

But all laws—even very good and just ones—are only a premise, a sine qua non, for the rule-of-law state and a socially responsible life. There is one more task, a social and educational one: to foster law consciousness in the citizens, to raise citizens' consciousness of the necessity of rule by law. The solution of this task is the cornerstone of education for democracy and a very complicated task in current Russian society.

There is a close interconnection between consciousness of law and social responsibility. During the transition period from a totalitarian regime to a rule-of-law state, it is impossible to develop responsibility without taking into account the lack of a social and personal vision of the principles of law. Neither can we expect an individual to have a positive attitude toward public establishments and social institutions before these institutions are good enough, as judged from the perspective of law.

During a transition period, it is vital to keep in mind that our goal in the sphere of education is *not* a *positive* social attitude in the student, but a *constructive* attitude. There is an important difference between the two. Each determines specific traits. The difference is decisive with regard to the relationship between conservation of traditions and innovations, between the observance of law and the creation of new laws. In other words, *creative activity* plays a vital role in the formation of social responsibility; this is of crucial importance under present Russian conditions.

One important problem is the relation between collective and personal responsibility. There is collective responsibility when each member of a collective, or of a group, is responsible. Hence, collective and personal responsibility are not separate phenomena; collective responsibility is based on responsibility of the individual.

Collectivism as an Educational Goal

The perspective that individual responsibility is the basis of collective responsibility is especially important for our country and for the theory of our education. Russian philosophy and pedagogy have regarded individualism as a negative phenomenon, opposed to humanism. According to such views, collectivism is the only possible system for interpersonal relations, the only system useful for education. Supporters of such ideas believe that collectivism always opposes individualism. This attempt to counterpoise collectivism and individualism leads to a very dangerous form of collectivism based on individual irresponsibility. We saw this phenomenon, for example, in the Soviet administrative apparatus, where, as elsewhere in the Soviet society, it was the ground for the development of bureaucracy and monopoly.

The Need to Cultivate Individualism

To eradicate bureaucracy and to counteract monopolization in all sectors of social life, we need to cultivate individualism. This view is connected with such values as self-confidence, strength of will, perseverance, and earnestness of purpose.

Individualism can be both positive and negative, depending on the individual's choice of goals and tasks to solve in concrete activity. Therefore, there is responsible and irresponsible individualism. If we succeed in combining individualism with social responsibility, we will help to develop not only a responsible individual, but also a person who is able to interact efficaciously with other people.

It is clear that the formation of social responsibility is not an easy task under the circumstances in our country. To solve the problem, we have to overcome serious obstacles connected both with specific features of Russian history and with the negative influence of Communist ideology.

To educate new, responsible generations is nothing less than to reconstruct a mentality injured, often destroyed, by totalitarian power, by demoralizing terror, and an all-embracing fear. The task of creating genuine democratic habits and attitudes is enormous.

The Role of the School

In this transition period it is important to develop preconditions for molding a new political, legal, and ethical mentality. No perestroika can guarantee spiritual changes. A goal-directed effort by all democratic social institutions is necessary. The most essential among these institutions is the school. What can the school do, and what does it do, to solve this task?

First of all, the *new, democratic school* has to avoid implanting in children political and ideological stereotypes. It must contribute to the pupils' development of free thought and creativity.

Most teachers understand well that new approaches are necessary with regard to content and methodology, especially in history, literature, geography, and social studies. The most difficult task may be to decide what, and how, to teach about society.

Some teachers and scholars have tried, and still try, to preserve the fundamental basis laid down by Marx, Engels, Lenin, and Bukharin as the main principles of history teaching, social studies, and social education. But there have been important changes in the interpretation of these fundamentals. According to official ideas, many Marxists tried at first to modify old dogmas, to combine them with principles of the rule-of-law state, universal human rights, and universal moral standards (e.g., standards independent of class consciousness). These ideas about universal rights were repudiated by the founders of Marxism.

Attempts to "correct" some of the statements by Marx or Lenin (e.g., about violence and its positive role in history; class struggle and dictatorship; ethics and the essence of human being), all the attempts to "decorate the facade" of the old ideological building, are, in my opinion, vain endeavors. At the same time they mark dangerous tendencies that are but other forms of the outmoded and "old way" of thinking noted by Eva Nordland in chapter 1. Even a modified Marxism is directed toward subordinating individuals to a collective; some individuals are taught to rule, while others are taught to be submissive.

Some collectivist ideas are positive, but to learn about these we do not need the aid of Marx. So-called scientific socialism is neither a general philosophy nor a methodology of cognition. We have to teach about Marxism, but then interpret Marxism as a stage in the history of human daring and errors (see chapter 9).

We must integrate, into teaching, the ideas and conceptions of humanism, social peace, cooperation, tolerance, and different political and economic systems. We have to reject ideas of sociopolitical or national messianism. Our schools should not be places for the training of "fighters for a happy future," "fighters for peace," "fighters for national revival." Children do not have to fight or struggle; they do not need lessons of hatred; they do not need indoctrination of any kind. So our schools (and educational system in general) need a radical reconstruction. This reconstruction has started, but we are at the very beginning of a long path.

Russian Schools in Transition

The following are some illustrations of current school experiments in changing content and methods with regard to nurturing responsible and creative individuals.

Humanization

One task is what is called the "humanization" of education. This concerns all subjects and student activities in school and out of school. In the sphere of school education, it is necessary, first, to take into account the students' personalities and their specific possibilities; secondly, we need a school curriculum that is more human. (See the chapters by Robert Zuber [chapter 9] and Sergei Polozov [chapter 5]; both underline the responsibility of human beings as part of nature.)

In changing the content of education, we must turn to the teaching of the humanities. We have to place human beings in the center of all humanitarian subjects, showing human beings as persons, with interests and needs, successes and failures. In history teaching, this approach presupposes the rejection of economic determinism. Not economic relations but human life should be the main content of history teaching.

This is the sole way to demonstrate that always, during all historical epochs, persons have had opportunities to influence society's development. The results of this influence can differ; the study of historical topics and historical facts can help students to realize that these results depend on individuals, on their responsibility or irresponsibility, on their attitudes toward social life.

It is now popular in our country to teach history that pays more attention to human lives, both of well-known persons and of so-called ordinary people. The question how to put these ideas into practice is being worked on with special interest by many organizations, including researchers and teachers involved in the project "SCHOOL." The main idea of this project is to show that the content of historical development is *creative activity*. A teacher has to explain that every part of history has its own value; there are not "more important" and "less important" epochs and civilizations. Always, in every epoch, it is possible to contribute to the improvement of social life. There are always various possibilities of development. To *choose the course* is always the most important task. These ideas are very stimulating in the educational system and help to encourage students to develop an active social attitude.

The new structure of historical courses and new curriculum ideas proposed by the project SCHOOL can not only improve knowledge and skills, but also foster creativity and responsibility, for every issue is connected with contemporary life.

For example, when discussing the emancipation of serfs in Russia in 1861 and reforms directed by Alexander the Second, a teacher can compare the problems of that period with today's problems. When students can study changes in real life in a historical epoch, as seen through the eyes of ordinary people, they can become involved in the remote as well as the recent past compared to the present. Studies of teachers engaged in the practical testing of new curriculum ideas document that the new approach has increased involvement by the students. One study describes how students discuss human nature, universal needs and hopes—the changes in, and at the same time constancy of, human reality. The students discuss how social changes cannot abolish the fundamentals of human interrelations; changes may affect the external behavior of an individual, but basic attitudes and aims endure.

Thinking about the constancy of human nature entails realizing that humankind has common aims and may become a united, integrated whole—an idea that is essential to all the authors of this book. It is this unity of humankind that requires the universality of human rights, and it is one reason why human rights are an essential concern of our project. As a consequence of new thinking, students wish to know more about other nations, more about external obstacles, and more about what can be done to promote an integration process.

Another result of these studies is the realization by students that the human community is a unity not only in space, but also in time. The experience of previous generations becomes an important factor that influences students' world outlook. This is a significant factor in developing social responsibility; responsible persons act with caution, checking their own behavior against the experiences of earlier generations.

Another example is also connected with history teaching. World history displays many cases of how stubbornness and arrogance of historical figures can have tragic results. In the project SCHOOL, the teacher stresses such cases, showing how policies based on lack of responsibility came close to fanaticism and were fraught with danger. Examples from the activities of the Bolshevik party in the former Soviet society are especially relevant in explaining this idea.

As a rule, history teaching gives a teacher many opportunities to expose the mechanism of irresponsible activity in the political sphere. For instance, groups in Soviet politics tried during the First World War (1914–18) to put into practice their political ideas and to achieve their aims without paying attention to immediate results for families and individuals. Sometimes radical politicians—Stalin being only an example—believed that it was possible, and even necessary, to use destructive means and violence in social life to eliminate the old system; such policies of violence left social interconnections hidden. As a consequence, the principle "The worse, the better" was sometimes the basis for political activities.

Individual Needs

A task closely connected with the humanization of content in schools is the orientation toward individual needs. Individualized approaches have been analyzed in research reports and articles. One aspect is especially urgent in present Russian society: Besides traditional subjects, there is a need for a system of *optional* courses, starting with courses on previously "prohibited areas," topics officially forbidden up until 1985.

Curricula have already been worked out for some of these courses, including "National Interrelations in the Soviet (later Russian) Society," "Political Culture and Democracy," and "Social Surroundings and the Person." There are also many optional courses on ecology, history, economics, and literature. These curricula should be flexible and allow discussion of problems during lessons.

The content of such courses is important for the development of social responsibility. Also important is the fact that students are able to choose among a variety of courses. Most of the optional courses whose contents are connected with social problems are planned for students ages fourteen through seventeen. There are few optional courses for younger pupils.

There is now a growing wish for optional courses connected with various religions. Religious education is an important means of teaching social responsibility. Every child needs information about the main religions, their history and main ideas. Besides, parents should have the right to religious education for their children in accordance with personal beliefs. The first attempts in this area have already been made. An optional course, "History of World Religions," has been worked out as a secular course. In my opinion, we need a whole system of optional courses connected with various aspects of religion; every student should have the right to study one of them, according to his or her interests and beliefs.

Values in Education

One more task needs to be stressed: the study of traditional values of various world civilizations, using content and methods to counteract stereotypes and superstitions. There are two directions in this work. The first is the attempt to overcome both dogmatic and modified Marxism. The second is to have open discussion of national ideologies focused on the "exceptional nature" of the Soviet Union and later Russia. The accomplishment of this task is possible only under conditions of de-ideologization and a political pluralism at school. The first attempts at perestroika (reconstruction) in the late eighties were, in my opinion, a failure, because built on Marxism. So we continue our endeavors. The second attempt may be based on Russian nationalism, and that might be worse.

Legal Education

Education in law at all levels of the educational system is necessary. In the framework of education in law a teacher has an opportunity to encourage children's democratic consciousness. At the very center of education in law should be the ideas of universal human rights, the UN Declaration on Human Rights and all the UN conventions.

The Responsibility of the Family

Another important issue is cooperation between school and family. Educating an individual to be responsible is possible only with the family's support and assistance. Every family has to stimulate a feeling of autonomy in the child. To be responsible, a child needs to know and feel that she or he is a subject, an "acting person" in social life, not an "object of education." (See the chapters by Eva Nordland [chapter 1] and Sergei Polozov [chapter 5] and their concerns about "object" relations with nature.)

Parents also need to encourage the feeling of "being an owner," as mentioned above, and help their sons and daughters to become participants in "adult life." Respect for a child's privacy and private property, material as well as spiritual, means that the parents arrange for the child to experience personal responsibility, to experience being an owner. ("There is something for which I have the main responsibility; so I have to be careful—and to mind!")

The Learner as Member of Society

Each child is not only a family member and a student, but also a participant in social life, both in and out of school. Children and teenagers need to find their own forms of participation. Activity in various nonformal groups is currently typical for teenagers (see chapters 3, 5, and 8). Teachers should not (and in our society do not) have to impose upon students the "adult" forms of social activity. Teenagers need to get used to cooperating with others according to the rules of their age groups; this is particularly true of groups working with cultural and ecological problems.

Political Training

In today's Russia we have various democratic and social institutions, new political parties and movements. These institutions take part in education for social responsibility. Teachers contribute by helping to organize teenagers' political clubs or groups supporting, for example, Christian Democrats, Social Democrats, and Liberals.

On the one hand, it is important to encourage participation in political life; on the other hand, the educational system should take care to avoid politicization of the social life of children and teenagers. Ideologizing is dangerous, as it is so easily combined with intolerance and training in stereotyping.

We have not yet really started to create possibilities for children and teenagers to act as socially responsible members in the framework of the local community. Today's communities in Russian cities and towns do not have real social institutions. An urgent task is to reanimate communal life, and involve teenagers in it, as part of a general democratization of our society—and as part of an education for social responsibility.

CONCLUDING WORDS

The tasks mentioned in this article do not exhaust the problem, of course. Some approaches may seem disputable; better solutions will surely be found. I hope the experiences of other countries and the awakening of creative forces in our society will contribute to the molding of new generations, guiding them to becoming responsible, active in social life, and tolerant.

READINGS

Chalidze, V. 1990. *The Dawn of Legal Reform (April 1985–June 1989)*. Moscow: Progress Publishers.

Novgorodtsev, P. I. 1922–23. "Über die eigentümlichen Elemente der russischen Rechtsphilosophie." *Philosophie und Recht* 2.

Spectorsky, E. V. 1925. *Christianity and Culture*. Prague.

8
Peace Education, Social Responsibility, and Cooperation

Galina Kovalyova

COOPERATION AND NEEDS FOR COOPERATION

Some years ago people from different countries came to Oslo to start a project on education for a new time: the Project on Ecological and Co-operative Education (PEACE). Many of us did not even know each other. The task we set out to do—a common work on education on the basis of ecology and cooperation—was my first international project. To develop cooperative relations through really working together was one of the ideas of the project.

During the past three or four years of cooperation I have learned a lot from my colleagues. The most important lesson for me is a deep understanding that I am a part of humankind; I have my voice in a global society; I can make some contribution in the common endeavor to improve the prospects of our planet Earth.

I have chosen cooperation as my main topic because of the enrichment creative processes may induce. We feel the effect when we realize that the final product of a group of people becomes something much more than the sum of the results of the individual participants. In this chapter I give examples of the implementation in real life—in school and out of school—of the ideas of our project. I want to show some of the new approaches to school reform that have been tried out in the last four or five years in my country. I wish my reader welcome to a spiritual cooperation in sharing these ideas to find a mutual understanding.

Need for cooperation

Processes are making our world more and more interrelated. The contemporary community of states and nations faces the necessity of living together peacefully in this complex, diverse, and interdependent world, and of working out new ways of political thinking that correspond to the present historical situation and to the will of the peoples (Gorbachev 1987).

We are becoming morally and intellectually more actively involved in solving global problems of great significance to the whole of human-kind. The problem of peacemaking unites us spiritually and calls for the cooperation of everyone—men and women, children, teenagers, adults—to become creators of peaceful relations.

Peacemakers' effectiveness in their endeavors for creating peaceful relations is dependent to a considerable extent on the scale and quality of cooperation and interaction with governmental and public forces at the local, national, and international levels. At a time when contemporary policies and social relations are being reconstructed in many ways, work for peace is supported by new pedagogical thinking.

New Level of Consciousness

In education the main aim for the new ways of thinking is to develop individuals with a high level of consciousness, who realize themselves as persons with their own distinctive features, seeing themselves as members of society and as representatives of humankind, and learning to understand the interdependence between nature, society, and individuals.

A new level of consciousness means self-awareness that includes the ability to create a picture of the world; realization of one's own participation in world change and development; self-reflection and self-evaluation; critical thinking; ability to see multiple approaches to the solution of concrete problems; respect for other people who have different points of view; and ability to carry on a dialogue and resolve conflicts without using force. A high level of intellectual skill in a person comprises not only a developed intellect, but also a developed system of feelings and attitudes, of which social responsibility is a vital element.

Cooperation at Two Levels

The pedagogy of cooperation is a manifestation of new ways of thinking in education. It is founded on long traditions in the countries of all PEACE participants. Working out the ideas of the pedagogy of cooperation, we should take into account the interdependent character of, and the mutual enrichment gained through, cooperation. Cooperation is a comprehensive phenomenon and has two levels: internal and external (see chapter 3). The internal level corresponds to the experience of a country in its realization of child-adult cooperation in activities that are meaningful for both, aiming at educating young people for a vision of the contemporary world and responsibility for its fate.

At the external level, cooperation means the joint efforts of educators and all the people concerned to work out the theory of cooperative peace education and put it into practice—that is, the international cooperation of teachers, children, young people, and others in several countries. International cooperation could include working out new contents and new methods for education for social responsibility at all stages of human development.

SOCIAL RESPONSIBILITY AS THE INTEGRAL PERSONAL CHARACTERISTIC

Structure of Social Responsibility

Anatoly Golovatenko (chapter 7) gives a conceptual presentation of social responsibility. I will focus here on a psychological approach.

Russian educators consider social responsibility to be the integration of personal characteristics that determine a person's behavior and activity, based on his or her understanding of the society's values (Sidorova 1987). The structure of social responsibility, from the point of view of Russian psychologists, is the unity of three components: cognitive, motivational, and behavioral.

The cognitive component includes the system of a person's knowledge about social responsibility, including the essence, standards, and rules of responsible behavior. The base of the cognitive component is a scientific world outlook.

The motivational component is the system of motives for socially responsible behavior. In youth, a qualitative leap occurs in the development of self-consciousness: one becomes aware of problems connected with one's own place in society and one's responsibility for one's own behavior. Motives are developing for socially useful activity.

The behavioral component is realized in choosing and providing for definite lines of behavior that correspond to the standards of the socially responsible person.

The Level of Social Responsibility of Students

To understand the development of social responsibility in teenagers, it is necessary to reveal the level of development and characteristics of each of its three components, and then look at factors that can influence and strengthen social responsibility.

The psychologist T. Sidorova (1987) conducted a survey in which ninety-three students took part; they were students in the ninth and tenth grades of the general secondary school in Electrostal, Moscow Region. The results showed that most of the students were characterized by a middle level of knowledge of the content of social responsibility, and by an unstable position with respect to keeping the moral standards and rules. The students verbalized their understanding of the concept of social responsibility with great difficulty, but expressed a positive attitude toward social standards and rules of behavior in society. The students displayed social motives more often than they expressed them in their ideals. That indicates their practical aspiration to correspond to the social standards.

Most students had reached the middle level of socially responsible behavior and activity; that is, social responsibility was not stably manifested by them.

Sidorova's analysis of the data showed that the following variants of the social responsibility structure were the most typical for the students examined:

1. A structure with "isolated" cognitive components:
   a. a good knowledge of social standards and rules, and
   b. developed motives, in combination with
   c. unstable behavior; or
2. A structure of "irresponsibility," which included
   a. weak knowledge of social standards and rules,
   b. weak personal motivation toward socially useful activity, and
   c. irresponsible behavior. (Manifestation of social responsibility might occur in this group, but was not typical.)

The survey showed that socially constructive activities, when they were well organized by the educational system, had a great impact on the development of all three components of social responsibility.

Sidorova's study shows that the education of the socially responsible person needs organized activities that comprise all levels of the social responsibility structure. Such activities must also take place at all stages of education in school and out of school.

Age Problems in Developing Responsibility

Special attention should, however, be given to the activities of teenagers, as is shown in the research of Russian psychologist A. V. Zaporodzets (1964). A teenager is especially likely to engage in socially useful activity, as well as adopt standards of social behavior, when the activity is appropriate to her or his age group. In the teenage period there is an intensified development of intellectual and moral characteristics of personality.

Other persons—their internal worlds as well as their behaviors—are a focus of teenagers' interest. Teenagers compare themselves with others and evaluate themselves. In this context a teenager becomes involved in self-education.

At this age it also becomes more difficult for educators and parents to communicate with the young person. It is a period of imbalance with fits of unprovoked aggression, even cruelty. The actions of teenagers do not as yet show integrity; teens' life objectives are not yet clear; their personal experience is limited, and their self-control is not as yet established. This should be taken into account when developing age-group activities to educate for social responsibility.

A NEW APPROACH TO EDUCATING CHILDREN

Impact of Current Reforms on Education

The changes in the political and economical spheres of Russian society require new educational approaches in the school. Current reforms, which started in the Gorbachev era, emphasize the ideas of democracy, self-government, human rights and freedom, openness, social pluralism, a law-based state, and social justice. The reforms are aimed at overcoming authoritarian stereotypes, which have deep roots in the minds of the people. Hence, democratization, socialization, and humanization of education are the main features of the new approach in educational reform.

In the past, the main aim of education was considered to be the transference of knowledge and skills to children. This led to an abstract, academic understanding of individual development and technocratic attitudes. The new approach gives priority to universal human values, the needs of children, and an all-round development of personality.

The theoretical basis of the old pedagogical theory was Marxism-Leninism. Emphasis was on the "historical advantage of socialism." The new approach rejects the notion that there is only one correct pedagogical model. Instead, a variety of views, ideas, and approaches are accepted. Broad experimentation takes into account both worldwide experience and our own best traditions.

Change in Students' Worldview

In practice the reform of secondary education in Russia is directed toward working out a curriculum that gives students an integral picture of the world in its dialectical, historical, scientific, and social development, while reflecting the problems of humankind and the interrelation and interdependence of nature, human beings, and society. We gradually learn to see humankind as an integral part of Earth's *noosphere;* every person realizes his or her own place and role. Each person is seen as a real force playing a role in preserving the natural environment as well as civilization. So, as Eva Nordland writes in chapter 1, a new worldview among students is needed and must be cultivated through the educational system (see also chapters 3, 4, and 6).

The Role of Science Education in Developing Students' Personalities

Science education has an important role in helping students become active citizens who comprehend the issues confronting society. Many of these issues are connected with the social use of science and technology. By emphasizing science/technology-related societal issues and person-related issues, science education can help students to develop values and develop decision-making skills.

Because societal and personal issues contain important moral components, students get opportunities to develop cooperation skills, respect for oneself and others, respect for environment and life, tolerance, and personal and social responsibility.

Table 8.1 illustrates the process of developing students' personalities in science classes through content, structure, and methods of learning.

TABLE 8.1 New Ways of Thinking in Education: Conditions and means for Developing Students' Personalities and Social Responsibility in Science Education

Curriculum Content Emphasis	Structure	Methods
• Nature of science	• Democratic,	• Brainstorming
• Skill development	stimulative, and	• Dialogue
• Human endeavor	emotionally	• Role playing
• Science-society-technology	supportive	• Problem solving
interrelations	environment	• Questioning
• Ethics of natural environment	• Decentralized	• Individualization
• Science in employment	decision making	• Cooperative learning
• Life management	• Meaningful	• Interviewing
• Societal values	community	
	participation	

As an example, the following section considers some practical material used by Russian teachers in their school work.

Positive and Negative Consequences of Science and Technology Application in Society (Risk/Benefit)

The main sign of a responsible person is the ability to foresee the consequences of one's actions. Science education can make some contribution to the development of this ability.

For science class issues, it is useful to emphasize the consequences of applying technology in society. For example, when studying the topic of nuclear physics and technology, students need to discuss the controversial nature of nuclear technology. It is very complicated to find the balance between the benefits and risks, for instance. Risks can be separated from benefits in time as well as geography. The use of X-rays for diagnostic purposes may obviously benefit a person in the present; in the future, however, it means an increased risk of cancer, depending on the amount of and age at exposure, among other things. While one region of a country has the benefit of electricity produced at a nuclear power station, distant regions may be the sites of the risk, where the nuclear waste is stored.

It is essential to give students the basic facts and help them understand science and the applications of technology, "for" and "against," benefits and risks. This aspect of students' learning process can be the basis for rational decision making that considers the future, other regions, other spheres of life. In such contexts it is obvious that a person's and a community's life prospects are connected with general knowledge and understanding—or the lack of it. Such discussions during lessons can help students develop skills in considering problems from a risk/benefit point of view.

Questions for discussion may include the following:

1. What examples from modern life involve the use of technology, with consideration for both its risks and benefits?
2. Using your examples, what risks and benefits are involved in the situations?
3. Is the risk separated from the benefit in time? In geography?
4. What may be the principles for application?
5. What may be done to diminish the risks?

Social Responsibility in Making Decisions about Technological Issues in Society

The possibility of nuclear accidents is one of the key risks for any society with nuclear production facilities. When studying science, students must realize that nuclear catastrophes could be global, that our Earth could be destroyed beyond restoration, that we all need special knowledge and training for understanding what are the real impacts of a nuclear accident upon society and individuals. We need intellectual training to understand how a nuclear accident may affect society and its development. We need intellectual instruments to find possible ways of minimizing the consequences.

The examples below represent materials I developed together with the American teacher Phil J. Davis of Pojoaqua Valley Middle School,

Pojoaqua, New Mexico, during the third summer institute of educators from the United States and the former Soviet Union. Two educators from different cultures and institutions collaborated to produce the following lesson plans. Because I am concerned with the practical implementation of the ideas presented above, I have attempted to illustrate the general pedagogical principles with specific classroom techniques and democratic methodologies.

Practical Implementation

The general objectives of this activity are the following: The students develop an ability to foresee the environmental consequences of group and individual actions and learn to analyze decisions using risk/benefit conceptualization. The students will feel a sense of compassion for the victims of nuclear catastrophes and a sense of empowerment and responsibility while taking action locally on these issues.

Russian and American students are asked to consider two cases connected with nuclear energy production in their countries.

Case 1

In the first case the students are given facts and readings concerning an environmental problem: people living near the Hanford Atomic Energy Plant were exposed to radiation that shortened many people's lives and severely damaged their health. It turned out that for a long time they did not know that there were any risks to their health. Scientists and government officials knew that there were people living near the plant and that they would suffer health risks. Scientists and the government knowingly used local residents as subjects for an experiment on the impact of radiation on humans. At the same time, the Hanford plant helped the U.S. government obtain temporary "national security" through nuclear armaments; local people got well-paid jobs and economic development that they could not expect without the plant. The scientists were able to increase general knowledge about the effects of radiation on different life forms. Nuclear waste was stored, and is still present, at the plant. The question now is: How should the waste be disposed of? Nobody has given an answer as yet.

Once the students understand what the issue is all about, they start to prepare their first role-play: a conference on the legal question of compensation for victims. Possible questions are these: What compensation, if any, should the conference recommend? Through what means should compensation be adjudicated?

The various roles in the play may be suggested by students; possibilities include these:

- Local Hanford residents who have suffered radiation-related diseases
- Local Hanford residents who have made a lot of money off of the plant and continue to expect to make money from it
- Scientists who defend the need to use human subjects in extreme cases
- Scientists who oppose the use of human (and animal?) subjects
- Law-related persons: constitutional experts favoring *and* opposing the right of citizens to sue the government through the courts
- Politicians representing various constituencies and ideas
- Journalists and other voices of public opinion.

The teacher might facilitate some general activities to elicit a risk/ benefit approach; the class may "brainstorm" to list risks and benefits from different points of view.

Another possibility is "the believing game": ask students to enter first into a viewpoint that emphasizes risks, then to take a new role emphasizing benefits.

Having finished examining the consequences of a decision in the past, the students turn to a contemporary issue. They consider the problem of the nuclear waste still present at the Hanford site. In that discussion a useful approach is looking at risks and benefits along the dimensions of time and geography.

Important questions include these: What solutions to the nuclear issue are better in the short run, and which are better in the long run? (Many critics claim that in American political and business culture, decisions are slanted toward short-term solutions, like getting elected as a politician or showing a business profit at the end of the year.) Should nuclear waste be shipped to a general storage area in New Mexico, or is the issue the responsibility of the whole nation?

As a result of studying the problems, students write a paper such as a letter on the issue of nuclear waste to the editor of a local newspaper. Whether they send the letter or not is up to the individual students and does not affect their evaluation program. What counts is the general quality of a student's contribution.

Case 2

In a second case, students form research teams and collect information themselves. For instance, they collect information and describe what happened in the 1986 Chernobyl nuclear catastrophe. Besides researching the events, they are expected to develop their own individual opinions regarding the following questions:

1. Who should make decisions about where, when, and if nuclear power plants should be built, how to dispose of the nuclear waste, safety maintenance, and plant closures?
2. Who is responsible for the consequences of disasters such as Chernobyl?

Sources of information may include not only written and video materials, but also the oral testimony of witnesses, scientists, officials, and the general public.

After the information has been collected and discussed by the research team, each student is expected to form an individual opinion; then the entire class meets for discussions and formulations of opinions. To clarify and challenge personal opinions further, the students are given a list of opinions and asked to examine them and see if their own opinions fit into one of the listed categories; if not, they are asked to create a new category. The given categories of opinions might be these:

- Scientists and engineers should decide, because they have the training and the facts that give them a better understanding of the issues.
- Scientists and engineers should decide, because they have the knowledge and can make better decisions than government bureaucrats or cooperatives—two groups that have vested interests.
- Scientists and engineers should decide, because they have the training and facts that give them a better understanding; but the public should be informed and consulted.

- The viewpoints of scientists and engineers, other specialists, and the informed public should all be considered in decisions that affect our society as a whole.
- The government should decide, because the issue is basically a political one; but scientists and engineers should give advice.
- The public should decide, because the public serves as a check on scientists and engineers. Scientists and engineers have specialist and narrow views on the issues and thus pay little attention to the general consequences.
- None of the above statements seem to describe my personal position. I will summarize my view in my own words.

When the students have classified their own arguments into categories, they have a full class discussion in which each voices his or her own opinion. Next, the students will be asked to role-play a position opposite to their own, an important part of the democratic process being to understand differing viewpoints. Each student, then, will be asked to play the part of someone who has a viewpoint other than her or his own.

After the students have all had the experience of defending their own original viewpoints, plus differing viewpoints, all the students are asked to drop their roles and vote. Before they vote, the teacher emphasizes that the majority *does not win* in the sense that the majority vote is *the correct solution*. A single individual may actually be defending the best idea against everyone else. The teacher reinforces and encourages the idea of having differing views, and also the flexibility involved in having changed viewpoints during the process.

At the conclusion of the full-class discussion, students break into smaller groups and talk about their feelings. They voice how they feel about the different groups concerned: the victims, the scientists, the engineers, the politicians, the officials.

The students are then given the task of expressing their individual feelings and opinions on the Chernobyl issue. Choices of ways to express themselves include essays, paintings, posters, group drama, political speeches, and letters to a newspaper or official.

Finally, students decide what concrete actions they can take to exercise social responsibility. These might include the following:

- A fund-raising activity where students make some craft items, and parents buy them. The funds are sent to the victims.

- Individual students write letters to newspaper editors.
- The students invite Chernobyl children to have a holiday at their school.
- The students demand action from the government.
- Other possibilities.

All the students together may choose one of these activities; groups and individuals may choose differently. The important principle is that each and every student learns to select some kind of socially responsible activity.

PEDAGOGY OF COOPERATION

An Example of the New Approach in Education

The *pedagogy of cooperation* is an example of the humanization and democratization of education as a basis for the development of social responsibility. The main ideas of such a pedagogy were declared by a group of teachers well known in the USSR in 1986 as the "teacher-innovators." Launched as a protest against the old authoritarian and bureaucratic system of education, this approach is based on cooperation, in all spheres of the educational process and human relationships, among teachers, students, parents, and school administrators.

The core idea of this pedagogy is the personal approach—the consideration of a child as a personality, as a subject of activity and contact. Education is interaction of teachers and students, including cooperation and spiritual and moral contact and communication. In the pedagogy of cooperation, all of these interactions are imbued with creativity. Creativity combines the cultivation of intellectual and social knowledge and skills, and so supports the development of personality as a whole.

Among the many ideas of the pedagogy of cooperation are the following:

- To teach students cooperation through collective cooperative activity
- Free choice of forms and content of activity
- Individual and collective creativity of teachers as the basis for individual and collective creativity of students

Cooperative Learning

Betty Reardon writes about various aspects of cooperative learning in chapter 2. My intention is to add some practical, concrete ideas. In the process of learning cooperation, one develops the abilities to do the following: to express thoughts precisely; to give grounds for one's point of view; to formulate questions precisely; to avoid categorical statements; to listen to opinions that contradict one's own point of view; to show self-control and empathy with the members of the group; to understand reactions of the group's members; to try to overcome disagreements through getting a broader outlook; to work out a common group opinion; to evaluate the significance of one's participation in the group activity.

Many works in the pedagogy of cooperation are devoted to *education for dialogue* (*dia:* "getting through"; *logue:* "message"). Students' attitudes toward facts and phenomena become apparent in a dialogue; their positions become clearer and develop. Dialogue helps to further mutual understanding and respect, when participants have learned cooperative ways of addressing and responding to one another. Only a dialogue in the broad sense can lead to a constructive discussion. A dialogical interaction is effective only if all the participants are active; passive members of the group do not gain much.

The dialogue interaction is at the base of all group forms of education. In group cooperation, everyone's actions are interdependent. Each person gains from the role she or he plays in a cooperative endeavor; all participants are ensured learning and development of their views and attitudes.

The demands of efficient cooperation are the following:

- The group members share their knowledge and thus help each other to achieve success.
- The group works together for some time in order to establish work rules required by the group members.
- Each group member is responsible for the group result.
- The quality and quantity of the group product (not the knowledge or skills of the individual members) are the main factors in evaluating it.

The teacher's role in organizing the group activity is complicated. The teacher is needed to help formulate the problem, organize the students' interaction, help establish a definite structure and control, and continually assess the group activity (Tsvetova 1989).

Examples of cooperative techniques are role playing, brainstorming, and discussion. But these techniques also work in only businesslike cooperation, without influencing any personal development. To develop the personality as a whole, it is necessary to carry cooperation into students' social life, combining businesslike cooperation with social and personal creativity. As Robert Zuber says in chapter 9, to educate is to provide challenges for the young within a wide variety of learning contexts, in the community as well as the school.

Communard Methodology

For our society to manage to further its economy, production system, science, and culture, we shall need a new methodology in our education. We shall need—through our school system—to develop in young people active participation in society's reconstruction. We need, that is, students with the ability to cooperate and participate in creative activities that are directed toward improving the spheres of social life. For this purpose we are, in Russia, as we were in the former USSR, developing the *communard methodology*, which has been spreading in our country. This methodology combines cooperation and social and personal creativity.

The main idea of the communard methodology is *self-education through the process of activity for the benefit of others*. Socially useful activities develop in the students an assurance that they can find a meaning in life. This methodology helps solve problems connected with the lack of assurance of solidarity, and also the feeling of uselessness, that seems to torment young persons of today, as pointed out by Eva Nordland in chapter 1.

The theory and practice of this method were originally launched by A. Makarenko and continued by I. Ivanov (1980, 1989). Makarenko used the experience of school communes in the twenties, after the First World War, when groups of children, often children without families, studied and worked together and spent their free time together. Communard methodology is a social phenomenon that appeared as a response to the situation of our society at the end of the forties, fifties, and sixties, and now again at the beginning of the nineties.

Ivanov worked out a theory of communard methodology on the basis of the creative activity of students and teachers. His basic idea is that of continuous personal and social development: throughout life a person should keep in mind the idea of human improvement.

According to Ivanov, education is *improvement of life* through creativity. Activity without creativity is not education; it is a waste of time and therefore destructive in the child's life. Ivanov worked out a system of collective creative activity—in the cognitive field, in practical work, in aesthetics, games, sports. He worked out a vision of the whole process of children's development from the moment when an idea comes to somebody's mind; then to its realization in practice, to analysis of the results and the birth of a new idea.

Educators together with students creatively solve common problems; they are improving their common life, their surroundings, their natural environment—for the benefit and joy of each other and people around them. The students learn to look upon themselves and others as creators of common benefit for the group, the class, the school, the community. This theory and the corresponding practice is communard education.

To use communard methodology means to create real situations for practicing cooperation for the common good. It is our experience that this pedagogy turns out to be attractive for the students, for children as well as for teenagers. They experience that they live a social life; they do useful things; they are working in real-life situations during the whole day.

Central to the practice of communard education is the organization of an assembly for a whole day of "being together," as we say: at a common *zbor*. The *zbor* is not a lesson, not an excursion or a march, not a meeting or a party. It is activities that can demonstrate a better life. The students are mastering these activities themselves; they have got, in Betty Reardon's terms, co-power; they are immersing themselves in this better life—cooperating for progress.

The assembly, the *zbor*, takes place three to four times a year, as useful collective work at a farm, at a firm, at a hospital. The work is planned to benefit people; the assembly continues as collective fun and games, and meals. The activities of the *zbor* are planned, organized, and analyzed by all the children and teenagers involved. The educators convey to the children an image of a better life, not a system of requirements.

A concentration of educational efforts takes place during a communard assembly. A great number of creative activities have produced a new phenomenon—collective relations among children and teenagers. This effect is difficult to create when activities are spread out over a long period of time.

During the day each student participates in many different activities: useful work, discussions, competitions, amateur concerts, sports, games, and so on. Often the day has a theme, such as "A Day in the Fifteenth Century," "A Sports Day," "A Day in Greece."

The *zbor* assembly day always ends with an evening party (*ogonjok*); the participants discuss everything that happened during the day—the good as well as the bad, the satisfactory and the unsatisfactory. What did we feel good about? What were the results? What was helpful?

The idea is that each person develops his or her own personality through positive models, persons that are a little older than themselves. The models influence through relations and attitudes: friendly support, mutual concern, understanding, sympathy. The educators emphasize the development of children and groups of children, or emphasize the organization of the particular activity. The students themselves suggest many practical, aesthetic, and social activities. Thus everyone's creativity and individuality are encouraged. Meals, for instance, are characterized by inventions and surprises.

During the day of working together, real cooperation is going on. Each participant contributes in his or her own way; each child develops abilities in collective creativity. In this way the *zbor* affects the children physically, morally, intellectually, and spiritually, and contributes to their all-around personality development (Soloveichik 1989).

When the people's work and their aspiration to new relations and attitudes link together, the performance becomes moral. In this case, as Berdjaev (1990) writes, the new spiritual human being, the essence of whom is high morality and creative aspiration, is developing.

A New Model of Interaction between Individual, Family, and Society

The role of school in bringing up young people is essential. At the same time, extracurricular activities, including the children's physical activities, are more effective when they take place out of school, in children's "everyday life" where they themselves are the principal innovators. The school cannot be the center of the whole process of upbringing. Broader models of social upbringing are needed, including the interactions among the individuals, the family, and society.

Researchers from the Russian Academy of Pedagogical Sciences under the guidance of V. Bocharova have worked out new models for upbringing in "the open social environment" (Barsukova and Dudorov 1990; Bocharova 1990; Galee and Rjabov 1990; Dashkina 1990). Responsibility for this type of upbringing belongs to the family and the social surroundings outside the school system, often in cooperation with the school system.

The characteristics of an "open social educational environment" include the absence of formal structures. Informal organizations are created voluntarily; the environment is common for children and young people, and in addition schools and adults from many walks of life participate. This kind of educational environment has a positive influence on the personalities of the young people, with great possibilities for contacts, communication, amateur performances, and initiatives.

But an open social environment is open also to a broad range of negative influences. So the main task of educators is to contribute to improving the environment, taking steps in a positive direction; at the same time educators must support the young person to withstand negative influences in the environment.

An important asset of this sphere of upbringing is the great variety of activities. What happens is largely dependent on the creativity of individual children and adults themselves. The main task of the educators is to follow developments and take the initiative when things do not ensure that everyone is included in a positive way.

The challenge is to create a microsociety—a society that is small enough to develop on the basis of self-government. Families, neighborhoods, organizations, and enterprises located in the microdistrict are, in these recent endeavors, expected to contribute socially and financially. An important feature of this environment is that children of all ages have possibilities of contact and of common initiatives and that parents and other adults are expected to help.

The idea of including all the different age groups of children has been accepted by parents. We often find sports clubs, studios, workshops, and the like organized across age groups. Entertainment at local festivals is often organized with children performing, parents supporting. At workshops, children repair such items as bicycles, musical instruments, clothes, and shoes, again with the help of parents, grandparents, or other adults. About eighty regions in the country have these types of social-pedagogical complexes. All age groups help in organizing social events, playing together, going to the cinema or theater together, organizing holiday parties, and having discussion clubs and sporting events.

In some pedagogical complexes there are also organizations for young people where they produce commodities and services, the main principle being that the activities are voluntary and express common interests and good relations. This social-pedagogical complex has a special group of people, the project committee, that is responsible for making the necessary decisions. The committee organizes different activities and connects all the formal and informal organizations in the complex.

But how do we train educators to stimulate, encourage, and organize this type of development? We need special educators, mediators between children and adults, between the developing personality and society. Social educators help the children in their social development and career choices, and defend their rights. Their work is directed toward creating the conditions for interesting activities and helping to create good personal relations. Social educators will sometimes work with the families or in the neighborhoods or with children or teenagers with special personal and social problems.

Pedagogical and developmental work going on in our country shows that social education through cooperation of young people with parents and adults has great influence on the development of children and teenagers. Practical and educational problems have a better chance of being solved when children are helped to solve immediate problems in their surroundings. Children learn to understand themselves and other people and to develop educational abilities on their own.

CONCLUSION

Pedagogy for social responsibility as part of culture has several layers: common pedagogical theory, common pedagogical consciousness, and educational practice for the common good. Pedagogical theory reflects the demands of the social situation in the country; at the same time, the theory reflects the understanding and acceptance by educators in and out of school. The new task of these educators is to spread the ideas of new ways of thinking in pedagogy—the ideas of democratization, socialization, and humanization. To work out a corresponding pedagogical practice—for the good of Earth, humankind, and nature—is the new, enormous task for educators—and for all people concerned, young and old.

REFERENCES

Barsukova, V., and V. Sudorov. 1990. "Alternative poka net" (There is no alternative yet). *Narodnoe obrazovanie* 4:58–62.

Berdjaev, N. 1990. *Sudjba Rossii* (Russia's fortune). Moscow: Sovetsky pisatel.

Bocharova, V. 1990. "Podrostki i vzroslie: zona doverija" (Teenagers and adults: the zone of trust). *Narodnoe obrazovanie* 9:41–47.

Dashkina, A. 1990. "Tretj puti" (One third of the way). *Narodnoe obrazovanie* 4:56–57.

Galeev, R., and I. Rjabov. 1990. "Sotsialnaja pedagogika: Almetjevsky variant" (Social pedagogy: Almetjevsky variant). *Narodnoe obrazovanie* , no. 3, pp. 31–37.

Gorbachev, M. 1987. *Perestrojka i novoe mishlenie dla nashej strani i dla vsego mira* (Perestrojka and the new thinking for our country and for the whole world). Moscow: Politizdat.

Ivanov, I. 1980. *Dva podhoda k vospitaniu i problema vospitatelnih otnosheniy. Aktualnie problemi kommunisticheskogo vospitanija schkolnikov* (Two approaches to upbringing and the problem of communicative relations: Actual problems of communistic education of students). Moscow: Moscow State Pedagogical Institute.

———. 1989. *Enciklopedia kollektivnih tvorcheskih del* (Encyclopedia of collective creative activities). Moskow: Pedagogika.

Sidorova, T. 1987. "Osobennosti sotsialnoj otvetstvennosti u starsheklastnikov" (Peculiarities of social responsibility of secondary school pupils). *Voprosi psihologii* 5:56–62.

Solovechik, S. 1989. *Vospitanie po Ivanovu* (Upbringing according to Ivanov's ideas). Moscow: Pedagogika.

Tsvetova, M. 1990. "Issledovanie uchebnogo sotrudnichestva v pedagogicheskoj psihologii v SShA" (Studies in cooperative learning in pedagogical psychology in the USA). *Voprosi psihologii*, no. 2, pp. 148–55. Moscow: Pisatel.

Zaprodzets, A. V. 1964. *Detskay psihologiia/pedagogicheskay Ensiklopedia* (Child psychology/pedagogic encyclopedia). Vol. 1.

9
Ecological Leadership in an Age of Diminishing Superpower Prerogatives

Robert W. Zuber

The essays in this book have been inspired by three important and related factors: the enormity of the ecological crises that threaten the current and future quality of life on Earth; the transformations in hostilities between the United States and the former Soviet Union, and related, volatile changes in the politics and economics of Eastern Europe; and the evolutions of educational policies and practices exemplified by, among others, the Project on Ecological and Cooperative Education (PEACE). Our world continues to provide abundant, if shifting, cause for hope and alarm. The long-awaited end of the cold war has occasioned the resumption of numerous ethnic hostilities in Eastern Europe. The extraordinary Earth Summit in Brazil took place at a time when many of our critical ecosystems are showing new signs of strain. This is a time of great irony and great anticipation, and our educational institutions have an important role to play in clarifying problems, inspiring commitments to thoughtful action, and helping to provide the skills needed for cooperative living and ecological repair. As educators, we must display courage and humility to predict the future and to identify the skills that will be needed to manage the planet wisely. But even more, we need to tell our young people the *truth* about the world, and about those educational policies crafted "on their behalf," as a major contribution to their own empowered choices. PEACE pedagogy must be grounded, above all else, in a fundamental, personal honesty.

This world, which we are still fortunate enough to inhabit, continues to rock uneasily as the winds of political and social change blow in many and varied directions. In the West, there has recently been a preoccupation with the "pro-democracy" movements that have sprung up around the world within nations that seemed committed (or resigned?) to life in accordance with sometimes idiosyncratic interpretations of Marxist social doctrines. This striving for greater economic and political participation has been gratifying to watch, even if Western interpretations of recent events have been unduly filtered through our own longings and prejudices. Chief among these longings in the United States is the longing for a renewal of United States influence within a global community that, the Gulf War notwithstanding, is still less inclined to look to New York and Washington for meaningful patterns of economic and political life. We in the United States, in our desire to reassert the primacy of our culture and social philosophy, seem to be overlooking the obvious—that changes in Eastern Europe and elsewhere symbolized not only the retreat of communism as an imperialist force, but the calling to account of hegemonic control in *all* its various manifestations. We have been witnesses to what many feel is the irreversible decay of "superpower prerogatives"—the once taken-for-granted ability of the United States and the former Soviet Union to make "rules" for the international community in accordance with their own security needs, economic interests, and perceptions about the nature of the world.

In the midst of these various changes and realignments, the developed world is witness to a burst of well-intentioned ecological concern. In the West, the media have inundated those who watch, listen, and read with images of environmental corruption and public response. From oil spills and toxic leakage to acid rain and deforestation, ecological issues have become, once again, aspects of a growing public interest. The *Christian Science Monitor*, a leading U.S. newspaper, speaks openly and often of the "environmental bandwagon" to which persons from a variety of walks of life and political affiliations are hitching their social concern. And, as perestroika became more a cultural struggle and less a symbolic invitation, the media in Moscow could be seen exercising their journalistic responsibility by bringing local environmental problems to light in the public domain. From the aftereffects of Chernobyl to industrial and agricultural pollutants, officials in Moscow had begun to acknowledge the depth of their own ecological crisis. Officials such as Vladimir Petrovsky (1989, 39) candidly acknowledged the "grave situation" within what was then the Soviet Union, a situation that still requires the creation of a "concerted national program" to counter environmental neglect. Petrovsky, like others, saw a massive infusion of capital, coupled with a reversal of official policies of secrecy, as necessary to reverse a process that could well create "300 million ecological refugees" within our lifetime.

The environmental concern reflected in the public discourse of governments and the media in the United States, Russia, and elsewhere has given much of the world cause to take notice. Despite recent realignments of influence among former ideological combatants, these countries and others will continue to play crucial roles in determining the effectiveness of local and international efforts to stem the tide of environmental abuse. Within the United Nations system, the permanent members of the Security Council can utilize their political capital and veto powers to broaden and toughen international sanctions against those who deliberately threaten the existence-potential of life on this planet. These nations can, by force of political will, reduce their voracious appetites for military hardware, thereby securing needed funds, human labor, and mineral resources for the difficult and expensive task of environmental rehabilitation. They can, by virtue of long-standing commitments to research and teaching, help lead the world in the search for new conceptualizations of our ecological problems, as well as those massive changes in life-style and thinking needed to address them successfully. Finally, these nations can take the lead in fulfilling an initial wish of the United Nations Environmental Program's World Charter for Nature—that ecological education become a viable and integral part of the general education programs of the schools of our community of nations. The children of the world perceive much about the environmental catastrophes that threaten, from Kuwait to Brazil, and enlightened industrial powers can do much to stimulate formal and nonformal educational structures—what Galina Kovalyova elsewhere in this volume refers to as "pedagogies of cooperation"—that help children process and live out what they have already begun to understand.

Much of this chapter will focus on problems of thinking, of knowledge, of education, since it is clear that our failure to implement many potential solutions to persistent human problems arises not from a lack of technique, but as a consequence of failed or superficial perception. Betty Reardon's essay in this volume reminds us that we have created habits of thinking and acting that are akin to addictions—to abstract, instrumental, materialist conceptions of the planet and of those persons, especially the elderly and the children, who seek to inhabit it meaningfully. In the process, we have failed to see prospects for care in our midst, while severely restricting public discourse about those very categories of human existence—realms of values, of beauty, of love and care, of feelings and passions—that make life aesthetically rich and emotionally worthwhile. Simply put, we need to learn to see the world in less burdened and manipulative ways, and to substitute expressions of reverence, gratitude, and cooperation for the categories of use and control that permeate our learned reactions to the created order.

Perhaps no nations on the face of the earth have worshipped more fervently at the altar of science culture than have the United States and the former Soviet Union. It is not science as a method for testing and explaining the material world that we revere, so much as science transformed into technological artifacts of control, entertainment, or power. If the United States, Russia, and those who follow, through education and self-examination, could break these epistemological addictions, could banish their unseemly reverence for technological idols, they might be more successful in enlisting the cooperation of other nations and peoples for the great ecological struggles that have already taken shape. The age of the superpowers has been transformed, but these and other powerful nations retain significant conceptual influence as a corollary to their continued military power. There is leadership and responsibility to be exercised, of a sort that can no longer be easily coerced by military force or other means, and the United States, Russia, and other powerful nations can facilitate many important changes in the international community, if only they will dare to take more of the risks associated with their evolving roles in a shifting world.

THE WARMAKING PROBLEM

> Plant a tree on the soil of your enemies, and see if you can still call them that.
> —Nancy Carter, "An Anti-Recipe for War"

The age of nation-states, as is well known, can be characterized in part by its obsessions with security questions. We spend at least as much of our collective energies protecting things as we do creating them. Our geographic borders, our "standards of living," our "national interests"— these and other concerns preoccupy political leaders and the military machines that have supported their policy choices. Any discussion about the responsibility of the great nations for the environment must begin with military-based questions, since the military mind-set has, for so long, been the "fuel" for an entire range of options and understandings in the pursuit of national and personal security. Even with the end of the cold war, this mind-set remains needlessly influential.

The military mind-set has also provided the backdrop for a wide spectrum of political and educational responses in the name of peacemaking. Critiques have been offered, both in print and through direct-action initiatives, against the current system of nation-states, the proliferation of nuclear weaponry, excessive levels of military spending, interventions by global powers in the affairs of less-developed nations, even the pervasive presence of militaristic thinking in the upbringing and education of children and in the life-style choices of adults. In many and varied contexts, communities of educators and other peacemakers have attempted to witness to the numerous ways in which personal and social conflicts are subject both to militaristic interpretations and to various forms of violent resolution.

In this period of environmental concern, the warmaking dilemma has taken on new meaning and greater urgency. Noting the increasing stockpiles of so-called weapons of mass destruction—nuclear, chemical, and biological—the United Nations General Assembly (1988, 34–35), along with the U.N. Environmental Program, has spoken clearly and boldly about the "far-reaching, even irreversible, changes in the global environment" that the use of these weapons could bring about. Scientists in the United States and elsewhere have called dramatic attention to both the devastating ecological consequences of nuclear attack (nuclear winter) as well as the long-term storage and maintenance problems posed by increasing quantities of nuclear waste products and ever-more-toxic chemical and biological weapons (Warner 1988, 2–8). In many and varied ways, we have scorned the counsel provided in the World Charter for Nature, that we must study carefully the consequences of the genies we plan to release (especially those arising from military and "security" needs) before letting them out of their respective bottles.

There is another obvious context in which military and environmental concerns converge, and that is regarding the nature and scope of military spending. Technological and monetary "fixes" for environmental neglect are ultimately shortsighted and misguided. Nevertheless, it is clear that a reversal of environmental decay and a reorganization of national economic priorities will require extraordinary applications of public and private funds. Some estimates of the cost of waste disposal, reforestation, ozone replenishment, and the other aspects of environmental repair run as high as $150 billion per year over a substantial period of years, and these estimates were made prior to the devastations resulting from the Gulf War. For many who have surveyed this funding dilemma, the obvious source for ecological capital is the military itself. Certainly, the easing of old cold-war tensions has opened up possibilities for reallocation of funds that did not exist several years ago. However, the so-called peace dividend is a long way from being acknowledged and apportioned, especially as military "crises" continue unabated in the Middle East and elsewhere, and there are chronic human needs around the world that loom large as funding priorities are painstakingly reestablished in the more affluent nations.

There can be little doubt that the persistence of a militaristic mentality and its spending consequences robs both the environment and the poor of this world of needed capital for repair of broken lives. This robbery, capably and steadfastly catalogued by Sivard (1989) and others, represents a profound moral blight on the record of twentieth-century policymakers. But there is another dimension of militarism, often overlooked, that will require some attention as new environmental priorities emerge—the effects of militarism, and the *poverty* that it so often leaves in its wake, on our ability to *affirm* personal, ecological responsibility. We will return to this avenue of thought in a following section. For now, it is important to pose these questions: What does it mean for people to organize their lives under conditions of poverty and/or the pervasive effects of militarism? What does it mean to live within paradigms of insecurity, to cope with daily prospects of enemies, real and imagined, to worry constantly about basic resource availability in a world gorging itself endlessly on military hardware and other technological "miracles"? And, most essential to the purposes of this chapter, how can one educate for environmental responsibility, interdependence, and cooperation when so many in this world cannot afford to see much beyond the fulfillment of their own material needs?

There can be no facile listing of the effects of these kinds of anxieties on world populations. Suffice to say that, in the current, uneasy international climate, life-styles of short-term satisfactions and self-protected actions are likely to predominate. When crisis threatens, we are likely to revert to those attitudes and behaviors that are most familiar to us, even those proven to be destructive of self and others. The familiar, in this instance, might well refer to reaffirmation and reappropriation of national sovereignty or, to the extent that this is still possible, superpower preeminence. It might refer to a preoccupation with maintaining one's standard of living, or to values and ideas that are personally comfortable, even if unsuited to the challenges of an evolving world. It might even refer to the reemergence of harsh, military-centered resolutions to international disputes. Despite the environmental demands of the moment, there is a chance that militarism will command its ultimate performance—in the minds of people ready to sacrifice the world and all that is in it, but unwilling to sacrifice a single opportunity for personal gain (Berry 1987, 101) or prerogative of political power. We need very much for the great nations to do their part to reduce international tensions and military options for dispute resolution. The warmaking problem must be solved. But, clearly, we must also learn to think better and understand more about ourselves, to supplement policy knowledge with a broader, personal knowledge—one that transcends self-protective habits and affirms the skills, values, and attitudes of cooperative living at its core. It is this task that presently beckons.

ECOLOGICAL REASON AND THE JOURNEY HOME

> Farmers became convinced that it would be better to own a neighbor's farm than to have a neighbor.
>
> —Wendell Berry

In the introduction to this chapter, I noted that the United States and the former Soviet Union have, perhaps more than any other nations, worshipped at the shrines of technology and technique. That is, they have made a series of choices to make economic, social, and political policy dependent upon a certain kind of analysis of the world—a certain way of knowing, if you will. This "way," aptly summarized by Douglas Sloan (1983), Owen Barfield (1988), and others, seeks to reduce the realm of the known to those aspects of the material world that can be quantified or understood definitively in terms of their categorical representations. Such knowledge is inherently *abstract*, since it is less concerned with particulars and more concerned with classifications. It is *instrumentalist,* in that it tends to accept for definition only material objects, and only in terms of categories of *use* to which something can be put, including the *power* to manipulate the world in accordance with some preconceived need or urge.

This type of knowledge is not "scientific" in the pure sense, since it is less about empirical methodology—that all-important skill of reality testing in which most of us are quite deficient—than it is about "science culture," the statuses and technological manifestations of scientific inquiry to which so many in the developed world pay homage, including many of the persons who teach our children. Put more simply, this "knowing" is less about the process of science and the important skills and insights it provides for life in this world, than it is about the fruits of science labor and the public acclaim accorded those persons who create and maintain technological commodities.

The "culture" of science can be seen to have infected many aspects of social and political life, places where science, pure and simple, would properly be relegated to a supporting role. This culture can be found in schools where people learn *about* things rather than *from* them, schools that dodge significant questions of value, meaning, and feeling under the pretext of objectivity or order. This culture can be found in religious institutions that restrict the pursuit of the divine through the use of language that is more idolatrous than mysterious, language that too often accommodates to "modern" worldviews that cannot apprehend religious meanings. This culture can be found in the "adult" world, where status takes precedence over effort or risk, where ownership becomes an end in itself, where categories of beauty and friendship are transformed into functions and benefit. This culture has even taken root on the farm, where technology replaces human insight and where "competence" and "expertise" drown the rhythms of life and care under rubrics of efficiency and productivity. This denial of the personal allows us to ignore, as Wendell Berry (1987) and his Russian counterparts remind us, that it takes many more hands to nurture and sustain our land than it takes to make that land "efficient" and "productive." In a similar light, it takes much more of a personal investment to help our children grow that in takes to make our children behave.

Our energies in support of environmental regeneration are stifled in face of pervasive epistemological biases of the great nations of the world, including the United States and Russia. Categories of ownership and control, of authority and expertise, of consumption and use, all impair human abilities to acquire and promote what the U.S. Green movement calls "ecological wisdom." This wisdom seeks to counter the abstract and manipulative characteristics of our ideas and our language, to refocus human communication and thought within the natural and cultural rhythms of local communities. It attempts to understand the ways in which our notions and expectations about things get in the way of an integrated, respectful, even reverential perspective about our human place within a complex ecological order. It reminds us that we are becoming victimized and endangered by the very abstractions that gave rise to our most substantial technological achievements, the "demons" that we can no longer control (Berry 1983, 65; Razuvayev 1990). As Berry (1987, 15) notes, "Humans have mental appetites that can be far more gross and capacious than physical ones. Only humans squander and hoard, murder and pillage because of notions"; and our notions are becoming ever more conducive to this kind of self-destructive response to the created order.

This "kingdom of abstraction" that the "developed" world has crafted for its own amusement and satisfaction creates problems for living, thinking, teaching, and communicating that cannot be minimized. Often, concepts that seem to provide some hope of breaking us out of our ecological dilemma take on lives of their own, restricting conversations that they were originally designed to inform and promote. One such concept, which has almost become a cliché among the environmentally sophisticated, is that of a "sustainable development." As defined by the United Nations General Assembly (1988, 7), such development must meet "the needs of the present without compromising the ability of future generations to meet theirs."

This concept, like others of its kind, has several important components to its message. It is significant that intergenerational consciousness can be promoted in this context—to be found in those persons willing to consider the future requirements of our progeny on a rough parity with the needs of present populations. Such a consciousness could lead to social policymaking dominated by preventative, rather than merely reactive, stances (Pianta and Renner 1989, 17), and to leaders willing to consider a broad range of *human* consequences, even to succeeding generations, prior to launching policy initiatives. Economic enfranchisement must surely be a goal of peacemakers, given our knowledge of the appalling poverty, disease, and hunger that infect larger and larger portions of the world populations. That this development can be undertaken alongside genuine concerns for quality of persons and ecological sensitivity should be cause for rejoicing in the nations of this world.

Unfortunately, "sustainable development" without a commitment to ecological wisdom might be another in a long series of misguided attempts to pour new wine into old wineskins. In a special issue of *Teaching Peace,* F. H. Knelman (1989, 6) explores the limitations inherent in any developmental model, even one that attempts to provide hope for impoverished humans and their ecosystems. Put directly, Knelman understands current policies of sustainable development as advocating "sustainable growth modified by technological fixes to reduce environmental impacts." Growth, in this scenario, is embraced as an unchallenged good. Technology is understood as a healing force in the world, despite the many unchecked demons it has already unleashed on our societies. Negative impacts, in environmental terms, are to be analyzed and minimized, but broader issues of global healing are dismissed, and the alleged goodwill of industrial, political, and military leaders in the proper assessment of these impacts is deemed above scrutiny. For these and other reasons, Knelman is properly dubious that this new policy path is anything more than antiquated thinking masked by humane intent.

Knelman and others are certainly aware of the commonplace collisions that are sure to occur between the economic needs of human underclasses and the urgent requirements of a damaged ecosystem. According to a series of recent Associated Press reports in the United States, efforts by the governments of the United States, the Peoples Republic of China, Romania, and other countries to clean up our air and water have met with stern worker resistance. One report had workers in Romania vigorously protesting a government decision to close a synthetic materials plant deemed a "national eyesore" (Smale 1990). Conflicts of this sort can be expected to escalate, especially in locations of considerable industrial damage to our ecosystem, as many millions of new consumers and legions of disenchanted workers express their economic demands in the uncertain and evolving global market. There are many more persons wanting their slice of a shrinking economic pie, and Earth does not seem ready to support those desires in the wasteful and avaricious forms that characterize living in so many of our most powerful nations.

It is difficult to see how economic elites and the increasingly vast and complex technologies they control can ever be counted on to promote the sorts of distributive justice demanded by increasing numbers of the world's people in this ecologically sensitive time. We have not repented of the sins resulting from the ideologies of progress and national sovereignty. We have not grasped the momentousness of resource scarcities, mountains of untreated waste, and depleted forests that groan to sustain our basic oxygen needs. We have not forsaken greed for the sake of interdependence nor narrow anthropocentric worldviews for the sake of inclusive ecological responsibility. And, most sadly, we have not yet created forms of curriculum and teaching that address the needs and skills of cooperative living in an ecological age—an age in which, as Willard Jacobson notes in chapter 4, ecological relationships remain uncertain, resistant to our facile certainties. Actually, we have begun the process of public review and education for many aspects of our environmental dilemmas, but we continue to neglect hard thinking and harder institutional and personal life-style choices at the risk of burying ourselves under the product consequences of our own creative desires and illusions of omniscience. In short, we have crafted environmental policies in advance of the state of our ecological wisdom, and this is anything but comforting news.

It might well be that the kinds of wisdom that can motivate persons in the developed nations to make foundational changes in thinking and life-style as a prelude to environmental healing are locked in images and metaphors close to home. Indeed, one of the most significant features of ecological thinking is a willingness to understand the world less as *resource* and more as *home*. To have a home means to be mindful of its gifts and its needs, its rhythms and its idiosyncrasies. To have a home means to see the self as connected, nurtured, and participant in a larger tapestry of life. To have a home means to see the effects of others' work on your own life, and to understand something of the effects of your work on theirs.

To have a home means a commitment to a world and a vision born in common with others. It may even, as Anatoly Govalenko suggests elsewhere in this volume, involve some healthy sense of ownership—the kind that motivates us to take responsibility for things, and for each other. The metaphor of *home* can provide vision both for policy and for a pedagogy grounded in cooperative and interconnected living. This planet was once perceived as being too formidable, too frightening, too vast to ever be home for us. In this moment of history, the world must be understood as too fragile, too needy, to complex to be grasped as anything less.

In our "kingdom of abstraction," where nationalism, power, and consumption play such important roles, place is just another business opportunity, just another context for manipulation and self-promotion. One place is as good as the next, and all are, increasingly, good for less and less. In the developed world, we are increasingly unlikely to live our lives where we make our "deals." We are less likely than ever to experience, firsthand, the effects of shoddy policy planning and implementation. "Everywhere, everyday," Wendell Berry (1987, 50) reminds us, "local life is being discomforted, disrupted, endangered, or destroyed by powerful people who live, or who are privileged to think they live, beyond the bad effects of their bad work." We make more and more flawed bridges we will never cross, flawed automobiles we will never drive, flawed dwellings in which we will never raise or educate our children. Through policies of war and trade, we decimate countries we will never, ever visit. We continue to promote sloppy thinking and shoddy work-manship in the false hope that we can perpetually escape having to face the judgments they render, as well as those young persons whose futures have been undermined by our negligence and downright laziness. In the throes of these abstract arrogances, allegedly "humane" policies for envi-ronmental responsibility can only be viewed suspiciously. Experience and education train us, too often, to assume that such policies can only be crafted to the benefit of some and to the inconvenience or detriment of many.

Clearly, we have much to learn as well as much to do. Ironically, this is especially true in the most powerful nations, including the United States and Russia, which still control so much of the academic and policy discourse. The educational role in ecological reform is a significant one, especially given the urgency of the problems we face. We need prompt action and wise policies, but we also need wisdom to sustain them and keep them on their right paths. The schools of the ex-"superpowers," despite their many achievements, embrace many cultural and epistemo-logical flaws, some much too willingly. Transformation and renewal in the educational systems of the major nations must take place if schools are to service new global forms and priorities. It is to the learning goals and objectives associated with this foreboding and challenging task that we now turn direct, if not sustained, attention.

THE SCHOOLS AND ECOLOGICAL HEALING

Repentance and good intentions alone will not atone for the ecologi-cal sins of the past.

—Vladimir Razuvayev

Global healing, the kind of multidimensional healing that Sergei Polozov speaks of in chapter 5, is not likely to appear magically on the wings of capital-intensive technology, without a commitment to thinking and feeling adequate to the new world we wish to create. We cannot, though we try our hardest, cling to reductionist and functionalist views of reality as though these can bring us closer to a world more in harmony with its own rhythms and long-term needs. The addictions of value and knowledge that control our social interactions need to be challenged, and quickly. The children of the world's nations wait for some word from us about prospects for their future, about the life path upon which they are expected to embark willingly and gratefully. In the midst of duties and rules and responsibilities and deadlines, fundamental questions remain, for them and for us. Does life have a chance? Is there beauty worth grasping, love worth risking for, happiness worth pursuing? These are not the questions that have grounded the curricular life of our schools, but they need to start being posed in school settings, and without delay. In the process of teaching the young about alternative worldviews and knowledge forms, we might also be able to teach ourselves something about our urgent and multifaceted responsibilities for children's futures and children's questions in a troubled world.

The following pedagogical remarks are meant to be suggestive rather than constitute a definitive proposal for curricular reform. The goal is to make suggestions for learning objectives that are consistent with the new world community that is struggling to evolve—one constituted by extreme ecological crisis and a diminishing dominance of the United States and especially Russia in the political, economic, and military aspects of global life. The assumption of this section is that there is a need for schools to reconstitute their offerings and agendas in a manner consistent with a vision of the world for which students are being prepared, a world that must actively affirm the skills of cooperative living. In other words, schools need to look into the crystal ball, to make some judgment, albeit tentative, about the kinds of social and economic options the planet will likely present when the young people under their care begin to assert adult prerogatives. That this judgment must be made at all is mandated by a need to provide students with experiences that will permit them to make effective and appropriate responses to the societies they will actually encounter. That this judgment can only be made with humility is also apparent, given that, as Wendell Berry (1987, 84) suggests, those who teach are preparing the young for a world essentially unknown to all of us, a world that never completely confirms our techniques and predictive capacities. We must be guided by some vision of the future, but we must also cherish the hope that our vision has some relevance to the world that actually emerges in the developing presence of our young people.

Pedagogical Goals

One of the most significant learning goals of schools dedicated to ecological healing and cooperative living is *intergenerational sensitivity*. there can be little doubt that the age-segregated learning environments in which most of us are currently educated rob us of significant experiences essential to human development and meaningful participation in the issues and processes of life. Put simply, we need to teach each other things that we cannot learn in isolation from those who have come before and who come after. The elderly need contact with the potentials for transformed life represented by the young. Persons in the middle years need to be reminded of how many more significant things there can be in life than careers and economic security. Youths need to understand the cyclic nature of personal successes and failures, the lights that exist at the end of the darkest, longest tunnels, the pain and loneliness that can quickly turn to love and joy. Children need to understand that the world into which they have been born is the fruit of many caring initiatives, and that they mean much more to us than strangers in a strange and hostile land. Indeed, as Valentina Mitina reminds us in chapter 3, children can learn that there are, truly, no strange and distant problems, or strange and distant persons. In these and many other ways, persons across the life cycle have their stories to tell and their responsibilities to share. Schools need to do more to assist in the promotion of this valuable, life-affirming communication across the increasing spectrum of human aging.

A related educational objective might be described as ecological *life-style training*. One of the most significant contributions of the environmental movement to the human rights community is its bequest of life-style concerns as legitimate components of human rights analysis. What we consume, what we waste, how we spend our leisure time, how we set personal priorities, how we understand the demands and responsibilities of friendship within a multicultural tapestry—these and other matters have profound significance both for human rights work and for ecological healing. Included in this analysis, notes Eva Nordland in her fine contribution to this volume, is some willingness to explore the effects of our life-styles on our common, planetary system of support. Awareness of the basic connections between the life-styles we protect and covet and the world environment that we have chosen to defend and sustain should be a component of every school's basic mission. It is ironic at best for us to utter concern about rain forests when our lives have become addicted to the products (and their low prices) that the rain forests make possible.

Such awareness has, as one of its benevolent consequences, the empowerment of the learner. To speak the truth about personal and social situations allows people to make informed choices and conscientious commitments. It allows people of all ages to live with "their eyes open" (Greene 1989), to participate intelligently in decisions that need to be made and that affect basic qualities of life that they, themselves, can discern. Such participation, what the Green party's Committees of Correspondence (1985, 16) call "grass-roots democracy," is another essential learning component for our schools. At issue here is not the teaching *about* democratic processes, as important as this might be, but rather opening eyes to the possibilities of, and obstacles to, reform of institutions and communities close to home. It is also about rights for students, spaces of integrity that we must help build into young lives, spaces that are respected and acknowledged in ways that are not subject to adult conceptions of order and convenience.

In the final analysis, it is educationally impotent to speak of "rights" to students who do not experience them in their own school lives. In the same way, it is difficult to make convincing arguments for change in the world when change close to home and soul is so frustrating and elusive. One piece of the ecological, educational truth has been provided by Betty Reardon (1985). Speaking of the insidiousness of sexism and its connection to the war system, she notes that "if we cannot change ourselves, we cannot hope to change the world." There is, whether we wish to acknowledge it or not, a concentric-circle paradigm that defines and motivates our caring proclivities. We must learn the tools of effective response to immediate problems as a prelude to a more universal and comprehensive commitment. Indeed, as Susan Ahearn reminds us elsewhere in this volume, comfort and power in familiar surroundings are necessary for identity formation and general mental health. Lives that seem out of control or out of economic and personal options are poor candidates for global, ecological citizenship. We need, as a starting point, tough and compassionate personal skills for coping with local challenges, as prelude to a larger and more comprehensive set of commitments, and schools can be conduits for their development.

Another categorical challenge posed to school officials and curriculum planners is a confrontation with *vulgarity*, by which is meant the ugliness and triviality that characterize the lives of too many persons in this world, including and especially those in the most powerful nations. Truly, there is much that is beautiful and noble about life on this planet that we largely refuse to acknowledge and appreciate, and schools can do their part to foster an appreciative and sensitive spirit. Gratitude, after all, does not preclude criticism and analysis, but merely provides their proper grounding. Gratitude provides an invitation for change. Its absence is too often a formula for personal humiliation and destruction, "attacking" the perspectives of others rather than trying to understand them as one more contribution to the elusive search for truth.

However, we must also understand that there is so much beauty and meaning in the world that we have yet to see in anything like its fullness. To borrow from phenomenological analysis, we believe that we know things well, that we have seen things and persons so often that they have become commonplace for us. In fact, we may have yet to see them for the first time. We have put too many human experiences "in their place," limiting their possibilities or potentially rich encounters by virtue of our expectations and values, our language and concepts. We "know" what things are for, we "know" where they go, we "know" how they are supposed to look. Our expectations and notions about things too often keep us from reinvesting in the aesthetic and ethical meaning of our own experiences, while they prevent us from entertaining important questions about the nature of beauty and its contribution to the quality of our lives.

Our lives embrace more vulgarity than they need to, and we can catalogue the effects of ugliness and triviality on many experiences of personal and educational significance. It is difficult to think profound and transformative thoughts when so many people communicate through clichés or routinely substitute credentials and authority for an honest search for truth. It is difficult to grasp the beauty of ideas within schools that are poorly designed or in constant disrepair, schools that simply "feel" lifeless and impersonal. It is harder to care about neighborhoods full of broken glass, broken windows, and broken dreams. It is a struggle to care about people within contexts devoid of basic respect, where persons have been cast primarily as means to others' ends. There is an impoverishment of the human spirit that must find some corrective analysis in our schools, for vulgarity in all of its forms has the disturbing habit of creating more of the same.

This concern with vulgarity leads to the next of our educational agendas, that of *craftsmanship*. As Wendell Berry (1987, 143) reminds us, one of the key elements in a program of ecological healing is the production of goods that do not quickly need to be produced again. "Our forests," he notes, "are more threatened by shoddy workmanship than by clear-cutting or by fire." At least in the developed West, craftsmanship conjures up images of slow, painful, production processes "made by hand." Such processes, though nostalgically pleasing, would seem to undermine the West's preoccupation with mass production as a means of lowering costs-per-unit to consumers, and thus raising the standard of living for persons of modest financial means (not to mention the profits of large corporations).

In fact, this learning objective has less to do with a critique of mass production than with overcoming several sets of abstractions that have made us adept at consumption but inadequate at responsible participation in our own economic lives. For *craftsmanship,* as the term is being used here, implies proven skill or expertise in the initiation and building of some particular product, service, or commodity. It implies some knowledge of the processes by which things are made on our behalf—where products come from, how they are made, what the economic and social conditions are of their creation. And, finally, it involves some responsibility for the product made—some notion of social and ecological consequences—creation as though the intended recipients of our products were the creators themselves (or someone they love).

In these and other areas, we have strayed far from the craftsmanship ideal. We consume without regard for the work that preceded our utilization, or for the effort that is required to dispose of what we no longer need. Too many of our children believe that chickens come from plastic wrappers and our milk from cartons, and we are not entirely sure how best to teach as a supplemental response to their abundant half-truths. We are oblivious to the cultures and nations of our products' origins, the sources of the raw materials we capriciously exploit. We know little of farming, or of the environmental compromises that are necessary to insure that fresh produce will appear on store shelves regardless of the time of year or distance from the farms that strain to provide it. We care little about lives in sweatshops making clothes for sale at discount. We have managed to block out all of the human and natural links to our consumption, and thus we feel free to purchase what we can as our incomes and personal tastes permit.

In the same vein, standards of living, especially in the West, have become driven by an increasingly complex set of technologies that make us increasingly vulnerable in the face of mechanical breakdowns of all sorts. Put simply, we not only don't know where things come from, we no longer know very much about how things *work*. We can't repair our water-softening faucets or our fuel-injected cars. We don't do much with our hands, and thus we don't know how the things we depend upon fit into the patterns of our increasingly technocentric residences. We are, too often, helpless when our gadgets fail us, dependent on a new set of technical experts to save us from a "home" environment from which we are, in some fundamental way, alienated and disempowered. Our gadgets are increasingly becoming masters of domiciles once presided over, and struggled over, by persons of some practical resourcefulness and skill, and it is not altogether clear that this represents a worthwhile trade-off.

Finally, there is this additional matter of craftsmanship—giving care and devotion to the building of things as though we were to be the ones destined to put them to use. It was mentioned earlier that we are less and less likely to live in the places that we make our "business decisions" about. It is easier and easier to build cars and other products without regard for the persons who will depend upon them. We don't know much about the drivers of the cars we manufacture, nor is our personal crafts-manship ever likely to become an issue for persons who witness our products driving down local highways. "Quality" is always and ironically a compromise within any business environment driven by contemporary consumer interests. Nevertheless, we can renew the process of personal-izing business decisions as a function of a broader community responsi-bility. The more we can picture friends and loved ones in possession of the goods we make and sell, the more we can imagine a world full of children longing for basic commodities that we have squandered, the more we can personalize the ugliness and triviality motivated by our "business interests," the better the world is likely to look for us all.

The final learning objective suggested here has been borrowed from Elise Boulding (1981, 82), someone who is concerned about needs for transformed thinking and social empowerment. She speaks of the "child's gift for making fresh and new connections" as something to which ecologically sensitive educators need to pay heed. These "connections" can be understood in at least two fundamental ways. First, educators can do more to stimulate within children the connections of thinking and feelings that hold such great promise for the future of the planet. We can learn to listen more attentively and less judgmentally. We can provide challenges for the young within a wider variety of learning contexts, especially in the communities beyond the walls of our schools. We can learn to appreciate what the promises and contributions of the young represent in a world that has been thrown off its aesthetic and ethical moorings. We can take the thoughts and feelings of the young seriously in their own right, rather than seeing them as temporary stages on the path toward thought, communication, and action "like our own."

But there is another meaning to be pursued in this vein, that of creating *networks*—of ideas, of persons, of interests, of action. We need to help the young to feel respectful enough of the knowledge and insight in their possession that they will want to see it mirrored in the world of which they are a part. Furthermore, the young will hopefully wish to locate and affirm persons of similar interests and commitments in a variety of social and cultural contexts. Of all the skills required of a future committed to ecological healing, networking may be the most important. In an age of changing political affiliations and power relationships, small groups of focused and determined persons may still be the most effective catalysts for those changes in social organization, thinking, and curricular priorities to which this essay has given some small testimony. Schools must help the young locate their communities of conversation, meaning, and protest, for these communities can best help to keep our global upheavals compassionate and honest.

CONCLUSION

This age in which we live, one characterized by the erosion and demise of global superpowers, is experiencing some profound birthing pains. Power, once taken for granted, cannot easily be made accountable to evolving democratic, political, and social interests. Thinking, often habitual, cannot easily alter either its forms or its assumptions. School life, reflecting in part the ideological priorities of the cultures that give rise to educational policies, cannot easily shift energies toward preparation for an unknown and uncertain future. These problem areas all stand at the beginning of some very formidable challenges. This essay and others in this volume have set some formidable, if tentative, agendas. What we now need to know is what kind of leadership we can count on, and what roles the Unites States, Russia, Japan, Germany, and others see fit to play in our common struggle against ecological collapse.

This essay was authored by someone who has much more direct access to the policies, thought processes, and curricular priorities of the United States than of Russia or other powerful nations. Having been witness to much "objective" Western reporting regarding the breakup of the former Soviet Union, I am convinced that for many analysts the struggles and evolutionary changes in Moscow confirmed the essential wisdom inherent and reflected in Western political and economic choices. However, the failure to grasp evolutionary changes in another nation and culture on their own terms is, from the standpoint of this essay, another negative consequence of abstract, ideological thinking. Just as the cold war mentality minimized the need of the United States to confront its own problems, so our "vindication" at the end of that "war" has served to blunt important discussions about our own revised role in the global community, a "new world order" that is more than a new motif on the theme of Western dominance of global affairs. Meanwhile, the environment cries out under the burdens of contemporary abuse, and people of the world search longingly for leadership with the ears to hear and the skill to help us fashion a responsible and comprehensive reply.

The United States and the former Soviet Union have, perhaps unwittingly, created a new, post-cold war political space for options and opportunities in environmental leadership. There are weapons to be dismantled, life-style issues to critique, resources to share, thinking to revise, school life to improve, children to inspire, people to empower, a planet to heal. It is not necessary for these two great countries to *do* all of this work or to *control* its processes and results. What is needed, instead, is for these nations to lend their considerable educational, technical, and economic skills to a self-reflective and humane series of social alternatives for a world suffering from poverty of possessions, of nature, of spirit. But even before this, the United States and the other major powers must heal their own wounds born of decades of cold war recriminations, militaristic policies, and competitive educational paradigms. Hopefully, history will judge kindly our responses to these demands of leadership.

REFERENCES

Barfield, Owen. 1988. *Saving the Appearances: A Study in Idolatry*. Middletown: Wesleyan University Press.

Berry, Wendell. 1983. *Standing by Words*. San Francisco: North Point Press.

———. 1987. *Home Economics*. San Francisco: North Point Press.

Boulding, Elise. 1981. "The Vision Is the Reality." In *The Spirit of the Earth*, edited by Jerome Perlinski. New York: Seabury Press.

Committees of Correspondence. 1985. "Ten Key Values." *Breakthrough* 6 (Spring).

Greene, Maxine. 1989. *The Dialectic of Freedom*. New York: Teachers College Press.

Knelman, F. H. 1989. "The Bruntland Report: A Critical Assessment." *Teaching Peace* 10 (Spring).

Petrovsky, Vladimir. 1989. "Pure Air, Money, and Secrecy" (interview), *New Times*, 2 August, 89.

Pianta, Mario, and Michael Renner. 1989. "The State System and the Consequences for Environmental Degradation." *IPRA Newsletter*, January 27.

Razuvayev, Vladimir. 1990. "Paying for the Past." *New Times*, September, 90.

Reardon, Betty. 1985. *Sexism and the War System*. New York: Teachers College Press.

Sivard, Ruth Leger. 1989. *World Military and Social Expenditures*. Washington: World Priorities.

Sloan, Douglas. 1983. *Insight-Imagination: The Emancipation of Thought and the Modern World*. Westport, Conn.: Greenwood Press.

Smale, Alison. 1990. "Small Steps Taken to Reverse Decades of Damage." Associated Press report, 30 March.

United Nations General Assembly. 1988. "Environmental Perspective to the Year 2000 and Beyond," 42/186, 30 March.

Warner, Sir Frederick. 1988. "The Environmental Effects of Nuclear War: Consensus and Uncertainties." *Environment* 30 (June).

10
Steps to a Renewal of Education: Concluding Words

Eva Nordland

The nine authors of this volume have listened to each other and discussed each other's contributions. The most important question, overall, has been : Will the next generation be able to work actively for sustainable development? In unison we answer: the next generation *can change their life-style* into an ecological and cooperative way of existence, and become responsible persons in a living world, respecting the diversity of life on this planet.

This change depends on the way the new generation learns—it must learn values, theory, and practice *as a unity*. Our answer also encompasses one vital aspect of change that concerns our own generation. We must be willing to take steps in education that concretely show the way; we must be ready to change in the direction of an ecological and cooperative education.

Traditional education in our time has cried out this message: "Even if we know a lot about the dangers and threats, we cannot take initiatives; our chief role and main obligation is to pass on knowledge and supervise our students!" The educational system declares: "Listen to what we have to say and then abandon our message." In this situation fundamental new steps in education are needed, redefining roles and obligations.

Ecology in the Center

The concept of *ecology and cooperation* is needed in the center of all educational institutions, using the school as a workplace for the theory and practice of aspects of sustainable development. The school must show that it really believes in the knowledge that it conveys and sticks to the values that it preaches.

Students must be stimulated to use their own experiences, and to listen to each other when they provide each other with examples of what they themselves see has to be changed or supported. Students will then be in a position to meet the knowledge of the school with their own personal knowledge and so be stimulated to reflect as they take steps to act on the basis of central values. Learning will then develop as a staircase—up many floors, leading from personal experiences to reflection and theory, and then to new practice, new experiences. Students will be prepared for, and open to, further theory and better praxis, in a continuous "spiral of understanding."

Practice-Theory in Learning

How can knowledge be used to turn into reality ideas of value: protection of nature, caring for each other, cooperation? Each educational institution can start with its own surroundings, as a first measure; all who are involved in the school can talk together about content and methods, about process and product. What are our values? What are our problems? What do we know? What can we do to improve things in our own environment as part of the ecological context? The students discuss common values, collect knowledge together, talk about what action to take, make decisions, and then—*act*. The surroundings give all possible help; especially important is the support of the school authorities.

The Framework Gives Meaning to the Content

An effective way to pass on the message about sustainable development is to proclaim the school, the college, the university, to be parts of an ecoregion, and so take responsibility for one's own part in it. Teachers and students together study traffic, buildings, water and electricity resources, protection of forests and fields, and attitudes toward plants and animals. Students and teachers work out common projects to improve the school system seen as part of an ecoregion. The program of learning combines theory and practice.

Students and teachers together become participants in a process to change their life-styles and the school institution as a whole. All take part in a process to make the institution a model with regard to taking care of each other, encouraging each other, and supporting self-respect and personal growth. The process also aims at becoming a model with regard to use of resources and ecologically better alternatives with regard to carbon dioxide emissions, reductions in the use of harmful chemical materials, improvement in energy efficiency, looking for renewable sources of energy, and so on.

When the institution starts to do something practical, imagination is liberated. One takes part in planning a new policy for running the institution.

What is meant by a sustainable economy at our place of work? And in a larger context? How can we in our school, in our district, and even on a larger scale, organize a program for protecting the future and coming generations? We at our institution are taking part in cooperative ecological endeavors to show that it is possible in real life to work for development leading in the direction of a healthy planet. The results of such studies can be included in the curriculum.

No student should leave the school or graduate from the institution without having taken part in practical work for environmental improvement on the basis of values and theoretical knowledge. Through continuous discussions of values, the people attached to the school aim at becoming conscious of their own life-styles, their own responsibilities, their own possibilities. What is the difference between development and growth, sufficiency and luxury, health and illness?

No Road to an Alternative—the Alternative Is the Road

Every educational institution needs appropriate evaluation systems that may turn the attention of teachers and students to those aspects of learning that are crucial: cooperation and ecology. We have many new forms of evaluation that concern knowledge and skills (i.e., tools for change), but we have not much experience when it comes to evaluation of reflection on values, capacity for cooperation, communication skills, or initiatives for ecological and cooperative improvements.

A satisfactory system of evaluation is characterized by a series of criteria—measures that stimulate students to take part in important practice where relevant knowledge and skills are needed. The students must work in cooperation for a humane and healthy environment on the basis of values, theoretical knowledge, and their own practice.

New forms of evaluation must accordingly include documentation that students have been participants (have used their time) working with the different aspects of what is declared important in their education. Basic requirements will be these:

- Consciousness of, and discussions about, values
- Knowledge about humans, society, and nature
- Reflection on experience in relation to book knowledge
- Making practical use of relevant knowledge and skills

The evaluation system must include descriptions of how the students have shown ability to take responsibility, using appropriate knowledge and skills. In practice this must include measures that students over some time will:

- get training in projects for cooperation and ecology,
- get education in communication and conflict solving,
- get practical training in social skills,
- have guidance in group cooperation,
- use personal experience in connection with theory,
- use theory and reflection in connection with praxis, and
- get experience in being evaluated in relation to the educational objectives.

Because those who work in these institutions for learning will be engaged in cooperating for protection and caring, they will acquire important knowledge and relevant facts and figures. They will also—because they are engaged with relevant praxis—generate habits, attitudes, and expectations, that is, acquire a core of personality traits that are in harmony with the educational objectives: unity of nature, cooperation between humans, equality, responsibility, caring. These values are practiced and reflected upon.

Because this education will increase the harmony between different aspects of the learning program, students will experience confidence and assurance and through this education develop self-respect and the ability to take initiatives for an ecological and cooperative future.

Questions for
Reflection and Discussion

NEW WORLD—NEW THINKING

1. What is your personal assessment of the "new mode of thinking" versus the "old mode of thinking"?

2. Is the New Thinking, to your mind, influencing the life of modern society (globally, locally)? If so, in what way? If not, why not?

3. How will you illustrate your understanding of new thinking by concrete examples in your own country and in the world?

4. How do you think the new moment should affect education? If you are an educator, what, if any, changes has it made in your own teaching? Has your school system taken it into account? How would you propose they do so?

5. What problems and needed changes in your own society are affected by the New Thinking? How should education direct itself to the problems of your society as they affect and are affected by the rapidly changing global situation?

6. How would you define security? What do you think makes for security in human society? How can education contribute to a more secure global society?

7. How does power affect the possibilities for ecological and cooperative education in your community? From what does the power base in your community derive? How is it exercised? How does it affect, and how is it affected by, education? Are these effects positive?

ECOLOGICAL AND COOPERATIVE EDUCATION IN THE CENTER

1. How does "ecological cooperative" education differ from present educational practices? What are the major obstacles to its implementa-

tion? Is such an approach relevant in some form or another to most of the world's educational systems and needs?

2. Could ecological and cooperative education make a contribution to education for democracy and justice in your community's schools? If so, what might that contribution be, and how might it be undertaken?

3. Outline a policy for your government for the repair of the environment of your country. In view of the changes in world politics, which spending priorities would you change to help get the resources needed for this repair?

4. Think about yourself in the role of environmental activist. What kinds of skills and knowledge do you think you would need to be effective in this area? Are these the skills and knowledge that are currently being taught in school? What are the similarities and differences?

5. What differences would ecological cooperative approaches make in your own thinking? Would such differences make you more or less effective as a local and a global citizen?

6. How would you advocate we educate for social responsibility on the local and global levels so as to make citizen action more effective as an agency for the achievement of a peaceful and just global order?

PRACTICE—THEORY—ECOREGIONS

1. What would you consider to be your deepest personal convictions? Where did they come from? Who were influential in their development? Would you recommend these convictions to others? Why or why not?

2. How does life inside of your home differ from the life you lead outside of home? Do you think that people take better care of things, themselves, and other people, in their own homes? Why do you think this is so?

3. Think about the things in your home, the food you eat, the water you wash with, the furniture you relax in. Where does it come from? Who makes it? Why might it be important to know about the sources of the products and services we consume?

4. Think about the things you have around your home that you can fix and maintain yourself. What do you know how to build, to repair, to keep in good working order? Are you intimidated by the complexity of things? Which ones? How dependent are you upon them? What do you do when the things you depend upon fail to work as you require?

5. What do we need to find out about the community/ecoregion in order to plan for an expanded concept of school?

6. Who is part of your community (human and nonhuman elements)? How are they related? Who decides how they are related?

7. What are the natural boundaries of our ecoregion? How might we prepare regional materials? What problems do we see in our landscape? What are contributing factors?

8. What ecological and indigenous knowledge do members of the ecoregional community have, and how can we use it effectively?

9. What people-to-people citizen diplomacy efforts between planetary ecoregions can create new knowledge of resource use?

10. How can learners devise ways to celebrate relatedness of all ecoregional members?

11. How can I weave ecological relationships into my teaching in an appropriate way?

CONTENTS AND METHODS—A UNITY

1. Why can the involvement of youth in the problems of environmental care be considered one of the most effective means of teaching the young generation social responsibility?

2. What are the backgrounds defining the acceptance or repudiation of anthropocentrism and biocentrism by society?

3. What are the specific advantages and drawbacks of formal curriculum and nonformal (extracurricular) education?

4. How should activity in small groups be organized to give every participant the opportunity to be responsible for group results?

5. What concrete activity will involve teenagers in the PEACE project and the practice of genuine cooperation?

EVALUATION AND REAL LIFE

1. What has "the new moment" meant in your own life, personally and socially? How has it affected the way you live your daily life and do your work?

2. Do you happen to know any new educational initiatives explicitly or implicitly based on the new-thinking principles?

3. Have you (as a student or as a teacher) any experience in cooperative education? What kind of methods would you suggest be used for reaching the new-thinking aims?

4. What obstacles do you see in organizing cooperative learning at school, and cooperation in the social life of the students?

5. If you were a participant in the PEACE project, what kind of approaches would you use to make it more effective?

6. What approaches to structuring social responsibility can you suggest on the basis of your own experiences?

About the Authors

Susan Ahearn is an American who at the time of the writing of these essays lived in the boreal forest area at the easternmost point of North America, on the island of Newfoundland. She was then an assistant professor of science and environmental education at Memorial University of Newfoundland. She is the author of numerous articles and materials in her field. She has directed two international film festivals on issues of peace and the environment and has worked for several organizations involved in natural areas preservation and environmental education. Currently she is one of the coordinators of a subgroup of PEACE, known as Practical Ecology in Education, which organizes outdoor expeditions to Russia and the United States for future science teachers of the two countries. Dr. Ahearn is a 1988 graduate of Columbia University's program in International Educational Development, specializing in Science and Peace Education. She organized workshops for citizens in her Newfoundland community to help prepare them to participate in national decision-making efforts related to defense, common security, and a sustainable environment. She is married and the mother of two six-year-old sons.

Anatoly Golovatenko was born in 1959. From 1976 through 1979 he studied history at Moscow University, and in 1982 he graduated from the Department of History of the Moscow Pedagogical Institute. From 1982 to 1988 he worked as a researcher at the Research Institute for General Problems of Education, Academy of Pedagogical Sciences. Since 1988 he has been the associate editor-in-chief of the journal *History Teaching in School*. A. Golovatenko is the author of articles concerning legal education in the schools, the methodology of history teaching, the history of school and education, as well as problems of modern social life and the theory of culture.

219

WILLARD JACOBSON is professor emeritus of natural sciences at Teachers College, Columbia University. He has worked and studied in eight countries and was the U.S. national research coordinator for the second IEA science study. He is author or coauthor of about seventy books and many articles. He has three children and two grandchildren. Dr. Jacobson is a former president of the Association for the Education of Teachers in Science, the National Association for Research in Science Teaching, and the Council for Elementary Science International. He is a fellow of the American Association for the Advancement of Science and the New York Academy of Science.

GALINA KOVALYOVA is a senior researcher at the Institute of General Secondary Education, Academy of Pedagogical Sciences, Russia. She previously worked for ten years as a secondary school teacher of physics. She is the author of articles on science education. Dr. Kovalyova is especially interested in the development of new ways of thinking, the humanization and socialization of science education, and science education in a nuclear age. Being a member of the school council of the Moscow secondary school where her son studies, she tries to implement the ideas of peace education in practice.

VALENTINA MITINA has an M.S. from the Pedagogical Institute in Moscow, Russia (1950) and an Ed.D. from the Academy of Pedagogical Sciences, Moscow (1974). Dr. Mitina has been teaching English for the past twenty years at all levels. Since 1971 she has been a senior researcher, specializing in comparative education, working for the Department of Comparative Education at the Research Institute of the Theory and History of Education, Academy of Pedagogical Sciences. She is the author of more than fifty works in comparative education, peace education, and related fields. She is on the board of the Movement of Educators for Peace and Mutual Understanding.

EVA NORDLAND has been a professor of education at the University of Oslo, Norway, since 1963 and was professor of psychology at Aarhus University, Denmark, 1971–72. She received her Ph.D. in 1955 from the University of Oslo. She has four children and two grandchildren. Dr. Nordland was a member and chair of the Council for Norwegian Broadcasting, 1955–60; chair of the National Council for Teacher Training, 1960–69; member and chair of the National Council for Peace and Conflict Research, 1966–68; and consultant for several government ministries, 1960–79. She has led official delegations to many countries, was a Scandinavian representative at the Council of Europe in education, and has lectured at universities in Europe, the United States, Africa, and Australia. She has written about forty books and several hundred articles. Dr. Nordland's main areas of work are social education, peace, and environmental work, and she has done a study of Norwegian UNESCO Associated Schools Project (ASP). Dr. Nordland is a leader of the council of Kornhaug Norwegian Peace Center, a member of the Research Council of the Nordic Alternative Future Project, and a representative of the University of Oslo in the Ecovalley Project at Sandnes, Norway, a community practicing ecological and cooperative education. Since 1990 she has been an adviser in social education to the Russian educational authorities.

Sergei Polozov, born in 1955, is an associate professor of zoology and ecology at Moscow Pedagogical University. He is the author of more than fifty papers in the fields of ornithology and environmental education, the coordinator of the Russian association Educators for Ecological Culture, and director of the ecological center Ecopol. His scientific interests include ecology, the behavior and protection of rare species of birds, the development of new approaches to the environmental education of university and high school students, the global problems of development, and the interrelations of science, education, and business. He is an organizer of field expeditions for studying ecosystems in various natural zones in Eurasia and North America. His hobbies are sports, photography, and communication. Dr. Polozov is married and has an eight-year-old son.

Betty Reardon is director of the Peace Education Program of Columbia University of New York's Teachers College. She previously served as director of the School Program of the Institute for World Order and executive secretary of the World Council for Curriculum and Instruction. Her main endeavors, even while serving in these administrative capacities, have been in the development of peace education. Consequently she has worked in curriculum design, teacher preparation, and the elaboration of a theoretical basis for peace education. Most of her substantive work has been done in a transnational context. She was a founder of the Peace Education Commission of the International Peace Research Association, has served as a consultant to UNESCO and other U.N. Agencies, and has participated in many international conferences and projects. She has published widely in the field, taught in several countries, and spoken at educational meetings the world over. Her best-known works in the field are *Comprehensive Peace Education,* a set of theoretical essays, and *Educating for Global Responsibility,* an edited volume of curricula for elementary and secondary peace education.

ROBERT W. ZUBER holds a doctoral degree in religion and the foundations of education from Teachers College, Columbia University. He has published in academic journals on issues ranging from human rights to the philosophy of education. He is currently senior program officer of the World Order Models Project and works with an East Harlem AIDS ministry. He is a founding director of EARTH (Education, Action and Research Towards Holism) and has served as associate project director for the International Institutes on Peace Education, based in New York.

Suggested Readings

Bateson, Gregory. *Steps to an Ecology of Mind.* Ballantine Books, New York, 1972. The central idea of the book is that we create the world that we perceive, not because there is no reality outside our minds, but because we select and edit the reality we see to conform to our belief. Sometimes the dissonance between reality and distorted beliefs reaches a point when it becomes necessary to change the understanding of the world. The ecological crisis at the turn of the century, shows us that we need radically new perceptions and ideas about our life on Earth.

Bateson, Gregory. *Mind and Nature. A Necessary Unity.* New York: Bantam Books, 1979. Bateson probes beyond Western scientific facts and creates a model of human beings and the universe in which we can learn to "think as nature thinks" and regain our place in the natural world.

Berdjaev, N. *Sudjba Rosii* (Russia's fortune). Moskwa: Sovetskij pisatel, 1990. This book, by a famous Russian philosopher, also includes articles he wrote before the revolution. He discusses the main problems of Russia and goes into the political and social development of the country. The book helps the reader to understand the Russian people.

Berger, John J. *Restoring the Earth: How Americans are Working to Renew our Damaged Environment.* New York: Doubleday, 1987. The book tells how Americans in fifteen different locations have begun to repair damaged ecosystems through application of the new science of restoration ecology. These inspiring stories attest to the new environmental consciousness that has become an accepted part of American society.

Berry, Wendell. *Home Economics.* San Francisco: North Point Press, 1987. Berry's books are designed to enhance ecological and cooperative education. His writing is generous, critical, and perceptive, and builds its truths from local perspectives and life-styles. His writings on culture, farming, education and religion are challenging, and written with vigor and compassion, in a manner that invites comment and analysis on the part of the reader.

Bertell, Rosalie. *No Immediate Danger? Prognosis for a Radioactive Earth.* Toronto: Women's Educational Press, 1985. We have known for some time that we face extinction if nuclear war ever begins. Rosalie Bertell shows us that we face extinction even if these bombs never fall; the production alone of nuclear energy and nuclear weapons is initiating the death crisis of our species.

Capra, Fritjof. *The Turning Point.* Simon and Schuster, New York, 1982. A historical review of the *old paradigm*, the old way of understanding and acting, in science and society, with a comprehensive critique of the limitations of such dominating concepts as "specialization," "fragmentation," and "linear cause and effect." The book also provides a synthesis of the emerging *new paradigm*, a vision of reality as something whole, with parts being integrated, interconnected, interdependent, and cooperating.

Chalidze, V. *The Dawn of Legal Reform* (April 1985–June 1989). Moscow, 1990. V. Chalidze is a well-known Soviet dissident and scholar of the Soviet legal system. This book is about the consequences of antilegal Communist governing in the previous U.S.S.R. and about ways to overcome those results. The book deals with special features of the Soviet legal mentality.

Educating for New Ways of Thinking. U.S.-Soviet Institute. Cambridge, Mass.: Educators for Social Responsibility, 1989. An overview of ideas expressed by American and Soviet teachers during their work at the U.S.-Soviet Summer Institute on the problems of new thinking and educating for peace.

Eisler, Riane. *The Chalice and the Blade.* Harper and Row, New York, 1987. An examination of scholarly evidence that human society can be structured on the principles of mutuality and cooperation, specifically between men and women working in "partnership." This theoretical work has become the basis of an approach to social reconstruction called the "partnership way" that is complementary to an ecological-cooperative approach and to a feminist approach.

Erikson, Erik H. *Gandhi's Truth. On the Origins of Militant Non-violence.* New York: Norton, 1969. To read Erik Erikson on Gandhi is to experience the presence of two great innovators. One of the most ingenious spiritual leaders since Christ is recreated by the most original psychological mind since Freud. The book expands our grasp of some of the deepest questions of our time.

Ferguson, Marilyn. *The Aquarian Conspiracy.* Los Angeles: J.P. Tarcher, 1987. This work has been a ground breaker in asserting the growth of a planetary movement toward social transformation that evolves out of a transformation of human consciousness. It is based upon an understanding of the planet Earth as a single system and the human race as a single species. It places emphasis on grass-roots movements and actual experiments with alternative life-styles based on ecological principles.

Global Education Associates (G.E.A.), *Breakthrough* 10, no. 4 and 11, no. 1 (Summer/Fall 1989). This special combined issue entitled "Ecological Security in an Interdependent World," edited by Patricia M. Mische and Melissa Merkling, tells about the networks and resources that G.E.A. brings to environmental education.

It covers a wide range of ecological concerns, and includes statistical and ethical analyses along with curricular considerations. It is a comprehensive record of the contemporary environmental education movement. E. Sahtouris writes about Vladimir Vernadsky on p. 66.

Gorbachev, Mikhail. *Perestroika. New Thinking for Our Country and the World.* Harper and Row, Perennial Library, New York 1987. This book is a historic document. Mikhail Gorbachev, a world leader, addresses the world's citizens with his message about a world without violence. He exposes the difficulty in changing the foundations upon which international relations have been built to the present time; these are the foundations of nationalism and competition. "But," Gorbachev says, "the new thinking is knocking at every door and window."

Gorz, André. *Ecology as Politics.* Boston: South End Press, 1980. The book emphasizes how we—at the end of the century—have a chance, through our creative efforts, to link our concerns for the quality of life with the issues of ecology as politics.

Greene, Maxine. *The Dialectic of Freedom.* New York: Teachers College Press, 1989. The book focuses on developing opportunities for creativity and self-determination in our overly "administered" world. With a special sensitivity to issues raised by women, ethnic minorities, and the disenfranchised, Greene alerts us to be "mindful" in a world that seduces and dulls us into not paying attention. The book explores ways to see more clearly and to affirm creative uniqueness.

Gromyko, Anatoly, and Martin Hellman, eds. *Breakthrough. Emerging New Thinking.* New York: Walker and Company, 1988. This work is a result of collaboration between Soviet and American scientists. The approach used in developing the book is similar to that in *The Promise of Ecological and Cooperative Education—Peace.*

Ivanov, I. P. *Entsiklopedia kollektivnyh tvorcheskih del.* (Encyclopedia of collective creative activities). Moscow: Pedagogika, 1989. This book gives a description of the collective creative activity of students at school and out of school. It shows the technique of the organization of this activity—the conditions of involving children in activity for the benefit of people.

Jacobson, Willard J. *Population Education—A Knowledge Base.* New York: Teachers College Press, 1979. The book provides background knowledge in population studies that is of use to teachers. It also contains a large number of activities that can be used by teachers.

Kapto, A.C. *Filosofia mira: istoki, tendentsii, perspektivy* (Philosophy of peace: Sources, tendencies, perspective), Moskva: Politizdat, 1990. From the position of new political thinking the author considers the essence of peace as a universal humane value, and analyzes its political, social, legal, and ethical bases.

Lemkow, Anna. *The Wholeness Principle. Dynamics of Unity within Science, Religion and Society.* Wheaton, Ill.: Quest Books, Theosophical Publishing House, 1990. This book demonstrates that holism is emerging as a common paradigm for all human modes of thought within the academic disciplines, philosophy, and spiritual belief systems; that the general-systems approach characteristic of "global thinking" is also a form of holism. The book provides a scholarly contemporary argument that validates ecological and cooperative education.

Lovelock, James. *The Ages of Gaia: A Biography of Our Living Earth.* New York: Norton, 1988. In outlining the life stages of the planet this work illustrates the kind of organic conceptualization that characterizes ecological thinking. The author's previously articulated Gaia hypothesis—proposing that the Earth is one self-regulating, living system—is fundamental to the basic values and assumptions of PEACE.

Macy, Joanna Rogers. *Despair and Personal Power in the Nuclear Age.* Philadelphia: New Society Publishers, 1983. This book goes to the heart of the psychological and spiritual dilemma we are experiencing in a crisis-ridden time. We are invited to unblock our feelings about our threatened planet and the possible demise of our species; we are encouraged to be empowered by the realization of our interconnectedness with one another; we are stimulated to respond creatively to the crises before us.

Mendlovitz, Saul, and R. B. J. Walker. *Toward a Just World Order.* London: Butterworth, 1987. The book argues for the restructuring of the international system and for creating institutions of humane global governance that are grounded on values consistent with ecological and cooperative principles.

Myers, Norman. *Future Worlds: Challenge and Opportunity in an Age of Change.* New York: Doubleday, 1990. This book has been described in reviews as a toolkit for future choices, and indeed it is. It is a highly illustrated atlas focusing on three areas: Pressures and Processes, Impacts and Outcomes, and Creating the Future. It presents realistic possibilities that are dependent on a radical shift in our perceptions, spirit, and life-style.

Naess, Arne. *Ecology, Community and Lifestyle: Outline of an Ecosophy.* New York: Cambridge University Press, 1988. The author's premise is that individuals will have to develop their own set of ecosophies, or deep ecological evaluation for living, rooted in an ethical system valuing life and nature. The book describes the relationship of ecosophy to technology, economics, ecopolitics, and the unity and diversity of life.

Novgorodtsev, P. I. *Über die eigentümlichen Elemente der russischen Rechtsphilosophie;* and Gurwitsch, G. *Die zwei grössten russischen Rechtsphilosophen Boris Tschitscherin und Vladimir Solovjev. Russische Rechtsphilisophie.* Beilage zur Zeitschrift *Philosophie und Recht,* 1922–1923, H.2. The two articles by Novgorodtsev and Gurwitsch display some features of Russian legal philosophy. The latter was influenced by European ideas and theories (especially in the nineteenth century). These two and many other Russian philosophers (among them V. Solovjev), have found new approaches to answering the old questions of how to combine Christian values and human rights, and how to overcome the contradictions between collectivism and individualism, and between moral and legal norms and values.

Odum, Eugene P. *Fundamentals of Ecology*. 3d ed. Philadelphia, Pennsylvania: W. B. Saunders Company, 1971. One of the most widely used textbooks in ecology. An excellent source of background information.

Peace, Environment and Education. Publications of Department of Education and School of Education, Malmö, Sweden. Also functions as a newsletter for the Peace Education Commission, The International Peace Research Association. Edited by Åke Bjerstedt. The materials published in its issues are of value to the PEACE project, for they help in understanding the process of peace-related education in different countries.

Pembina Institute. *Peace Education News* 10 (Winter 1990). This special issue entitled "Re-defining Security: Education for an Ailing Planet" is an excellent resource for persons doing curriculum work in the environmental field. Rob Macintosh and his colleagues keep readers abreast of Canadian and U.S. efforts to create forms of curriculum and political advocacy that are appropriate to the state of environmental disrepair, disrepair that Pembina seeks to counteract.

Reardon, Betty A., ed. *Educating for Global Responsibility. Teacher-Designed Curricula for Peace Education, K–12*. New York: Teachers College, Columbia University, 1988. The book includes interesting and useful materials for teachers to use in school practice for peace education. The variety of topics and suggested methods make this book a resource not only for American teachers, but also for those of all the PEACE countries.

Reardon, Betty A. *Comprehensive Peace Education: Educating for Global Responsibility*. New York: Teachers College, Columbia University, 1988.

Sahtouris, E. *Gaia: The Human Journey from Chaos to Cosmos* (New York: Pocket Books, 1989). According to Sahtouris's account, Vernadsky gives a general picture of the origin and development of scientific ideas as a global phenomenon; the study of global-scale problems reveals a close link between nature and society.

Sales, Kirkpatrick. *Dwellers in the Land: The Bioregional Vision*. San Francisco: Sierra Club Books, 1985. One of the first writers of the last decade to describe the American movement known as bioregionalism. Sales envisions a world of ecological survival based on regional approaches that undo the disasters of American "giantism"; the ideals include the concepts of decentralism, participation, liberation, mutualism, and community initiatives.

Schell, Jonathan. *The Fate of the Earth*. New York: Avon Books, 1982. Uses an ecological approach in the examination of profound problems facing the inhabitants of the planet.

Schumacher, E. F. *Small is Beautiful. A Study of Economics as if People Mattered*. Great Britain: Abacus,, 1974. Shows how the pursuit of progress and profit in today's world promotes the growth of giant organizations and specialization that serves the short-term interests of powerful groups. The result is gross economic inefficiency, environmental pollution, and inhumane working conditions. Schumacher proposes a system of smaller working units, communal ownership, and regional workplaces that use local labor and resources. In this way he points the way to a world in which capital serves human beings instead of human beings remaining slaves to capital.

Shaposhnikov, V., ed. *Problems of Common Security*. Moskva, Progress, 1984. The book summarizes the results of the Scientific Research Council on Peace and Disarmament and the Soviet Peace Fund Study (a study of various aspects of international security and disarmament), and shows how they are related to each other.

Slavin, R., S. Sharan, S. Kagan, R. Hertz-Lazorowitz, C. Webb, and R. Schmuck, eds. *Learning to Cooperate, Cooperating to Learn*. New York: Plenum Press, 1985. This volume presents both research results and statements to increase our understanding of how cooperative learning groups work and why they produce characteristic results. The material attests to the continuing vitality of the field of cooperative learning.

Sloan, Douglas. *Insight-Imagination: The Emancipation of Thought and the Modern World*. Westport, Conn.: Greenwood Press, 1983. The historian Douglas Sloan takes the reader on a journey through modern intellectual history, pinpointing the ways in which science and the university have restricted knowledge and its pursuit to those things which can be quantified or measured. In the process, matters of faith and value, of quality and beauty, of the personal and the spiritual have been denigrated or ignored. Within our narrow-knowledge frameworks, the earth and the life forms that inhabit it are to be manipulated and exploited rather than revered, respected, appreciated and preserved. Also written by Sloan is *Toward a Recovery of Wholeness: Knowledge, Education and Human Values*. New York: Teachers College Press, 1984.

Solovejchik, S. L. *Vospitanie po Ivanovu* (Upbringing on Ivanov's ideas). Pedagogika, Moscow 1989. The author gives the basic principles and contents of the *communard methodology*, which were worked out by I. Ivanov through the experience of his friends. Attention is mainly paid to the application of this methodology in the practice of the Soviet school.

Spectorsky, E. V. *Christianity and Culture*. Prague, 1925. An interesting analysis of the role of Christianity in previous and modern society (the beginning of the twentieth century). The study connects main Christian ideas and spiritual life to a "secular" culture.

Thompson, William Irwin, ed. *Gaia. A Way of Knowing*. Hudson, N.Y.: Lindisfarne Press, 1987. The works presented in the book provide an analysis of modern approaches toward creating a new ecology of consciousness.

Turnbull, Colin M. *The Human Cycle*. Simon and Schuster, New York, 1983. The author reflects upon the stages of human life and their meaning in each society. The author describes how we all live within the same ecological laws and he draws on this unity to provoke thought on contemporary social issues.

USSR: *Sostoianie prirodnoi sredy v SSSR v 1988 godu*. (The state of the environment in the USSR in 1988). Moskva: Lesnaya promishlennost, 1990. This is a collection of systematically arranged official statistics on the quality of the environment and the threatening ongoing changes, the conditions of natural resources, the health condition of the population, and regional ecological problems. Such statistics are published for the first time in the history of the USSR.

USSR: *Ohrana okruzhaushei sredi i racionalnoe ispolzovanie prerodnih resursov v SSSR*. (Environmental protection and rational use of national resources in the USSR). Statistical report, Moscow, 1989. The collection contains statistics on the effect of humans on the environment and the amount and usage of the natural resources, and information on the ecological situation.

Vernadsky, V. I. *Nauchnaya misl kak planetarnoe javlenie* (Scientific thought as planetary phenomenon). Moskva: Nauka, 1977. This is a basic analysis and a general picture of the origin and development of scientific ideas as a global phenomenon; the study of global-scale problems reveals a close link between nature and society.

The World Commission on Environment and Development. Gro Harlem Brundtland, Chairman. *Our Common Future*. New York: Oxford University Press, 1987, and Moskva: Progress, 1989. An international commission devoted to the analysis of the reasons for the critical ecological situation on the planet and to finding ways to eliminate the global threats.

World Council for Curriculum and Instruction. *The Forum* 4, no. 1 (June 1990). Special Issue: "Caring for the Earth: An Educational Imperative." This volume represents the efforts of an international organization of educators to explore the implications of their common work for ecological repair. Included are curricular and more philosophical perspectives, including an essay by Eva Nordland, international coordinator for the PEACE project.

Yablokov, A. V. *Population Biology. Progress and Problems of Studies on Natural Populations*. Translated from the Russian by Pyotr Aleinikov. Moscow: MIR , 1986. An English translation of a very important Soviet book in this field.

Index

Ahearn, Susan, 71, 104, 121, 203
AIDS, 76, 78
All Union Teachers Congress (Russia), 55
alternatives, need for, 1
American-Soviet collaboration, 63–64
anthropocentrism, 101–3; in societies, 134
Apaches (Arizona), stories and legends, 129

balance, and change, 82–84, 96
Barfield, Owen, 195
Bateson, Gregory, 7–9, 13
Berdjaev, N. (Russia), 185
Berry, Wendell, 195–97, 201, 205
biocentrism, 102
biosphere reserves, 135
Bocharova, V. (pedagogical sciences), 186
Boulding, Elise, 36, 206–7

Canada, ecological documents, 133
capitalism, failures of, 15
Capra, Fritjof, 7
Carter, Nancy (poet), 192
Chernobyl, 179–81
children: desires for, 101; activities for, 108
climax condition, 31
Clubs of International Friendship (Russia), 52
Colegio de villa de Leyva (Colombia), 123
Committees of Correspondence (Greens), 203
Commonwealth of Independent States (CIS): member nations, x; social and economic difficulties, 1
communard methodology (Russia), 183–85; and the *zbor,* 184–85
communism, failures of, 15
competition, 14, 30
consciousness, ecological, 21; new level of, 170

cooperation, 61–64, 77–78, 95; among nations, 61–64; needs for, 169–70; and new approach in education, 181–82; two levels of, 170–71; in UN system, 61
cooperative learning: meaning and promise, 29–34; power and, 36–38; practical considerations of, 182–83
cultural evolution, 68
culture, ecological, 103–4
cycles, 78–80, 95; natural, 79; producer-consumer-decomposer, 80–81

DDT, unforseen effects of, 94
decentralization, examples of, 122–24
democracy, *viii;* and personality, 57
democratization, 55
Dialogue of Cultures (Russia), 58
Diamond, Irene, 55
domination, 36
Dubos, René, 78

earth; fragility of, 4
ecological education: areas of concern, 127; basis of, 100–101; educational promise of, 115–17; evaluation of, 213–14; framework and context of, 212–13; practical activities for, 108–10; and praxis, 124–26
ecological healing, 200–201; and craftsman-ship, 205–6; and fresh connections, 206–7; and life-style training, 202–3; and networking, 207; pedagogical goals, 202–7; and vulgarity, 204
ecological information, 106–7; in USSR, 106–7
ecological opposition, 111